I0197797

*Building structures
and skills for
fundraising*

Building structures and skills for fundraising

Elizabeth Westman Wilson

Practical ACTION PUBLISHING

Practical Action Publishing Ltd
27a Albert Street, Rugby, CV21 2SG, Warwickshire, UK
www.practicalactionpublishing.org

© Intermediate Technology Publications 2001

First published 2001\Digitised 2001

ISBN 10: 1 85339 534 X
ISBN 13: 9781853395345
ISBN Library Ebook: 9781780445014
Book DOI: http://dx.doi.org/10.3362/9781780445014

All rights reserved. No part of this publication may be reprinted or
reproduced or utilized in any form or by any electronic, mechanical, or
other means, now known or hereafter invented, including photocopying
and recording, or in any information storage or retrieval system, without
the written permission of the publishers.

A catalogue record for this book is available from the British Library.

The authors, contributors and/or editors have asserted their rights under
the Copyright Designs and Patents Act 1988 to be identified as authors of
their respective contributions.

Since 1974, Practical Action Publishing has published and disseminated
books and information in support of international development work
throughout the world. Practical Action Publishing is a trading name
of Practical Action Publishing Ltd (Company Reg. No. 1159018), the
wholly owned publishing company of Practical Action. Practical Action
Publishing trades only in support of its parent charity objectives and any
profits are covenanted back to Practical Action (Charity Reg. No. 247257,
Group VAT Registration No. 880 9924 76).

Contents

1 Studying the ground before the campaign

Imagine that your organization has been told by an international donor agency that its funds have been reduced by its parent government. As a result, it cannot promise you any increases in funding in the future and warns that the grants you have received in the past will probably decline. Another agency decides to focus its efforts in a few key areas, in none of which your organization falls, and tells you to expect no further funding from them after next year. Your board recognizes a financial crisis: the organization will either have to raise money from other sources or reduce its programs. Like most boards, it dislikes making difficult decisions. As a result, it does not decide to cut programs or staff. Instead, it turns to you, as the manager, and says, "Find more money." With international funding in decline, it looks as if much of that money will have to be found closer to home – from local individuals, corporations, and foundations.

Our biggest satisfaction right now is that we appear reliable to grantees and donors. Our biggest challenge is local fundraising.

United States trainers never say that before you start, you must get ready. You must establish a structure to deal with money. Even the smallest organization needs six months of work. They should not encourage small organizations by saying all it takes is a letter.

Tamas Scsaurszki, Hungarian Foundation for Self-Reliance

Some people in your organization believe bringing in more local money is a good idea. Some local fundraising may have been under way for years. But local support has not formed as high a percentage of the budget as will be necessary in the next decade. Ten to twenty-five per cent may be realistic if a new fundraising program is established. In the past it has been easier to get a grant for several years from an overseas donor than to find local funding, which usually must be renewed more regularly. Now that overseas option is less available. Attention must be paid to local fundraising.

Fundraising efforts are often described as campaigns. A "campaign", according to the Oxford dictionary, is (1) an organized course of action for a particular purpose or (2) a series of military operations in a definite area or to achieve a particular objective. There are two lessons to learn from these definitions. The first is the importance of a well-defined objective. The second is the importance of organization, or planning. A good general carefully surveys the ground before engaging in a battle. This chapter discusses major issues to examine before engaging in fundraising campaigns.

Two goals in local fundraising
The goal of local fundraising programs is not just to increase revenue quickly for particular programs. A second, underlying goal is to make friends whose

support will, in the long term, sustain the organization. A big effort on one or two fundraising projects may bring in lots of money, but friend-making is what brings success in the long run.

A single event or other fundraising activity may bring in more money than it costs in staff time and out-of-pocket expenses. Then everyone involved may be satisfied. But that should not be the only criterion for judging success. Effective fundraising recognizes the value of investing money to make friends even when there is no immediate or direct financial return. As a friend of mine used to say, "I'm using a small fish as bait for a big one."

One organization may invest in a newsletter or an annual report to tell people about its work, in the hope they will become donors. It may send free copies of the newsletter to government officials in hopes they will make policy decisions or give contracts or grants that will benefit the organization and the people it serves. A second organization may hold events that make a tiny profit or no profit at all to publicize its work, in the belief that within a few years those same events will grow better known and thus more profitable. It may also spend time and money trying to arrange publicity for a new program in order to tell potential donors about a new opportunity to invest in the community. A third organization may spend many hours and some money talking to local business people in the hope of eventually securing their donations. These organizations are investing money to make friends.

Making money takes commitment

Before a voluntary organization makes a commitment to raise funds locally, everyone involved – board members, senior and other staff members, and key volunteers – must agree to the programs that are being proposed. Otherwise there will be internal discord. They must also agree to take part in the fundraising enthusiastically. They must be aware of and commit themselves to the realities, not just the dreams.

That is easy to say. But when it becomes necessary to increase local fundraising substantially, many people back away from making the necessary effort. They want the results, but shy away from committing time and money. They find it difficult to take time from their own activities. They find it difficult to accept the idea that fundraising costs money – that "It takes money to make money." Staff members, board members, and long-time volunteers may protest or, worse, be silently resentful. They may say:

"Is money from my budget going to be spent on fundraising?"

"We don't want business people on our board. We don't trust them."

"We are a non-profit organization. If we take consulting contracts, we will become just a business. What will happen to our ideals?"

"If we take government contracts to survive, we are going to become a tool of the government."

It is difficult to begin serious fundraising if there is almost no money to invest in doing it – if the first job is to find the funds to raise funds. One way is discussed in Book 1 – making some kind of an alliance with another organization. Various ways of raising money at the lowest possible cost will be discussed in Book 3. Most of this book, however, is devoted to creating the structure required for local fundraising. This involves, first, analysing the current situation realistically (the subject of this chapter) and, then, gathering together a group of people to help you.

Start by looking backwards
Begin the planning by examining where your money has been coming from for the last two or three years and how much it has cost to raise that money. Only by looking at all the costs of fundraising will you get an accurate picture of your revenue. Some organizations consider only out-of-pocket expenses in this calculation. That is to say, they cover only the direct costs of each fundraising activity, such as buying donation boxes, or renting a hall in order to hold a fundraising event. But what about the cost of collecting the money regularly from the donation boxes? And what about the cost of a press release for the local newspapers and broadcast media telling the public how to get tickets for the event? Many organizations include a portion of the manager's time, and the time anyone else spends in fundraising, doing work such as recording donations or sending out thank-you letters. Will you ignore those costs, or include them in the total cost of fundraising?

All you need is a pencil and paper. A hand calculator or a computer would make the job easier.

The more elaborate approach will look complicated at first glance, but only because there are so many possible ways of raising money. At first, when fundraising is only starting, the calculations should be fairly easy.

Don't be frightened by the next few pages. Take them step by step. All you need is a pencil and paper. A hand calculator or a computer would make the job easier. Don't be afraid of making educated guesses, because any calculations are going to be only roughly accurate. What you are looking for is a sketch of your organization's funding, not a finished portrait.

Step 1
Make a list of the sources of your organization's income. The list might include the following headings, depending on your organization's history:
Overseas donors. International agencies (Ford Foundation, World Wide Fund for Nature, Oxfam, etc.), foundations in foreign countries, foreign governments, and government-funded development agencies
Local intermediary/umbrella groups, and other consortia
Governments at home. National, state or provincial, regional, and municipal governments and their agencies
Corporations. Businesses, local foundations, service clubs, unions, and other bodies that make donations, sponsor events financially, cooperate in certain programs, and match grants from their employees or others. (Different types of corporate support are described in Book 3.)
Individual donors. People who give money as a result of direct-mail requests, door-to-door canvasses, telephone campaigns, advertisements, tag/flag days, donation boxes, and visits requesting personal donations, people who sponsor events
Special events. Parties, concerts, long-distance runs, etc.
Income-generating activities. Sales of products (T-shirts, craftwork, food,

greeting cards, audiotapes and compact discs of local music, videotapes of local festivals and scenery, etc.), sale of services (technical assistance, training, newsletter subscriptions, ecotourism, etc.), rental of space
Annual memberships
Fees paid by beneficiaries
Religious contributions. Donations from a church, temple, mosque; donations made directly by members of a religious community as a group
In-kind contributions. From individuals and corporations – gifts of desks, food, computers, etc.
Volunteer time Other donations

Organizations don't put actual contributions in their budgets. If they get free space, they don't put that in their budgets. They think only of contributions of money. They don't value the time of people who are often working for nothing or for peanuts. Everything that is a saving should be in the budget – supplies given by the merchant next door – everything.

Ms Malvika, South Asian Fund Raising Group, India

Step 2
Once you have listed all the sources of funds, write down the revenue you have obtained from each source during the last two or three years. It is important to use the experience of more than one year in order to allow for any major variations in funding sources. Most of the amounts can be found by checking the annual accounts. Two categories of revenue will, however, require some estimation because they do not involve actual money. These are in-kind contributions and volunteer time.

The value of an in-kind contribution is simply what it would cost to buy a similar item. Volunteer time can be determined in much the same manner. Estimate the number of hours of volunteer time your organization receives for each task in which volunteers participate. Then estimate how much it would cost per hour to hire a staff member to do the same amount of work. If that is difficult to determine, calculate the cost based on the minimum legal hourly wage in your country, if one exists. Or ask friends or colleagues what they believe is usually paid for similar work.

The value of volunteer time will also be shown as income in the annual operating statements (See Book 1, Chapter 13) so recording it will not distort the financial picture. Why bother calculating it, then? One reason is to have some idea of the benefit being received from volunteers and what it would cost if that source of energy dried up. The other, and by far the more important, reason is to demonstrate to granting agencies and other donors the support your organization enjoys in your community.

Step 3
Calculate the average proportion of the total revenue coming from each source. To do this, find the total revenue for each source for the years being examined, by adding the annual revenues together. Divide that by the total revenue from all sources over the three years, and multiply by 100 per cent.

It's not as complicated as it sounds. Imagine a hypothetical voluntary organization called BestHealth, which sets up and manages rural health clinics. Its manager decided to see where its revenue had been coming from during the last three years. This is what he found.

For several years, BestHealth had been receiving, through a local inter-mediary organization, a sizable annual grant from a Canadian government-funded aid agency. For most of those years BestHealth had received Σ220,000 each year from that source.[1] Last year, however, the grant was reduced by 10 per cent, to Σ198,000, and BestHealth was warned that it would probably be reduced further in the future.

The year before last, BestHealth received a special grant of Σ70,000 from Oxfam to implement a special project in its village.

Three years ago, BestHealth began looking for more money from its community. It started distributing donation boxes in local shops, and the contributions from that source have been growing steadily, from Σ2,500 in the first year to Σ3,300 last year. It also ordered several thousand greeting cards that it could sell from its office. The cards were late being printed and arrived just days before the principal annual festival, so revenue from sales of them was disappointing in the first year (only Σ2,000), but it has grown since to Σ10,000 in the second year and Σ14,000 last year.

BestHealth has also been receiving regular contributions from a wealthy church in a nearby city. Those donations, after remaining steady for many years, have increased after BestHealth announced that its Canadian grant from the intermediary was being cut.

The manager of BestHealth calculated the average contribution of each revenue source in the manner described above. For example, he found the total amount of money raised through the sale of greeting cards (Σ12,000 + Σ10,000 + Σ14,000 = Σ26,000) and calculated that that was roughly 3 per cent of all the money BestHealth raised during those three years (which amounted to Σ763,000). The result of all his calculations is shown in Table 1. The numbers confirmed the organization's heavy reliance on foreign funds (93 per cent of the total revenue over the three years) but showed that there was a modest yet solid community support that might be tapped for further money.

Table 1: Sources of revenue

	Last year	Year before	Year before that	Total revenue over 3 years	Per cent of revenue over 3 years
Overseas donors					
International agencies			70,000	70,000	9%
Foreign governments	198,000	220,000	220,000	638,000	84%
Community-based campaigns					
Donation boxes	3,300	3,200	2,500	9,000	1%
Income-generating activities					
Greeting cards	14,000	10,000	2,000	26,000	3%
Religious organizations					
Local church	8,000	6,000	6,000	20,000	3%
Total	223,300	309,200	230,500	763,000	100%

Note:
1 In this chapter, currency is quoted in a universal currency called the sigma, represented by the symbol Σ. The sigma bears no relation to dollars, pounds, piastres, nairas, pesos, rupees, or any other actual currency, nor do the revenues or costs shown bear any relation to actual revenues and costs in any country.

Step 4

The next step is to estimate what it has cost to obtain your revenue. This will necessarily be a rough estimate, unless you have been keeping track in detail of expenditures in time and money for fundraising. Most organizations do not do so until fundraising becomes a major part of their activities.

For each category of revenue, try to calculate the cost of raising funds under several headings. The most important are likely to be:

Staff time of managers; of clerical staff involved in record-keeping, sending receipts, and other office duties; of staff involved in sales of merchandise or services

Staff expenses for travel, attending meetings, entertainment, training related to fundraising, meeting donors, attending craft fairs, etc.

Consultants' fees for advice on fundraising or for fundraising services

Project-related supplies including letterhead, receipts, computer paper, and printer ink cartridges used in a specific fundraising activity

Project-related promotional costs for writing, design, and printing of brochures, tickets, and other printed matter for a specific activity; mailing and distribution of material for that activity; advertising, press releases, and other publicity for that activity

General promotional costs for newsletters, annual report, publicity, advertising

Costs of merchandise sold for raw materials, manufacture, transportation of goods

Costs of services sold for supplies and other materials

Rent, property maintenance, and services for space devoted exclusively to fundraising or income-generating activities

Volunteer time spent in fundraising and income-generating activities

Volunteer expenses for transportation, food during working hours and at meetings, travel, honoraria, and other rewards

Board and committee expenses for travel, meetings, entertainment, training

Most expenses can be assigned to a particular category with precision – for example, fees paid to consultants for a specific project, the cost of printing brochures and invitations to advertise a special event, the costs of making greeting cards or other merchandise for sale. These are the "direct costs" of a fundraising activity.

Remember that only costs directly related to fundraising should be included. Try to keep the calculations simple. For example, if a committee meets especially to discuss fundraising, all the costs connected with that meeting can be assigned to fundraising. Or, to take another example, if an organization has a small retail store for greeting cards and merchandise in its own building, and that retail store takes up 10 per cent of the total building, then 10 per cent of the total costs of rent, property maintenance, and services (light, telephone) can be assigned to fundraising. On the other hand, it is not likely worth keeping track of the amount of time the board spends actively discussing fundraising programs (not just the need to raise money).

A few costs must be based on estimates. These include staff and volunteer time and general promotional costs.

Staff time can be calculated in two ways. The simplest is to estimate what percentage of his or her time each staff member spends in fundraising. Then assign that percentage of the employee's total wage package (wages plus benefits) to the fundraising activity. A manager, for example, may estimate that she spends 10 per cent of her time each year trying to secure grants from overseas agencies and foundations, and that her secretary spends 5 per cent of her time typing proposals and in other ways supporting fundraising. The cost in staff time is therefore 10 per cent of the manager's wages and benefits and 5 per cent of the secretary's wages and benefits.

The percentage used at this point will be no more than an educated guess. Once major fundraising gets under way, a more accurate method may, if desired, be used to record the cost of staff time, especially the time of the manager whose salary may be a large part of the organization's budget. A manager may spend – in fact should spend – a significant amount of time on fundraising. It is not unusual for a manager to spend up to half of his or her time on fundraising, especially when the program is just beginning.

Organizations need to count time as money. We should count people's time. It is like housework, no value is given and no respect.

GURINDER KAUR, SWADHAR FOUNDATION, INDIA

If they are spending a lot of time, staff members can be asked to keep track of the actual number of hours they devote to fundraising – writing letters, arranging events, and supervising volunteers etc. The number of hours can then be multiplied by the average hourly wage of the staff members, or used as an accurate percentage of the total wage package.

The average hourly rate can be calculated in the following manner: First, estimate the number of hours a staff member should be expected to be working in a year. Then deduct from that total the average time spent on vacation, sick leave, lunches, tea or coffee breaks, and other non-productive activities. Divide this smaller number of hours into the annual cost of the employee's salary and benefits. The result will be the average hourly rate. It is enough to use one average rate for all clerical and other staff. The average hourly wage of the manager and other senior staff may need to be calculated separately if they are paid significantly more than the office average.

Volunteer time can be given a value as an expense in the same way as for revenue. Calculate the number of volunteer hours that support each activity and the cost to have the same work done by staff members.

General promotional costs – the costs of producing newsletters, annual reports, and general informational brochures – may be considered part of the general operations of your organization. In that case, you may decide to charge none of the costs to fundraising.

On the other hand, if 15 per cent of the copies of a newsletter are sent to granting agencies and other potential donors, you might decide to show 15 per cent of the total costs of producing the newsletter (including staff time in writing, editing, and desktop composition) as a cost of overseas and corporate fundraising. If many members join your organization principally to receive its newsletter, an appropriate percentage of its costs could be shown as a cost of securing memberships.

Assigning general promotional costs to any category of revenue is very much a judgement call. If desired, the entire cost of producing such materials can be assigned to fundraising, but it would have to be clear that those costs will not likely ever be recovered from donations. Instead, an organization might call such general promotional expenses "educational expense." The reason is that brochures, newsletters, and annual reports do more than ask for money; they also educate donors and the general public about the needs of the community being served and the ways those needs are being met through the organization. In other words, these educational activities are seen as part of an organization's general program, not part of its administrative and fundraising activities. This convenient category of "educational expense" allows an organization to reduce the proportion of its total budget it appears to be spending on fundraising – even though the publications should help in fundraising. As a result, the organization does not look as if it is asking for money largely to pay for the costs of raising that money.

It is possible to divide the costs of any publication between education and fundraising – the cultivation of donors. What you do will depend on what other organizations in your area do, the wishes of your board, the policies of the major agencies giving you grants, and your own belief about the appropriate allocation of costs.

The manager at BestHealth decided to count all publications as educational expenses. He calculated the cost of raising money as follows. He figured he spent 5 per cent of his time each year completing grant applications to the intermediary for the Canadian aid agency and preparing quarterly reports for it on the use of the money. He spent another 5 per cent of his time looking for other grants from other overseas sources and from the intermediary. In three years, that effort had produced only the single grant from Oxfam. His annual salary and benefits amounted to Σ50,000, so he assigned a cost of 5 per cent of Σ50,000, or Σ2,500, to each of those categories. Since neither the manager nor any of his staff had had any substantial increases in pay or benefits during the three years, he used the wage packages currently in effect. This was, after all, only a rough estimate.

His clerk/secretary, who had to type the reports and gather many of the figures, estimated that he also spent about 5 per cent of his time on each category. His annual salary and benefits totalled Σ20,000, so Σ1,000 was added to the manager's Σ2,500 in each category. These were the only significant costs of raising the money from overseas donations.

The next source of revenue, the donation boxes, had been expensive to make. To ensure the safety of the money, they were built of wood and fitted with locks. The boxes were distributed by volunteers and the money in them was collected once a month by volunteers. It took three volunteers half a day every week. This amounted to 76 days out of approximately 250 working days in a year – or 30 per cent of one year. Using his secretary's wages and benefits as a basis, the manager assigned 30 per cent of Σ20,000, or Σ6,000 as the value of this work. The volunteers also needed money for transportation and snacks as so they could go from shop to shop collecting the money.

The bookkeeper or the manager's secretary had to count the money from the boxes each week and deposit it in the bank; that took about an hour and a half a week or 5 per cent of someone's productive time, so he wrote down $1,000 as the cost of staff time for raising this money.

The greeting cards were produced very cheaply. A local artist donated her drawings without charge, and a local printer said he would donate his time and would produce them at no cost except for ink, paper, and envelopes. He estimated that the cost of printing would have been $3,000, and the manager decided that the artist's in-kind contribution was worth just as much. Because the printer was doing the work for free, however, he printed the cards only when he had no other work, and that is why they were late in delivery.

The paper and envelopes for the cards cost $5,000 in the first year. The only other expenses in connection with the cards were small regular purchases of plastic bags to put the cards in when people bought them, a book of bills, and occasional advertisements and posters reminding people that the cards were available.

The greeting cards were sold to visitors by BestHealth staff members as part of their regular jobs. This took little time from their regular work, so the manager did not charge anything for staff time or office space against the greeting cards.

The donations from the local church took almost no staff time at all. The church officials counted the money and prepared it for deposit in the bank. The manager might have to spend a certain amount of time with them each week thanking them, and might have to make occasional visits to the church to thank the congregation. He figured that might involve, at the very most, $750 of his time. The manager summarized his calculations as shown in Table 2.

Table 2: Costs of fundraising

	Last year	Year before last	Year before that	Total costs over 3 years
Overseas donors				
International agencies				
staff time	3,500	3,500	3,500	10,500
Foreign governments				
staff time	3,500	3,500	3,500	10,500
Community-based campaigns				
Donation boxes				
manufacture of boxes			4,500	4,500
volunteer time	6,000	6,000	6,000	18,000
volunteer travel	600	600	600	1,800
staff time	1,000	1,000	1,000	3,000
Income-generating activities				
Greeting cards				
in-kind contributions			6,000	6,000
cost of merchandise	50	50	5,000	5,100
project-related promotion	200	200	200	600
Religious organizations				
Local church				
staff time	750	750	750	2,250
Total cash expenditures*	9,600	9,600	19,050	38,250

* excluding the value of volunteer time and in-kind contributions

Step 5
Calculate the ratio of cost to revenue for each category. Count only actual cash received and cash spent, including the cost of staff time. Omit volunteer time and any in-kind contributions. You will then see which activities were the most efficient in purely financial terms. If you brought in three times what you spent on a particular fundraising activity, that would be a ratio of 3 to 1.

The manager of BestHealth came up with the results shown in Table 3. Obviously the Canadian grant has been the most efficient method of raising funds, but BestHealth can no longer depend so much upon foreign generosity. The local church is the next most efficient, returning $\Sigma9$ for every $\Sigma1$ worth of time the manager must spend cultivating its minister, elders, and members. The greeting cards are doing well, and there are still some 2,000 cards still in stock from the first printing; when those cards are sold in the current year, the return will be more than 5 to 1.

Table 3: Ratio of revenue to costs in fundraising over 3 years*

	Revenue	Costs	Revenue/costs
Overseas donors			
International agencies	70,000	10,500	7
Foreign governments	638,000	10,500	61
Community-based campaigns			
Donation boxes	9,000	9,300	1
Income-generating activities			
Greeting cards	26,000	5,700	5
Religious organizations			
Local church	20,000	2,250	9

* excluding the value of volunteer time and in-kind contributions

Only the donation boxes have been disappointing. To date, revenue from the boxes has not caught up with total costs. That should turn around in the current year, however, because the cost of the boxes has almost all been paid and they should continue in use for several more years. The revenue from them will never be great, but the boxes place the organization's name and its needs in front of thousands of people in the community. The manager decides, at least for the time being, that making friends is as important as the small amount of money collected. He leaves the boxes where they are.

The value of the historical analysis
With this analysis, the manager of BestHealth now has the background to guide him, his board, his senior colleagues, and key volunteers in planning more active local fundraising. The results of the calculations suggest opportunities and may prevent a waste of money and time in unprofitable ventures. For example, the greeting cards look profitable. People seem to like them. The manager might ask himself and his colleagues, "Should we consider expanding card sales? If we do, will expenses rise because we will have to find places to sell them? Should we set up a system so that people can order

them by mail? To do that we would have to print a leaflet showing what the cards look like and mail it to people. We will almost certainly have to spend more money if we want to make a lot more money by selling greeting cards. Will it be worth it?" The donation boxes might eventually be withdrawn if a more effective use can be made of the volunteers' time that will also keep the organization in the public eye.

With the financial analysis of current fundraising in hand, you are now prepared to start asking questions about your own organization.

Were there special circumstances about some donations that distort the numbers? (Did you receive one large gift that will not be repeated? Did grant income alter dramatically?)

In view of the ratios of revenue to cost, which sources of funds should be given priority in the next few years? (But remember that some activities may have been undertaken more to make friends than to make money.)

How much can we count on renewed support from current donors?

What was the most satisfying part of our fundraising program?

What was the most frustrating part of our fundraising program?

Seeking "seed money" for fundraising

All business activities involve risk and require investments of time and money. The money for the initial investment may be difficult to obtain. Some donors, however, may be prepared to provide "seed money" to start a fundraising project. But they will first expect to see a business plan that includes a realistic budget and demonstrates how the organization will avoid possible risks.

They will want to assess the organization's financial state and management capabilities, to ensure that their seed money falls on fertile soil. They will want to see the general budget of the organization applying for seed money. They will also want to see a separate budget for the particular fundraising program they are being asked to support. That budget can be prepared using the same method as was used for the historical analysis – but this time looking forwards instead of backwards. The rigorous approach to cost and benefit in fundraising will help persuade potential donors that you know what you are doing.

Nevertheless, it may be hard to persuade a donor to invest in a fundraising program. The staff members of most donor agencies know next to nothing about fundraising. They may be able to evaluate your organization's service program, but few of them are able to judge the merits of a fundraising proposal. They may have spent their careers as project officers in development agencies without ever being exposed to the mechanics of a fundraising program. It is especially important therefore to be clear and persuasive when asking for seed money for fundraising projects.

General budgets were discussed in Book 1.

The Swadhar Foundation wants to emphasize simplicity of giving and simplicity of receiving. We want people to be informed. We now have 1,000 communities linked. There is a power in our way. People identify easily so the potential is great. We don't want to target just the middle class. We want support from the grassroots even if it will take longer than getting a grant from Ford or Rockefeller. That way we build a constituency and a relationship with the community.

GURINDER KAUR, SWADHAR FOUNDATION, INDIA

Closing gaps in the line

Before mounting a campaign, a good general ensures that his own defences are secure. An organization about to start a fundraising campaign must search for weaknesses in its positions. Financially, one of the most serious weaknesses is an appearance of wastefulness – indications that the organization could be more businesslike in its operations, or that it could reduce its expenditures. Outsiders who sense such weakness will expect the organization to change its ways before they are willing to support it.

Consider ways your organization has reduced its costs in the past. How can it save money in the next two years? Ask yourself:

Saving money is the quickest way to raise money for your program.

Ms Malvika, South Asian Fund Raising Group, India

Saving staff time
Could we get volunteers to do jobs we are now paying to get done?
Are we forming alliances for greater efficiency – sharing staff or functions?
Can we reduce the number of staff?
Can we eliminate a non-core program?
Do we ensure that no one wastes time?

Money saved is money earned.

Gurinder Kaur, Swadhar Foundation, India

Purchasing
Do we get discounts on what we buy because we are a voluntary organization?
Is there anything we could stop paying for that would not affect our work?
Are we asking for in-kind donations as often as possible?
Do we look for in-kind contributions that can be converted to cash?
Do we get several quotations when we have to buy something such as office equipment or insurance?
Do we order more copies of printed materials than we can use before they are out of date or damaged?
Do we use the barter system whenever possible? (In this system money is not exchanged for labour: labour is exchanged for labour. Local Exchange Trading Systems, as they are called, are especially useful where many people are unemployed.)

Overhead
Could we negotiate lower rent for our present space?
Could we lease cheaper space or share space without adding to transportation or other costs?
Can we reduce what we spend on memberships?
Do we have a program to encourage staff to save money?
Can we reduce what we are spending on travel?
Have we explored every way of saving on taxes, utilities, etc.?
Do we recycle paper etc. whenever possible?
How do we ensure that our money is always working for us? If donors permit it, do we ensure that money is always invested wisely and is never left in the bank earning a low rate of interest?
How do we monitor both large and small expenses?
How do we guard against bad debts?

At the same time, look for opportunities to gain income or other benefits that are being missed. Voluntary organizations can become so devoted to their mission of providing service that they fail to think about the real costs of their operations. They rarely attempt to recover any of these costs, even when it would be relatively easy. They give, without thinking, many kinds of services, advice, and products for which they could charge or, at least, ask for an in-kind favour in return. When we do a favour for an organization that is not one of our beneficiaries, how often do we say, "Please put me on your mailing list," or "Perhaps you would like to take out a membership in our organization," or "I assume that you will pay my expenses to come to speak at your meeting"? Think about all the work you do and how you might bring in some return for each of the components.

Inspecting your position

Finally, before thinking about specific goals for local fundraising, examine your organization and its people as it is now and as you and your colleagues hope it will become:

What are our dreams for our organization?

What are our fundraising dreams?

Is our work in the mainstream or do we fall outside the current areas of donor interest?

Are we committed to meeting specific local needs? Or do we aim to accommodate the ever-changing goals of donors?

If we have a written fundraising strategy, is it still relevant?

How well does our fundraising strategy reflect the current economic situation?

How are we facing up to the need to invest money in local fundraising?

Do we all truly believe we have the track record and stability to take on the job?

How does the staff feel about an investment in a fundraising program?

Will the staff support a fundraising program even if it means sacrifice on their part?

If the staff does not support such an investment, how can they be persuaded to do so?

Do we have a strong board that is committed to fundraising?

Do we have enough of the right kind of volunteers to give the support we will need?

What are the barriers to beginning fundraising that we cannot ignore?

Given that "right now" (rather than "later on when things improve") is always the best time to start fundraising, what conditions right now will make it easier for us to succeed?

In three years what percentage of the budget do we intend to raise from local sources:

    ☐ *5–10%* ☐ *10–25%* ☐ *25–50%* ☐ *50–75%* ☐ *75–100%*

In five years what percentage of the budget do we intend to raise from local sources:

    ☐ *5–10%* ☐ *10–25%* ☐ *25–50%* ☐ *50–75%* ☐ *75–100%*

Table 4: Fundraising activities - checklist of probable costs and revenue

	Year 1	Year 2	Year 3
Expenses			

Expenses
Management time
    ___ hours @ Σ ___
Other staff time
    Record keeping, issuing receipts
        ___ hours @ Σ ___
    Clerical
        ___ hours @ Σ ___
    Sales
        ___ hours @ Σ ___
Staff expenses
    Travel
    Meetings/entertainment
    Training
Consultants' fees
    ___ hours @ Σ ___
Rent and property maintenance
    In organization's offices
        ___ square metres/feet @ Σ ___
    In other space
        ___ square metres/feet @ Σ ___
Communications/fax/telephone/Internet
Other services (light, heat, water)
    In organization offices
    In other space
Manufacturing expenses (for goods to be sold)
Marketing expenses
    Publicity
    Advertising
Printed materials directly related to fundraising
    Stationery, including receipts
    Posters and other announcements
    Other (newsletter, fundraising brochure,
    annual report, etc.)
      writing/editing
      ___ hours @ Σ ___
      design and typesetting
      desktop composition (DTP) if in-house
      ___ hours @ Σ ___
      printing
      distribution/mailing/deliveries
Capital expenses
    Equipment, including computers
    Furniture

Table 4: Fundraising activities - checklist of probable costs and revenue *(continued)*

	Year 1	Year 2	Year 3
Expenses *(continued)*			
Volunteer expenses			
Time			
___ hours @ Σ ___			
Transportation			
Meetings/entertainment			
Honoraria			
Training			
Board/committee expenses			
Travel			
Meetings/entertainment			
Training			
Revenue			
Overseas donors			
International agencies			
Foundations			
Foreign governments			
Governments at home			
National			
State/province			
Regional			
Municipal			
Corporate program			
Sponsorships			
Donation boxes			
Partnerships			
In-kind donations			
Matching grants			
Community campaign			
Flag/tag days			
Donation boxes			
Product sales – greeting cards, etc.			
Sale of advertising			
Mailed requests for donations			
Annual memberships			
Fees paid by beneficiaries			
Special events			
Individual donations			
In-kind contributions			
Volunteer time			
Religious offerings			
Other donations			

Looking ahead

It's now time to begin mapping the fundraising strategy and building the organization to support it. Try to involve everyone possible in planning fundraising and income-generating activities. People who are part of the planning have a stake in its success. They understand the urgency of implementing the plans if they understand the financial situation. There is a danger, of course, that everyone will get so involved in the planning that nothing ever gets started. Deadlines are imperative.

Ease people's fears by starting small. Do only what is manageable. Unless you have been building credibility already, it would not be wise to expect much additional income immediately. Think about raising not more than 5 to 10 per cent of the total budget in the first two years of fundraising activity if you are starting without local fundraising experience. Don't expect to expand current fundraising capacities, if you have started already, by more than 5 per cent in the first year.

Eventually you will have to build a fundraising budget, showing anticipated revenue and the costs that are likely to be incurred in raising that money. The budget will show how much seed money you will need to invest in fundraising, what staff or space will have to be added, how many hours of volunteer work may be required, and what kinds of volunteers will be needed. As you make the fundraising budget, you will need to answer many specific questions about the future. At this stage, as you build the organization, you can do little more than think about all the possible sources of revenue and the categories of possible expenses. You can, however, start assembling the budget, filling in the numbers as information becomes available.

Every time you confront a problem, plan to build the remedy to the problem into your fundraising plan, in money or in time. If the board is not ready to take its proper responsibility for fundraising, how much time will be needed to strengthen the board? What ways can you raise money while you strengthen the board? If you need to recruit volunteers, how will you do it and how long will it take? What fundraising can you undertake in the meantime?

Table 4 is a checklist of probable costs and sources of revenue in fundraising. It is intended only as a guide. You will not use every line of it in the beginning, or perhaps ever. You may have only one fundraising activity at the beginning. You may have some additional costs or sources of revenue that are not included. The checklist should, however, help you think about building a budget based on the detailed plan for fundraising and income generation that you and your staff members, board members, and volunteers will create.

The checklist should be used in two ways. First, use it to plan the costs of each individual fundraising activity, whether it is the sale of merchandise or a special event or a direct mail campaign. Only a few of the lines will probably be needed at this stage. Next, use it to gather together all the costs of fundraising in a total fundraising budget. To do that, include all the costs you have estimated for individual activities. Add to them all the additional costs of fundraising that are not tied directly to a single activity.

You may find, for example, that you have listed printing needs for several activities; gather them together in a single total. You may also need printed books of receipts that can be used for many activities but are not tied to any single one of them.

Do not worry about being too precise in your estimates of time and money at this early stage. What you are trying to do is get a picture of the probable cost of possible fundraising activities and the probable revenue that will come from them. You may well find that some ideas must be discarded at an early stage because they are too expensive in time and cash, either because the return is unlikely to be great enough or because the resources simply are not available. Other ideas will seem more financially promising and should be pursued further.

One final important piece of advice. In looking ahead there are two important rules:

1 Be generous in predicting costs of time and money. Fundraising activities will almost always require more time than you expect. There will often be unexpected costs as well. It's a good idea to budget as if everything will take at least twice as long and cost twice as much as you think it will.

2 Be cautious in predicting revenue. Grant applications get turned down; attendance at events may be less than expected; the return from a direct mail campaign may be disappointing.

Following these two rules may make it more difficult to predict a highly successful fundraising campaign. But it will prevent unpleasant surprises. And if your planning is solid, and cautious, the money should come in.

2 Setting up the campaign headquarters

Your budget for fundraising will have to include the costs of setting up the fundraising program. Will you be able to make do with what you already have? Will you need a new desk? A filing cabinet? A new computer or a better computer printer? Will existing staff do the accounting? Will the board, volunteers, and the executive director be responsible for the planning, administration, and routine management involved in raising money? Or will another staff person be needed? How much will costs be likely to rise as a result of inflation during the life of the plan, say, over three years?

If it is difficult to predict the rate of inflation two or three years in advance – and it normally is difficult – it is reasonable to ignore inflation in making the initial plan. In other words, costs may be projected at current rates over the life of the plan. But if that approach is followed, it is essential to account for inflation each year in setting revised annual targets and budgets for fundraising. Otherwise, even if a target is met, an increase in donations that you sought to fund new programs may be eaten up by the rising costs of raising the money.

Personal contact at the office

The first impression many people will have of your organization will be when they visit your office and/or project, write a letter to your organization, or telephone your office. What impression will they receive?

- Is the message on your answering machine friendly and helpful?
- If your location is hard to find, do you have a map that you can send people before they visit so they will not arrive late and frustrated?
- Do you have a clear, attractive sign in front of your site and at all projects?
- Can people who are disabled visit your location easily?
- What immediate impression is presented to visitors? Is your office clean and tidy? Is it cheerful? Are your staff neatly dressed, clean, and polite? Do they show an immediate interest in visitors?
- Do you have a visitor's book where people can write their names and addresses? Are guests encouraged to include comments about their interest in or support of your organization?
- Have you trained your staff, board, and other volunteers who answer calls and letters and greet visitors to be friendly and helpful?
- Do these people always have up-to-date information about the organization?

- Can they talk easily and accurately about the organization?
- Do they know how to reach you if you are not present?
- Is correspondence answered promptly? Does it have all the qualities of effective print communication outlined in Chapters 12 and 16?

Every professional fundraiser has a story to tell about a large donation that was lost because no one answered the telephone, or appeared interested in the donor, or was able to answer questions. These things happen because staff and volunteers are human and humans are imperfect. But it is possible to guard against this kind of failure. It takes planning and training.

Your staff, board, and volunteers represent your organization. Every one of them does. Explain to them how important it is to represent it well. Give them the information they need to do so. Train them in business etiquette. It will pay off.

Someone I know, who was a staff member of an organization but not a fundraiser, once spent an hour talking to a man who did not look impressive, who never identified himself fully, but who asked interesting questions. A week later, the organization received a gift of two thousand dollars. That was money that could so easily have been lost if the staff member had been less polite or less patient.

Don't lose donations through indifference. Make the most of personal contact with anyone who approaches your organization. After all, they are already showing interest in your work.

What else will you need?

The amount of furniture, the type of equipment, and the variety of services you will need will depend on the type of fundraising program you plan. If you are distributing donation boxes to every house or to many businesses in your community, you will have to consider the needs of the people doing the delivering and collecting. They will not need much furniture, but you may need to pay the costs of their transportation and meals while they are distributing boxes. If you are mailing lots of letters, you may need a place for people to fill and address envelopes. Consider the following possible requirements:

- space for volunteers to do their work and to keep work materials and their own belongings safely
- one or more desks, with chairs for workers and any visitors
- a computer, printer, calculating machine, and other equipment
- filing cabinets and chests that will provide convenient, secure, dry, fireproof storage for records, donor files, fundraising materials, and products for sale
- access to an inexpensive photocopier
- a telephone
- a good commercial printer, not too far away
- a quiet place to meet with board members, donors, and others
- a display area for information
- a display and/or sales area for products for sale
- a secure place for visitors to park vehicles

Building credibility

Careful records, audited annually, are a sign to board members, volunteers, donors, potential donors, auditors, bank managers – anyone interested – that your organization is responsible and trustworthy. In other words, that it is transparent and credible.

"Transparency" does not mean the records must be open to anyone who wants to see them. You may need to restrict access for reasons of security and confidentiality. You can't afford to have records mixed up, damaged, or mislaid. Nor can you afford to annoy any donors who do not want the size of their donations known. Transparency does mean opening the records to those who have good reason to want to confirm your credibility.

The value of records for fundraising

Good records contribute to good planning. Good planning is essential for success. A winning general depends on intelligence reports. In a fundraising campaign, your records are your intelligence information.

I was recently at a fundraising committee meeting for our local theatre. One member had been phoned by a bank manager, asking for a letter that would allow him to release the donation promised by the bank for the year. The bank had promised a donation annually for three years but there was no written record of the request or the commitment that anyone knew about. If the bank manager had not phoned, the pledge might have been forgotten. Even if there had been a record, finding it would have been difficult. The records of the fundraising campaign were in the homes of three different people. There was no filing cabinet in the small office that had space for fundraising material. That evening the committee, all volunteers, decided the fundraising history was important and agreed to buy a filing cabinet.

Keeping detailed records

Most organizations that start fundraising programs cannot imagine the amount of information they will accumulate, even in the first two years. Their staff members may be accustomed to receiving occasional large cheques from foreign donors and paying expenses by cheque or cash. But they have never before had to receive and account for dozens, possibly hundreds of donations of relatively small amounts of cash. Nor are the systems they use organized to record all the information needed for effective fundraising.

Most organizations are accustomed to a simple method of bookkeeping – a ledger very much like a bank account book. At first, it is tempting to continue to keep the records simple, perhaps a drawer of cards, or a computer list, of donors with the date money was received and the amount. Organizations selling merchandise may keep a similar record of customers – at least, of customers buying large quantities.

Keeping systems simple always seems like a good idea. In fundraising, however, some complexity is necessary if the records are to do their job. This record keeping takes time and training. Good records are essential for four reasons:

1 to ensure honesty

2 to track the cost of fundraising and the revenue

3 to establish credibility

4 to plan future fundraising

Detailed records cannot guarantee that all money given is actually received by the organization, but they can go a long way towards achieving that goal.

What information about potential donors, actual donors, donations, purchases, and grants should you record? You will need to know as much as you can of the following information about each donor:

- his or her name, address, and phone number
- the size of the gift
- when the gift was given
- when the thank-you letter and receipt were sent
- how the gift came about (for example, the newspaper advertisement to which the donor responded, the mailing list used, the religious organization that asked its members to give, the volunteer or board member who secured the donation)
- the donor's motivation, if known
- the purpose for which the gift was given
- for individual donors: whatever special information you can gather about the person, such as family, religion, occupation, business, social, and family connections, political interests, other special interests
- for corporate or government donors: details of their interests, donation policies, names and personal information about decision-makers and others who might influence the decision-makers
- a record of all significant meetings with the donor, including what was promised or requested
- what sort of follow-up is needed, by whom, and when; for example, you may want to invite the donor to visit the office or a project.

Once, when I was raising funds for a school, I drove past the homes of the students to see how large the houses were, how well they were maintained, and what kind of car the family owned. My driving around did not tell me whether a family could give a big donation to the school, only whether the family could likely make a big donation to *some* organization. My job was to commit the family to supporting my cause, the school. It is always useful to have some idea of what a potential donor can afford before asking for a donation, and then to ask for that amount of money or for support for a project in a certain range.

The more personal information you have, the more accurately you can estimate what is appropriate. With good records you can also be more persuasive. If you can say, for example, that some of the business associates or fellow believers of a potential donor have already contributed money, you will have improved your chances of getting a donation. But you will not be able to do that without good records of donors and personal information about that particular potential donor. (In general, you must say only that the other people have made donations, never how much they gave. That is confidential information unless the donor has agreed that it may be publicized.) Good records also allow you to spot trends over several years. Is support coming from young or older people, or more from one religious group than another?

Once a file has been opened on a donor or potential donor, every donation and change in personal information should be recorded. Brief accounts of meetings with potential and actual donors should be included. The names of spouses and children should be kept on file so they can be mentioned when it is appropriate. (That is a trick good politicians know. Fundraisers often forget it.)

Every donation should be recorded, with the date of receipt, the name of the donor, and the amount received. Every pledge should be acknowledged in writing and entries made to ensure the promise is kept. Every time merchandise is sold a record should be made of the item, the quantity sold, and the amount received. Every time money is collected from a donation box, a record should be made immediately of the amount, the date, and the place where the box is held. (See Book 3, Chapter 10 on donation boxes.)

It is equally important to issue receipts promptly in every case – to donors, to customers, to the merchants or families holding the donation boxes. Keep duplicates of all receipts issued. In most countries, printed books of receipts, with carbon paper and duplicate sheets, are available in stationery shops. An organization that sells merchandise can use the forms commonly used by merchants who give customers one copy of a bill of sale and keep a second copy for themselves.

At the organization's office, the bookkeeper should enter the total amount received each day in a general ledger under the appropriate heading (donations, sale of cards, etc.). The same ledger should be used to record bank deposits of cash, cheques, and money orders.

At least two people should be involved in keeping records. One or more people should be responsible for collecting and receiving money. A third person should check the amount of money against the record the first two have made in the receipt books, and deposit the money in the bank. If money is being received by mail, the third person may issue the receipts; when the exchange is face-to-face, it is simplest to have the receipt issued immediately by the person who receives the money. Using this system does not mean you think people are dishonest; it provides protection for everyone involved.

The organization's auditor will look each year at how money is handled and may suggest, or insist on, improvements. It's a good idea to talk to an accountant before starting fundraising, to get detailed advice about setting

Recording revenue

To raise money, a British organization ran a shop that sold used clothing and household articles. The cash from the sales was recorded in a cash register, and the money was kept in a box or a drawer in the shop until it was turned over each night to the organization's bookkeeper. At the end of one year, the manager of the store was puzzled: the amount of money recorded by the bookkeeper was less than expected. The manager checked her cash register tapes and found that in fact more cash had been received than was shown in the bookkeeper's records. The staff member who carried the money to the bookkeeper did not bring with it a cash register total of sales. He brought only a note of the total amount and the money. Did the person who carried the money keep some of it? Did the bookkeeper keep some of it? Did the manager, in fact, keep some of it? No one really knew where the money had gone. No blame could be attached but the organization had lost thousands of pounds.

up a secure system for receiving, recording, and depositing donations and other revenue as well as for giving receipts.

Tracking costs

You also need to know what your fundraising program is costing you.

In the past, writing grant applications may have taken a great deal of time. However, you may never have counted the time and therefore the cost to the organization. It was just part of the job.

Raising funds locally is likely to be more expensive than getting grants, especially if you use the mail or paid advertising. Keep track of out-of-pocket expenses for items such as printing letters and fundraising brochures, postage stamps, advertising, and transportation to meetings. And count the cost of the time the manager and other staff members spend in fundraising. When I was running a development agency I spent half my time on fundraising. So half my salary was counted as a cost of fundraising.

Charities everywhere like to brag about how little money they spend on administration and how much they have left to spend on their programs. The truth is, many organizations don't spend nearly enough money on administration, and errors and omissions are the result. Try to find a balance. Once you start fundraising, you will have another set of administrative expenses, however tiny, to fit into your budget. You will have to begin to consider what costs should be included in your fundraising budget, which should be assigned to other lines in your administration budget, and which can be assigned to programs. The maximum amount that you can legitimately spend on administration, including fundraising, may be dictated by your donors or by regulations in your country.

If you have reliable electricity and some money, keeping records of donations is best done on a computer.

Using computers

Even with only a few donors, it will not be long before you have a large pile of cards or a large file in your computer. Eventually, you will have to separate the people and organizations that give large donations (with whom you will deal individually and preferably face-to-face), and the larger number of people who give smaller donations. You may want to keep records of them as part of a group – people who bought tickets to the last orchid show or donated to the organization through their church.

If you have reliable electricity and some money, managing this information is best done on a computer. You may develop your own system or use any of dozens of excellent software programs for fundraising. Make a list of the information you need to keep and store (see the list in a previous section). Estimate the number of individual records you will want to store. Consider whether you also want to manage information about events, what kinds of reports the board wants, and whether business activities will be included. Then talk to other organizations about whether people are happy with the system they are using. Talk to local computer experts about programs that might best meet your needs. Ask questions on a listserv if you have access to e-mail. Learn about the reputation of the software manufacturer. Check whether training, service, good manuals and warranties are

available. Buy carefully.

Once you have bought a program, be prepared to invest time and money in training the people who will run it. Expect it to take several days of training and several weeks of practice. Allow time to transfer the old records to the new system.

3 What are other organizations doing?

Successful fundraisers are always willing to try out a new idea or use an established technique in a new and imaginative way. In countries where few organizations are raising money locally, the opportunities for experiment and novelty are many. You can ignore what anyone is doing and go your own way. Or, you can draw all the possible lessons from the management, communications, and fundraising practices of other agencies and then go your own way.

In doing research for these books, I found many organizations unwilling to say much about the details of their fundraising activities in case they might be imitated. In Singapore, for instance, competition for funds is fierce. A fundraiser for a children's organization said, "It can get really ugly. I never talk to anyone here about fundraising." Where competition is rough you may need to do a bit of clever detective work. Recruit staff, friends, and family to watch for publications, letters, events, and other fundraising practices that you should know about.

Book 1 describes how an organization can find out quickly how it sees itself and how other people think of it. Armed with that knowledge, an organization can develop its own style of fundraising. However, that style will not be formed in an instant. Just as when a person chooses clothing, an organization may take a while to find what is suitable, attractive, and comfortable. The style may be quite personal, reflecting the tastes and intuitions of the leaders, as much as it reflects logical and businesslike decisions. Every organization has a personality. Each organization's personality is original, unique. Let it show.

A few years ago I was writing eight to ten fundraising letters a year. Hundreds, sometimes thousands, of each were mailed to current or potential donors. At that time, the fashion in fundraising was to write letters that were three or four pages long. Fundraisers believed that long letters drew in more money than short ones. But I knew I could never be bothered reading to the end of the many long appeal letters I received at home.

Some of those letters wanted money for cancer research, others wanted it to relieve famine, still others to teach people to read. No matter what the cause, all the letters looked much the same to me. All the paragraphs were only one or two sentences long, with many underlined single words and sentences. To me, short paragraphs with constant underlining are hard to read. I wondered whether there was a single giant computer cranking out all those letters to be printed on a single giant press.

The letters I wrote did not follow the fashion, but I thought they suited the organization's style. They were short and they were simple. They looked and read like a letter anyone might write to a friend or colleague. I counted on the impact of the words themselves. That was appropriate, because plain words – radio scripts – were our organization's business. Trendy looks were not important to us. We had always counted on attractive, simple presentation to get attention.

Was I right or wrong? Donors seemed to like the letters. Our response rate was usually higher than that of other organizations in the same year.

On the alert for good ideas

Effective fundraisers are always on the alert for new ideas that can be adapted for use in their own organizations. Possibilities are all around us. It's only a matter of keeping your eyes and ears open and your mind receptive. What are people talking about? What are other agencies doing? Which ones seem to be attracting new friends? Which ones seem to be successful in fundraising? What are the secrets of their success?

As you answer the questions that follow, try to analyse what others are doing. Reject any techniques that do not suit the personality and style of your own organization, no matter how successful they may be elsewhere. Think about how you can put the imprint of your organization on the successful techniques that are appropriate and make them your own.

What are people talking about?
When fundraising is talked about at meetings of civil society organizations, what have you learned that you can apply in your own organization?
- If you have attended local fundraising training courses, what did you hear from the presenters that could be useful?
- What did you hear from the audience that could be useful?
- What can you learn from the fundraising mistakes you hear about?
- What can you learn from the fundraising successes you hear about?
- Do you want to know more about what fundraising people are talking about? How can you arrange that?

Who is making new friends for their organization? How are they doing it?
- What successful publications – annual reports, newsletters, brochures, letters – are coming from other organizations? What lessons can you learn from them?
- Which organizations are getting media coverage of their organization and its fundraising activities? In what media? How do you think it was arranged? What can you learn?
- Who is holding events in local hotels, meeting rooms, and restaurants? What kind of events? Who is attending? Should you be attracting the same people?
- What organizations similar to yours seem to have strong boards and advisers with good community representation? What makes them strong? How do you think the people in them were secured?

- How are other groups finding and using volunteers? What can you learn?

Who is good at fundraising?
- How successful have agencies similar to yours been in attracting support from each of the groups listed below? What strategies and techniques have they used in each case? (Mailings? personal solicitation? special events? selling services? selling merchandise? other?)
  Members
  Individuals
  Corporations
  Local foundations
  Service clubs
  Religious groups
  Local governments
  Purchasers of services or goods
  Other groups
- What fundraising activities of other agencies might we want to adapt for our organization?
- Have these strategies been used long enough – possibly for several years – to be judged for their success?
- What are other organizations saying they want money for? Which causes seem to be fashionable at the moment? Are we in or out of fashion? Can we afford to follow another line or should we adapt our message to meet the current interests of potential donors?
- What words are organizations similar to ours using in their fundraising materials? What are they saying in their fundraising letters and brochures?
- Are other organizations talking about donations to them as an investment in the community, or are they talking only about fundraising?
- What fundraising ideas might we try that have not yet been used in this community?
- If we have read books about fundraising, what new ideas for possible programs have we discovered?

4 The role of the leader

The big question is why to raise funds, not just how. It is a question of reaching out to people who have more to give, to give them an opportunity to build society.

NGOs need more confidence. We are ashamed of what we do. It feels like begging. We need to always think of the why – the number of poor people in a village, for instance.

You need to learn to talk your story well.

NGO people must be an example. They should not have big cars and fancy offices.

DANILO SONGCO, CODE-NGO, THE PHILIPPINES

An organization undergoes a major change when it starts or greatly expands its efforts to raise funds locally. Leadership during this transition is essential. The leader must not only encourage others to follow into the new activity; he or she must persuade them that they *want* to be part of it. People will not follow where they do not want to go.

Every successful voluntary organization has a leader. Someone who does more than organize and administer. Someone who inspires. Many organizations have no paid staff members and depend entirely on volunteers for administration and program work; volunteers also raise whatever money is needed. When a full-time manager has been appointed, volunteers tend to look to that person to take the lead in fundraising. Eventually fundraising leadership may move to someone else – perhaps the chairman of the board as he or she gains experience in the field, or some other person who is highly respected by the group.

Most voluntary organizations have neither quite enough money nor quite enough time to achieve all the good that they can see needs to be done. A good leader encourages others, whether they are paid staff or volunteers, to overcome these twin obstacles. When extra effort must be put into local fundraising, these leadership skills become increasingly important. The manager must take time from a concern for core programs to inform, motivate, and lead fundraising efforts. To achieve success, a senior manager should:

- have a strong, clear vision of the purpose of the organization
- communicate that vision frequently and boldly to keep people inspired
- understand clearly which activity is the reason for the organization's existence and which activities only provide support (see Book 1, Chapters 11–13 on long-term planning)
- be specific about the objectives of the program and establish priorities
- involve people in planning any changes that will affect them
- build all the parts of the organization into one team

- always act ethically
- be ready to take bold action, to try something new
- be determined to succeed
- be well organized
- think always of what will keep people motivated
- act on fact, not opinion, as much as possible
- find and use professional advisers
- develop a strong board
- attract all the good volunteers required

Being a good leader takes experience and hard work. If necessary, managers should be prepared to ask for training or for help from other, more experienced managers. In the next few pages, we will consider some of the difficulties that beset the leaders of voluntary organizations. Board members and volunteers who have managed businesses themselves can be important allies to a manager who faces these problems.

Looking credible to the local community

Since the 1960s, many organizations have not had to account for their money except to their own board and to foreign donors – sometimes only one or two, sometimes a dozen. Nearly all their money has come from those donors. Very few donors have had local offices in the countries where the organizations work, and some with local offices have been closing them. Organizations have typically had no regular direct contact with major donors. Representatives visited infrequently, and often only for a short meeting and a picture-taking session.

All this changes with local fundraising. The potential donors are part of the community. If they do not actually live or work in the place where the organization is active, they live in the same country. They are close at hand; the organization is always being observed. If there are signs of waste, that will become known. If the organization appears to have enough money already, whether or not it does, people will be reluctant to give it more. Salaries and benefits, especially of the senior manager, come under the microscope. In many developing countries, local people resent the apparent wealth that can accompany international grants. They see the big white vans that are bought with the grants, and the offices in large houses in leafy suburbs. But as long as they are not themselves being asked to support these expenses, they feel detached; it is not their money that is being spent. When they are asked for money to maintain an organization's program, they are far more concerned.

Good managers therefore must always try to find a balance between their desire for the highest quality in their programs and the need to keep costs low. As long as grants came from outside the community, these two goals may not have been in conflict. Donor agencies have developed detailed systems to evaluate the performance of an organization on the basis of its results rather than its appearance. If the evaluations are done well, these donors recognize success (or failure). They recognize that success is a result of skilled management – either volunteer or staff – and may encourage the manager to develop those skills further. (Even large agencies with complex evaluation systems are not entirely objective, however. Their decisions also can be influenced by an appearance of extravagance. One executive director I know was seen driving a luxury car, lent him for several weeks while a friend was out of town. The executive director felt that his major funder, an international agency with offices in the same city, never had the same enthusiasm for his organization after that.)

A manager must, in the first place, appear credible to board members or to whatever group oversees or advises the manager. (Board operations are discussed in the next chapters.) It is not enough that board members respect the manager's abilities. With the decline in foreign funding, they are likely to have become much more involved in the finances of the organization than before. They will want to review all salaries carefully. So will donors. Questions will be asked.

On the board to which I reported for seven years, some members had never worked for a living and some had never had a salary as high as mine. They probably thought I was overpaid. Other members who were business executives thought my salary was shockingly low. At one annual meeting, a donor asked about the salaries of the staff. The chairman refused to give numbers because, he said, he was embarrassed that the salaries were so low. The chairman's firm statement satisfied the donor, at least for the moment. Such an answer would never have been credible if it had come from a staff member rather than a volunteer.

ILLUSTRATION: MARK LITZLER

LITZLER

"The ideal fundraising executive will know a little bit about estate planning, tax law, marketing, and hypnotism."

What would the donor have thought if the chairman had, in fact, given numbers? Would he have thought the salaries were too low or too high? The answer would likely have been affected by the donor's own salary. The donor wanted it both ways. The donor wanted to know that the organization was well managed, but he was clearly concerned that we were all overpaid. In my experience, most donors think exactly that way. They want the managers of voluntary agencies to be efficient and professional but, at the same time, they want the organizations to operate on a shoestring so that most of the money goes to the program.

A manager of a small non-profit organization must excel to survive, but must do so almost secretly. The manager must often play down publicly an investment in professional management for fear of looking like a big spender. I used to hesitate to talk to donors about the visits I and other staff members made to beneficiaries and potential partners in other countries, for fear of making the organization seem rich. Yet it was essential to the success of our program to see how recipients used the information we provided and to understand the conditions in the countries we served. We had to travel.

Donors scrutinize annual reports to see how much is spent in areas such as travel and administration. They stop giving if they suspect the amounts are too high, even when they have no basis for an informed judgement.

Organizations are praised when they keep their administrative costs low. That can mean not enough training, low salaries, difficult working conditions, and perhaps poor morale. In many cases, low administrative costs should not be a source of pride. They may be too low for truly effective operation.

One of the challenges facing the manager is to motivate other staff members in the face of these difficulties. Another is to convince board members and potential donors that the organization is truly efficient. A third, if justified, is to convince the same people that the organization will be even more efficient if more money is invested in developing the organization's own human resources – its staff and volunteers.

Avoiding the trap of just trying to break even

An organization that has depended on overseas or government grants, or on earned income from an endowment, can generally predict income and expenses with reasonable accuracy for several years ahead. Granting agencies often give advance warning of probable cuts. Interest rates may rise unexpectedly, but they do not often fall rapidly or without warning.

As the dependence on local giving increases from almost zero, it is still easy to predict expenses. Most continue as before. With careful planning, even the costs of new local fundraising can be predicted. It is far more difficult to predict the *income* from fundraising, because the organization still lacks experience and historical records.

Probably the organization has always tried to break even – that is, it has tried to ensure each year that its expenses are no greater than its income. Perhaps it has even tried regularly to have some money left over at the end of the year, to build a reserve fund for emergencies. Once an organization becomes dependent on local fundraising, however, its income becomes more uncertain each year; the goal of breaking even grows correspondingly more difficult.

A non-profit organization has a bottom line that is just as real as the bottom line of any corporation. But breaking even is more difficult than trying to make a profit. If a budget is built to break even, any disappointment is serious. If a corporation aiming at a 10 per cent profit earns 4 per cent less than budgeted, it still has a 6 per cent profit – not what was wanted but at least it remains in the black. If a non-profit organization that has planned to break even has unforeseen expenses or less revenue than expected, it will be inevitably in the red. Hence it is important to budget conservatively – anticipating that expenses will be slightly higher and revenues lower than first imagined, and planning to end up with a little more revenue than expenditures to permit flexibility.

Boards and donors may question this kind of conservative budgeting. They will be eager to slash at any "fat" they imagine may be in the numbers. The manager must be able to convince them the budget is realistic – prudent, not extravagant.

Organizations that are trapped in a rigidly break-even budget find it difficult to adapt to changing conditions. In those with small budgets, managers cannot afford to make even one mistake. They become afraid to experiment, to branch out in new directions. They may want, for example, to diversify their fundraising programs to minimize the risk of loss. But they do not have the money to do it, or the experience and knowledge that might convince their boards to make the effort. They may be forced by policies and poverty to avoid taking the calculated risks that could bring success later on. The shortsightedness of such policies is recognized by Peter Drucker, one of the most famous management experts in the world. It is not recognized by the boards of most voluntary organizations.

For far too many boards of directors, a good manager is one who has not overspent or underspent the budget by more than 5 per cent at the end of the year. These boards do not recognize the damage to the program caused by not having enough money to do enough work and do it well. The leader is trapped. If the only way he or she can convince the board that the organization needs to raise more revenue is to run a deficit, and a deficit appears, then it's likely the board will simply decide the manager is incompetent. On the other hand, if there is no innovation and the funds are not completely spent at the end of the year, the organization is seen as financially secure, the manager is considered competent, and everyone relaxes. The board asks: "Why do we need to start fundraising? We broke even last year."

This dilemma can be resolved only if the leader talks freely to the board about possibilities and problems and does not try to appear superhuman, on top of every situation, with the answer to every question. Boards must be made clearly aware of the limitations imposed by lack of funds – that so much more service could be given with even a little more money. They must be convinced that additional revenue will be well spent, and will produce benefits that will repay the effort of raising funds. They must recognize that the bottom line is not the only important line in the budget.

Maintaining enthusiasm

Worrying every day about money is exhausting. Managers spend much of their time wondering whether the budget can be met, whether a grant will be approved, whether a fundraising campaign will be successful, whether bills will be higher than expected. Even if money has come in as planned during the first half of the year, what will happen during the next six months? It is hard to keep smiling. You can never forget you have to raise money to deliver your program and pay the salaries on which your staff and their families depend. Yet you want always to seem confident and reassuring to your staff and to the people you hope will give your organization their time and money.

A staff member of a rural development agency in south India told me the foreign grant on which his organization depended would be cancelled in two years. He said, "Some of us have been saying for 20 years that we will have to stand on our own two feet. But I am not the manager; I am only an employee. It is a crisis for the organization because many of the staff are older and will not get other jobs." Junior staff members had been meeting about the crisis, which was not even acknowledged by the leadership. The leaders needed to act before the downward slide was irreversible. They needed to discuss the situation with all the staff openly, consider everyone's ideas about fundraising, reduce the program if necessary, and give responsibility to a small group of people to get on with fundraising. Because the organization had ignored what was happening in the world beyond its doors, it was forced to launch fundraising programs without having ever attempted to build its credibility. In such circumstances, it is hard to maintain enthusiasm. Managers of voluntary organizations get tired, depressed, burned out, even when fundraising has been carefully planned and carried out. Few can keep up the interest and energy level of their first years in the job. Here are some ways to combat fatigue and discouragement.

- Cut your program before you get into financial difficulties. Nothing causes sleepless nights more than feeling the organization slipping behind financially but doing nothing about it except worrying. A small retreat is not the end of the world. Chances are that you will be able to recover the lost ground next year or the year after.
- Remind yourself that if you ask enough people for money, you will bring in enough money to meet a sensible goal.
- Keep your sense of humour. Take a few minutes every day to share something funny with people around you.
- Take regular daily breaks from your work.
- Don't skip holidays.
- Take advantage of opportunities for professional development.
- Share your problems with colleagues.
- Delegate jobs you know you can do better than anyone else, jobs you want to keep for yourself. The jobs may not get done quite as well or as quickly, but they will get done – and you will have time to move on to more important activities.
- Finish at least one thing each day that you do not want to do.
- Set realistic goals.
- If one fundraising activity is likely to bring in more money than several others, focus your time and attention there. Forget the other activities or let someone else do them. You cannot do everything.
- Take pleasure in small victories.

Measuring your fundraising success
You will have done a great job if at the end of a fundraising activity:
- the money you wanted to raise is actually raised
- the board and volunteers congratulate each other on the wonderful job they did
- staff members recognize that they also performed well, mostly behind the scenes.

5 The role of the board

A board should be composed to ensure smooth functioning without too much conflict, but diverse enough in terms of gender, age, and disadvantaged communities to reflect different interests. Members need to have expertise in fundraising, auditing, and publicity. Board members have a role to play in raising funds for the organization through personal reputation and contacts.

Pushpa Sundar, Indian Centre for Philanthropy

As we have seen, voluntary organizations may expect international and government funding to be reduced, making them increasingly dependent on their own efforts to raise funds from other sources – most of them local. In these circumstances, an organization's most important resource will be its board, which is responsible for the financial stability of the organization as well as its policies and programs. But setting up a board that is both willing and able to attract significant local investment and funding is not an easy matter. Even the idea may be a surprise: I have heard an experienced Indian fundraising consultant profess astonishment at the idea of board members having responsibility for fundraising.

A strong board committed to raising money is essential to fundraising success. Yet most boards are slow to adapt to the changing state of affairs. Many are accustomed to an environment in which voluntary organizations existed because support came from outside. They are accustomed to receiving grants from international donor agencies and governments. When necessary, board members helped staff, or took the initiative themselves, in writing to these established donors and playing host to their representatives. They did not call this fundraising; it was "getting grants" and it conferred prestige, especially if overseas visits were involved. In fact, it was fundraising by another name. It just happened to be directed to a few outside sources; it was not visible in the community, nor did it involve the community deeply.

As reliance on local funding increases, new demands will be placed on boards that have been working smoothly, carrying out limited responsibilities to everyone's satisfaction. Few are likely to act decisively at the first signs of financial trouble. By the time they are ready to act, a looming problem may have become a financial crisis. At that point, the board may be paralyzed by arguments about who is responsible for finding the necessary extra money.

When other sources of revenue dry up, many boards look first to government, usually with limited success: governments these days are cash-strapped too. Gradually, board members may come to recognize they must undertake a more direct role in ensuring that the organization survives. They

34

may begin by recognizing the need for local fundraising and for income-generating projects. Then they may come to realize that they need to give their own money or their company's money, and that they must ask others for personal and corporate donations. Many board members will resist such an active role in fundraising. If they do, the organization for which they have accepted responsibility is likely to wither and die.

With encouragement, boards can change their roles. An adviser to a Caribbean voluntary agency described the evolution in his organization:

Our board is several years old. Boards have a tough time in Haiti. The original board members thought they might get paid or get jobs. So we had to start fresh with people who could be visionary and make good decisions.

At first we wanted the seven members just to get to know the program. They are professional people. Only one is a businessperson. We never mentioned fundraising when we asked them to serve. We assumed that board members would have names we could use for fundraising and that we could use their influence. We did not think they would actually solicit. They are very busy. It is hard to get them to come to meetings.

It is hard to get the "poorest of the poor" on boards. [And then] they may not have the capacity to choose the right people [to be members] and they don't know a pool of people from which to choose. We had to draw in outside people whom the poor people did not know.

We meet every two months for a half a day on a weekend. We also had a week-long leadership seminar. Board members gave up a week of their holidays. It was exciting.

We are trying to get financial support from the Haitian community outside the country, primarily in the United States, and in particular in the Miami area which is only a two-hour plane ride away. We got a grant to send some board members to Honduras to learn about microcredit. They stopped in Miami for a week to talk to churches who might support us. Each year we should do something exciting like that. Probably we can find funding.

> *In Thailand, organizations are not asking for money directly. They feel like beggars. We need to train people to ask for money naturally. Asking directly is the best approach. Start small. Get ten people on the board to write to their friends. Sounds good but no NGO has the capacity to get the board to do this. You need a staff person to motivate them, to get the lists together, and to do the letter.*
>
> CHANIDA CHANYAPATE BAMFORD, FOCUS ON THE GLOBAL SOUTH, THAILAND

Here is another example of board members tackling a funding crisis as reported in the *Chronicle of Philanthropy*. A women's organization found its board members reluctant to raise money. "They are all working women, and they did not come on this board to raise funds," said the director. "They came on to work with the programs, to do policy, and they thought that the role of fundraising was up to the executive director." To ease members into fundraising, the director persuaded them to give small parties at their homes and then make the case for supporting the organization to their guests. The charity went from 120 to 800 donors in two years.

Why not let the executive director and the staff do the fundraising?

When an organization's income is falling or standing still, the board may tell the manager: "Go out and raise some money!" Board members don't offer to help, and often are offended if the manager asks them for help.

The debate about whether staff should do the fundraising has gone on for years. Some people say that a highly motivated, well-trained staff can run a successful fundraising program. They say that it is not worth the time and effort it takes to turn board members into donors or fundraisers. They say that staff members should use that time and effort to approach outside donors to bring in money.

I have observed and tried fundraising both ways – relying on staff and on board members supported by staff. In every instance, the success of the staff was limited if the board did not get involved. The staff of an organization can raise money successfully. But it alone will not come close to raising all the money that could be raised over a number of years with active board support. Staff members may make a huge effort to raise local funds, but they will find sustaining that effort difficult in the long run. It is rare for an organization to rise above its board.

It is important to persuade board members, and to persuade them to enlist other volunteers to raise money, because with more people much more can be done. With active board members and a group of other volunteers, it will be possible to reach much further into the community than if all the fundraising is done by staff. The campaign will have a strong, broad base of workers, rich and poor, of different races and religions, from a range of occupations, locations, and political positions. Without all these volunteers, the staff is the hub of a wheel that is missing its spokes.

I know this from painful personal experience. In seven years of running a development agency, I failed to stimulate my board to raise funds in a major way. Successive chairmen believed the board was there to govern, not to ensure the financial health of the organization through their efforts. Board members did make personal contributions because the chairman wrote to each member every year. And several members did see themselves as fundraisers; they attracted modest support by writing letters to friends. At the same time, I was spending half my working life desperately hunting for money. I realized the extent of the board's failure, and my own, one day during a board meeting, when one of the members told us about the success of a fundraising campaign at her church. She was thrilled at the size and number of contributions she had obtained by calling on people. Her own gift to our organization was modest and she never raised any money for our work. Had she put the same effort into raising money for our agency as she had for her church, and if other board members had followed her example, the agency would have been much healthier. But she didn't and they didn't.

I think that our staff members were too successful. We did not make our dependence on the board clear enough nor did we talk enough about its fundraising responsibilities. What happened? Members took the easy way out and left it to us. Had the board ever become a fundraising board, it could have raised much, much more than we raised, and with a lot less effort. I was not alone. In a survey of 1,200 US charities in 1997, only 2 per cent of the executive directors responding said they considered fundraising to be a strength of their board. In fact, fundraising topped the list of weaknesses.

The role of the staff in fundraising

Ideally, an organization has several fundraising programs and its board and staff members work together, complementing each other's efforts. Staff members can and should play several roles. The most challenging is the one at which I failed: training and stimulating the board to raise funds. To be successful, staff members must first train themselves by taking courses, reading guides to fundraising procedures, seeking advice by e-mail and the World Wide Web where possible (see Chapter 24 in this book and Book 3, Chapter 20), and picking the brains of anyone who knows anything about the field and is willing to talk about it.

The board is supposed to fundraise but it pushes fundraising onto the staff.

PATMA RATNAYAKE, SOUTH ASIA PARTNERSHIP, SRI LANKA

Staff members play other important parts in any successful fundraising campaign. They may be expected to:

• support the work of board members who don't have the time or inclination to write proposals, draft fundraising letters and put them in the mail, plan brochures and arrange for them to be printed, edit and publish newsletters, and keep detailed records of contributions. The board should be able to rely on the staff (or other committed volunteers if there are not enough staff members) for the support it needs to raise funds.

• carry the major responsibility for direct mail campaigns once the organization begins soliciting large numbers of donors

• conduct some direct fundraising activities. Staff members can, for example, place collection boxes in local shops. (But imagine how many more boxes could be placed on public display if board members were also willing to approach the local merchants they patronize.)

• make their own financial donations to the organization they work for. The donations may be modest, but they should be visible. Every organization I know that raises a lot of money includes staff members in its published list of donors. That tells the public that the employees believe in what they do.

It is a good idea to get the division of labour between board and staff clear from the start. Who does what best? There are some advantages to having staff members take the lead at first. They may have had some training in fundraising. They may understand that in seeking funds the important thing is not to talk about what the organization needs but to *listen* to what the potential donor wants. They know the organization best and are relaxed when talking about it because they have the facts at their fingertips. They know stories about people that can make the organization come alive for potential donors. When carefully planned, staff fundraising can be effective. The Kenya Farmer's Community Development Club plans fundraising a year ahead. Its 50 staff members each spend seven hours a week on fundraising. At first, staff members were reluctant but, because fundraising was carefully planned and could be conducted efficiently, they came to agree that it was a good idea. Undoubtedly, one of the reasons for the success of staff members was solid support from board members who organize fundraising events, write letters, and approach corporations for in-kind donations.

At the same time, staff members are often at some disadvantage in raising money. They may see themselves, or be seen by others, as asking for money to pay their own salaries. This never bothers people in submitting a grant proposal. Yet somehow when it is local people who are being asked for support, the salaries assume more importance. This appearance of self-interest makes people – both the askers and the givers – uncomfortable. Staff members, who earn little money themselves, may also feel nervous about approaching rich people; they may expect board members to do that job. They may be equally reluctant to approach the people they serve, for fear they will be seen as trying to take away what the organization has just given.

The role of the board in fundraising

An American consultant, Renata Rafferty, says: "I make it abundantly clear that the ethical imperative of stewardship is such that service and commitment to the board and the organization should be one's fourth highest priority in life for the period of service to the board. That is, fourth after family, faith, and (possibly) profession. Placing that priority on your role as a steward requires an equivalent commitment of personal resources: time, energy, expertise, and money." Nevertheless, a 1997 study by the US National Centre for Nonprofit Boards said 68 per cent of the 1,028 organizations reporting did not require trustees to make a contribution. Of the 32 per cent that did, more than a third did not have an explicit, written policy. However, things are changing. Many United Way organizations in the USA now require the board members of all the agencies they support to be donors. The question is: Can an organization legitimately raise money in the community if even its own board members do not give it 100 per cent support? Any board member can give at least a small donation.

If an organization is conducting fundraising programs, its board members must be donors. They must lead by example. They should also be prepared to ask others to give money to ensure the organization's financial strength. That dual commitment is the first step in fundraising success. It should be spelled out clearly when a person is invited to serve on a board. But that is not done often enough anywhere in the world. Organizations that expect financial support from board members rarely talk about their expectations. What are the results? Staff members feel frustrated because board members balk at assuming an obligation they did not know they had when they agreed to serve. The staff members feel that the board does not support the organization. And board members resent having been kept in the dark. They may feel they have been misled. If new board members understand exactly what is expected of them, later misunderstandings and disappointments are less likely. A happy and enthusiastic board is one of the best demonstrations of an organization's credibility.

Unfortunately, many volunteer board members are unwilling to give money or to find it. They are afraid of approaching other people and businesses for money. Or they think asking for money is undignified. They believe the people they approach will see them as beggars, not as what they are – selflessly committed to a good cause.

The chairman of a Canadian board said recently: "We are a policy board. We are not a fundraising board." No board members have ever been asked to contribute to that organization, although some have done so without being asked. Board members do volunteer considerable amounts of time. They serve on committees of volunteers running fundraising events. They buy tickets and work at the events. They come up with clever ideas to promote the sale of greeting cards, posters, and raffle tickets. They worry about the costs of running a gift shop they own and wonder how more customers could be lured in. They suggest where in-kind donations may be found. They take an interest at budget time in the costs and the income resulting from staff-led fundraising.

Grants from government are getting smaller every year, however, and fundraising is not making up the difference. The board members look carefully at the bottom line. At the end of each year they see no deficit and everyone is relieved. But what is the cost of having no deficit when revenues are dropping? The answer: shrinking service and overworked staff.

Board members help especially on the corporate side mostly but also with individuals. The chairman is writing a letter. His secretary is going through the phone book looking up names. Five hundred letters have been sent out so far.

CHARLENE HEWAT, ENVIRONMENT 2000, ZIMBABWE

Giving time and ideas is not enough. The water vendor or the electricity company cannot be paid with time. Money and time are not the same. Those board members could make a huge difference if each made a generous donation, as most could afford to do. They could make an even greater difference if each wrote a letter to ten friends asking for a donation. Together the board could raise as much money in a few weeks as is raised by running events throughout the year.

Board fundraising for the future
Once the board is ready to raise funds, what will you expect members to do?

Members should do what is most suitable and interesting to them, but all should contribute – not just money, but also time, contacts, and expertise. We have already talked about a few activities board members can undertake early in the fundraising process. Gradually, as the organization expands and diversifies its fundraising programs, board members can:

- call on potential donors, individuals, corporations, and foundations to develop their interest in the organization or to solicit a contribution
- suggest more people who may donate or open doors
- write letters asking for donations
- write letters to thank donors or phone to say thank you
- advise about opportunities to earn money through commercial activities
- advise on management issues
- approve all fundraising plans, no matter who is implementing them—board, staff, or consultant

As you gain more confidence and the board gains experience in fundraising, the expectations can be more specific. A target can be set for the whole board and individual targets for each member. It should be put in terms of what percentage of the budget can be raised by board members. That does not mean each person must actually go and ask for that amount of money. It means the board member is expected to facilitate, in one way or another, gifts that meet a certain target.

Building a board that will raise funds

A voluntary organization that is about to start raising funds locally must often revise its structure. Perhaps it has seen no real need in the past for a formal board. It has only an advisory committee, with no official or legal responsibility for the organization's financial affairs. The advisers may have provided useful technical expertise or suggestions about ways to make the day-to-day operation of programs in the community more effective. They may be the organization's only group of outside volunteers. Their responsibilities and activities may be limited, and they may be unwilling to do more. At the same time, they may be insulted and think their role has been diminished if the organization forms a new board of directors with legal responsibilities. To keep their good will, it will be important to retain the advisory committee as a formal body alongside the new board, and perhaps to give it a grander status than it had previously enjoyed.

At least some of these committed, experienced volunteers – technical and program advisers – may be persuaded to serve on the new board. They will bring balance and depth to it because of their expert knowledge and their familiarity with the organization's history. They may also have contacts that were not thought much about when fundraising was not a priority. If enough advisers can be enlisted, they may form the nucleus of the new board.

The transition can be tricky. It will require diplomacy and time. Advisers who have been working together comfortably for years will have to fit with newcomers from different backgrounds and have different perspectives. They will be expected to be active in areas beyond their spheres of special expertise and to give and find money as well as advice. Nevertheless, with the addition of new members and good leadership, an advisory committee can be transformed into an effective official board.

Other organizations will already have a fully constituted board, but not one that has had any major responsibilities for fundraising. Perhaps the board consisted originally only of the founders, or was intended principally to give moral support and some technical advice to them as well as some indication of community support. Over the years, the original members may have re-placed themselves with friends with similar backgrounds. Perhaps the board helped to secure foreign funding. But local fundraising would not have been mentioned or even considered a board priority. There was enough grant money for the board members to feel relaxed about the financial survival of the organization for which they were legally responsible. In such cases, an executive director and chairman, or the chairman alone, should meet with each board member individually to learn that person's view of the board's role in fundraising and the role of the director. The key questions to be asked are: Can we count on you for introductions to people who might invest in our work? Are you willing to help find people who will donate? Will you help us get them interested in our organization and go with me to ask them for support? The answers to these few questions will show a member's degree of interest in fundraising.

If such a board is governing the organization well, and is reluctant to do more, there may be no reason to force fundraising upon it. A more prudent strategy may be to form a special committee devoted exclusively to fundraising, and give it enough authority to operate on its own under the least possible board supervision. Board members may still be willing to do occasional fundraising behind the scenes, and to encourage others to be active in this respect, but they will not be required to undertake the full responsibility for raising money. To ensure effective communication between the two bodies, some members of the board could be appointed to the fundraising committee and vice-versa. (Various ways to reinforce the board in this manner are discussed in the next chapter.)

It is also possible that the chairman and some other influential members of the board will be prepared to begin raising funds seriously. After all, there is little real difference between calling on the representative of an international foundation and calling on a local donor. If you are fortunate enough to have such an adaptable board, it may only be necessary to reinforce it with new members whose talents and contacts are especially suited to local fundraising.

"Committee work? Fund raising? Public accountability? You didn't tell me it was going to be that kind of board!"

Whichever route you follow as you begin local fundraising, it will usually be necessary to bring new members into your organization's governing structure to strengthen its fundraising leadership and broaden its community representation. Finding and enlisting the first members in each of these categories will probably be difficult; once aboard, these new members will be able to attract others. Advisers and friends in the community may be able to suggest candidates. One strategy that often works is to ask the very people you would like as board members to recommend names. Once their interest has been caught in this way, they may agree to serve on the board themselves.

Organizations that are starting activities they hope will earn income – such as selling merchandise, running training programs, or offering consulting services – will have a special need for board members with business experience. These organizations are going into business, whether they realize it or not. They will need people with good community connections and experience in financial management, marketing, and communications. These are exactly the qualities and skills needed for all fundraising, so those board members will be doubly valuable.

Set a schedule for building a fundraising board. If the transformation is slower than planned, carry on with fundraising anyway. Use the board members who are willing to be active in this respect. Just do less than originally expected – but don't delay and don't give up.

Attracting effective new board members

Board members, new and old, must be credible and respected, both within the community and within the organization. Finding such people and getting them to say "yes" can be difficult. You may believe you have no access to the level of people you think you need. Don't be discouraged. Of course it helps if people are well connected locally, but commitment to an organization's goals is just as important. You don't need an entire board of effective, active fundraisers, people who will go out and ask others to invest in the organization. It is only necessary to have all the members committed to the fundraising program, and a few of them ready to take the lead in seeking out donors.

It may take a year to identify the people you want as board members, capture their interest, and secure their commitment. It can take another year, perhaps longer, to weld them into a cohesive, effective team.

The boards I know about tend to think about finding new members (or renewing old ones) just before the annual general meeting. But attracting good board members should be a year-round activity. The chairman should ask at every meeting for suggestions of who could be board members, or volunteers. Once board members know they are expected to suggest names, they will get in the habit.

This section talks about the personal qualities of good board members, with an emphasis on the characteristics of good fundraisers. The kinds of representation you need are discussed in the next section.

Ideal fundraising board members would have as many as possible of the following characteristics. They should:

- have full faith and confidence in the worthiness of the cause
- share a vision of what the organization can achieve
- believe strongly in the service the organization provides today
- recognize that private support is essential
- understand the role of a board of directors (see Book 1, Chapter 7)
- have served previously on other boards
- have gained your trust because they are known to some staff or board members already
- have a good reputation in the community
- show intelligence and foresight
- have common sense
- be able to communicate clearly and precisely
- be open to new ideas
- enjoy learning new skills
- make only promises that can be kept
- have demonstrated that they keep the promises they make
- have friendly, outgoing personalities
- know lots of people
- enjoy an optimistic view of life and not be easily discouraged
- be able to arrange some free time
- have a sense of humour
- be willing to spend time helping the organization without pay

- dress appropriately for every occasion
- be hospitable

List these characteristics in order of their importance to you. Then ask yourself:

How many of the characteristics does each of your present board members have?
What important characteristics are missing?
Which of these missing characteristics are most important to your organization?
List them in order of priority.
What will you do to improve the situation?

Building an effective fundraising board

The first people to ask to join the board are people who have already shown that they are committed to your organization. Then look to groups with whom you may have had little contact but want to involve. Ask yourself to what extent you want the board to represent a cross-section of the community. Will it be enough to concentrate solely on adding people who will be helpful with fundraising?

While broad representation is useful, it should not be at the expense of the people who are already the organization's recognized public face. Donors want to see the names of people they know. If necessary, expand the board and council or patrons in a way that will to continue to give these essential people a significant place. In India, the law dictates that one-third of the founders must be on the board permanently.

Several types of people may be approached. The most important are considered in the following paragraphs.

If our circles of acquaintances are not diverse, we may have a large segment of potential supporters who no one in our group knows and who don't get asked by us. Therefore, it behooves us to make sure our boards of directors and our staff and volunteers represent the broadest possible range of demographic possibilities in our community.

JOAN FLANAGAN,
THE GRASS ROOTS FUNDRAISING BOOK

Local donors

No one is more likely to agree to serve on the board than someone who is already supporting the organization. In the beginning, there may be few donors to approach, especially if your organization has never had an active fundraising program. You may in the past have received donations from only a few friends of the board or of staff members, and perhaps one or two local business people. Those donations may have been mainly in the form of advice, a service, or in-kind contributions. But these people have shown their interest. If they also have some knowledge or experience you need, then they are excellent candidates for board membership.

Local members

Even though your organization has not been actively raising funds, it may already have members who pay a small fee each year to belong. These people are donors, in effect. Many of them may know each other already and may perhaps have served on the board or done volunteer work. They know the organization and are committed to it. Who better to serve on a board that will do fundraising?

Representatives of the people you serve

The people who benefit from the organization's work, or members of their families, can bring an important perspective to the board. They can also be effective fundraisers because they know at first hand the value of the organization. Often they can tell a deeply moving story of how their lives have changed for the better. These board members can speak from personal experience about what is needed in their communities and can help to establish priorities among those needs. Sometimes language barriers make it difficult for beneficiaries to participate in board discussions, but even then efforts may be made to involve them through translators.

Their presence on the board is also an effective way of building credibility. When beneficiaries are appointed to the board, it shows donors just how committed the organization is to the people it claims to serve. It also shows the commitment of those people to the organization.

Business people

The most difficult group to approach may be business people – not necessarily because they themselves are difficult but because of the discomfort, even suspicion of them, that is common in so many voluntary organizations. Some times this suspicion is justified – in the case of major polluters, for example. Sometimes the suspicion is simply prejudice – a belief that all businesses are concerned only with making a profit. The business people in turn may be suspicious of any invitation from an organization they consider, rightly or wrongly, to be left wing, anti-capitalist, or subversive of the social order.

The financial, entrepreneurial, and managerial expertise of business people, their reputation as good citizens, and their contacts are essential for fundraising. But what you want most of all from them as board members is commitment. Without commitment, there will be little benefit in having them join the board, no matter how important they are. Committed business people can open doors. They can also carry the organization's message to communities it may not be reaching now, and in a positive way.

As an organization succeeds in its fundraising programs, it will want to recruit more business representatives from higher and higher levels of management. It is never too soon to take the first small steps in this direction. Approach first the companies with whom you already do business – your printer, a local merchant, your bank or credit union. Next approach companies you know, and then companies you want to be associated with – large retailers, other banks, insurance companies.

It is not necessary to aim for the chief executive officers of big corporations. Junior employees can be a big asset. They are keen and on their way up the corporate ladder. They can be of great help.

Be careful, however, that you do not appear to be selling board seats. Sometimes a business will want one of its employees to serve on the board of an organization. It may want to be seen as doing public service, or may think it will gain respectability through the association. It may be quite willing to contribute to the organization as well. That is fine if the interests of the business and the voluntary organization are the same. If they do not coincide, a promise of support may influence an organization to move in a direction it did not want to go.

A glassmaking factory is a major industry in a town in India. Several years ago, an accidental leak caused major pollution in the stream that passes by the factory. Repairs may have solved the problem but no one is sure. A new state-wide advocacy organization working to clean up the environment is starved for funds. The chairman of the glass factory offers help. He is willing to sit on the board and to contribute to the new organization.

Should the organization accept the chairman's offer? How will his presence on the board affect the organization's public image? Is the possible damage to its credibility more important than the benefits to be gained from the chairman's knowledge and contacts and the factory's money? Will the chairman's presence on the board influence the organization's policies?

The board has some serious questions to answer before it can respond to the chairman's offer.

Be cautious about inviting people just because they are rich or important. If they say yes, they may not do anything, having said to themselves, "It's a good organization. I'm really just lending my name. I don't need to go to meetings." Get board members who will work.

We are encouraging outreach to NGOs within the business community. It is not common to have business people on boards. This is a new idea. It will need work to present it to NGOs.

PETER NIZAK,
DEMOCRACY
NETWORK, HUNGARY

Young people

Most of the boards I have worked with have had few, if any, members under the age of 30 years. That would seem to make sense in fundraising terms because older people have more money than young people. Charities everywhere in the world get most of their money from older people. But it does not make sense in the long term.

Young people have ideas very different from the ideas of their parents about how their communities should develop and what their own roles should be. Because young people are hard to reach in old ways, a whole generation of possible supporters, both present and future, may be missed. In fundraising, young people can approach a group of possible donors that no one else in the organization may know how to reach. They can talk to them as peers in language they understand.

A young person who joins a board gains as well as gives. Think of young people as career seekers who might want to work in a field that is wide open everywhere in the world. Being a board member and fundraiser can launch them on a professional career in the relatively new field of professional fundraising.

Women

Women are holding more and more economic power and yet continue to be underrepresented on boards. They are a minority on the board even of some women's organizations and some organizations that serve mainly women.

In some countries, a major role for women on boards may be unacceptable or inappropriate. In most countries, women can take a more active role than they have been offered. Women reach audiences and potential donors that male board members don't even know. They can also present the case for the organization effectively. In my experience women board members usually take their responsibilities more seriously than the men. If they say they will raise money, they will. At board meetings I have noticed that it is the women who are more likely to have read the material beforehand. Men often seem to be shuffling paper, trying to read about an item just before it comes up on the agenda.

Politicians and civil servants
Like business people, government officials may be suspicious of an invitation to join a board, especially if the organization has opposed government policy. Where officials are willing and permitted to join boards, however, they can be valuable assets. They know government policy. They can also open doors. They may lend credibility. On the other hand, they may link the organization too closely with the government in power and arouse suspicion among beneficiaries and donors. A decision on recruiting board members from government must therefore be taken carefully. Obviously, it is unwise to be too closely associated with one political party, however powerful, unless, of course, there is only one party.

Members of minority groups
Many boards are criticized nowadays for not reflecting their community in their membership. Be sure to include representatives from all segments of the community, including minority groups.

Issuing the invitation
An invitation to join the board is a serious business. Potential fundraising board members should be approached with sensitivity and care; treat them as important in the community and important to you. They are being asked to play roles they probably have never played before. You will have to walk a fine line between scaring away good people and not being honest about what you need from them.

Make sure the right person does the asking and does it in person. The right person is likely the chairman, if there is one. If not, then the invitation might come from someone who has been associated with the organization as a volunteer for a long time. A senior staff person and perhaps another board member could go along if that will improve the chances that the candidate will agree to serve. Don't overwhelm a potential board member by bringing along too many people. The staff person should stay in the background; someone who is being asked to volunteer time and money is more likely to be impressed favourably by another volunteer.

The manager may need to brief the person making the approach before the meeting. Here are five golden rules to follow in inviting someone to join a board to help it raise funds:

1 Before ever issuing the invitation, be absolutely clear about what you want the new board member to contribute to the board's activities, and

for how long. All volunteers, no matter what their role, have a right to know what is expected of them before they agree to help. Briefly, people willing to serve on boards want to be part of a cause that is larger than their own lives, to feel useful, and to know exactly how the work they are being asked to do would help the organization. They also want reassurance that they will not be wasting their time by being involved in a sloppily run organization. They want to be able to talk with pride about any organization in which they are involved and about the contribution they are making. Your organization also wants this important contribution to its credibility.

2 In issuing the invitation, don't just offer a seat on the board. Start with the service – the work the organization is already doing – and go on to describe the opportunity to be part of that work. Make it clear why the person is particularly well qualified to help your organization. Sound excited and exciting. You are not asking a favour; you are offering a chance to improve the lives of hundreds or thousands of people.

3 Don't play down the importance of what you are asking or the degree of commitment that you require. Be specific about the help you need, the time required, and how, in particular, the person can contribute to the fundraising program. The chairman should emphasize that the organization expects that board members will attend meetings regularly.

4 If the response to this point is favourable, ask for a specific commitment to participate in one of the fundraising programs. Ask the person to do one or more of the following:
- thank donors
- solicit in-kind contributions
- help with events
- visit potential donors
- find new donors
- write to foundations and corporations and meet with their representatives if advisable

5 Be clear that you expect board members to consider making a donation to the organization. It is not necessary to press the point too hard, but the expectation should be expressed. Many people will ask what the organization considers an appropriate donation. Have a figure in mind: "We hope you will consider making a donation of ...."

If they are willing to consider serving, potential board members should be invited to tour projects, visit the office, meet other board and committee members, perhaps attend several board meetings as observers. They should be given an orientation package about the organization, which could include:
- the history of the organization
- the role of the board and what is expected of each member
- the by-laws and articles of incorporation
- the legal responsibilities and liabilities of board members and the protection provided by the organization
- past annual reports
- recent detailed financial statements

- the minutes of board meetings for the past year
- current brochures describing the work of the organization
- major policy documents, such as a three-year plan
- any fundraising plans and materials that already exist
- a list of senior staff members with their positions, and how to reach them both at the office and at home
- a list of the members of the board and committees, their positions, and how to reach them
- the job descriptions of the executive director and of senior staff

Once a person agrees to serve and is elected to the board, the chairman should write a confirming, welcoming letter. The letter should include a clear statement about the term of office. It is a good idea to appoint board members to three-year terms. This makes it possible to attract new people continually. Valuable members can always be reappointed for a further term or appointed to an honorary board, a council of patrons, or a special executive committee that may have less responsibility. Don't lose good people who know your organization. But if people don't take their membership seriously, they should be replaced.

Motivating fundraising leadership in the board

The board chairman, perhaps with staff help, has recruited new members from various sectors of the community. As part of the recruiting, the new board members have come to understand the full range of their responsibilities for the organization's finances – to give money and to get money as well as to govern. But understanding is one thing; action is another. What methods can be used to get board members moving and raising money? Here are a few.

1 Experienced fundraisers find that general appeals at board meetings, especially for help in fundraising, often fall on deaf ears. It is more effective to approach the board members one at a time and privately, asking them to do a specific job or to make a specific donation according to their means and talents. Board members usually respond to this personal, special treatment.

2 Consider a board retreat, during which all the members go away for a day or two to plan the future of the organization. The retreat, if possible, should be held in a hotel, conference centre, or other suitable site away from everyone's office so as to minimize interruptions. The retreat will accomplish several things. It will result in a plan. Equally important, it will provide an opportunity for board members to get to know one another better and learn more about the organization itself. Board members need to feel comfortable talking about your work to their friends. It could take a year or more before a new member feels confident enough to be fully persuasive.

3 Meanwhile, don't leave any board members out of the fundraising picture. Here are some ways you can involve board members in campaign planning and at the same time help them to feel more comfortable about asking for donations.

• Make a wish list: "If we only had enough money, we could ...."
People get excited when they see possibilities for improved service, and then they are more willing to work. Vague wishes are not enough: the possibilities must be expressed as clearly described projects, showing what would be done and how lives would be changed. At this point, the board should be thinking about the ends, not the money. Once the potential for service is seen, the many ways of achieving it can be explored – not just by raising cash but through in-kind contributions, by volunteer help, or by reducing expenses in other areas to make cash available.

• Engage the board in putting together a statement of why people should support the organization. That statement should set out the needs of the community that are the concern of the organization and show why the organization is best able to meet those needs. It should look to the future, to the benefits to the community that will come from the investment of donors. (See Book 3, Chapter 2.)

By working on the statement, board members will come to know the strength of the case for support. They will learn the language of the organization so they can talk about it enthusiastically, without fumbling or hesitating.

• Involve board members in planning the overall budget, which in cludes the fundraising budget, however tiny that may be at first. In the process they can learn the priorities and just how little money there is. Be sure members understand that a break-even budget does not mean success. Let them see how the balanced budget has been achieved. Too often managers are praised for avoiding a deficit when all it means is that they have reduced needed services. (See Chapter 4.) Restoring those services may then become a powerful motivation for raising money.

• Start board members making lists of names of possible donors. Most everyone has family, neighbours, and friends. Some are close by, others have moved to cities. Some will have good jobs. They should be put on the list. After that, encourage members to add people they know through their business and religion and through so cial and service clubs. Ask them to list former schoolmates, their bank manager, their doctors, dentist, a lawyer to whom they once paid a fee, and everyone who ever asked them to donate to other causes.

• Involve members in volunteer work in the programs. Give them a chance to learn at first hand what the organization is all about. They will talk from the heart after that. Ask them also to help at any special events the organization holds, to sell raffle tickets, greeting cards, and other income-generating products, and to undertake local speaking engagements once they are familiar with the work of the organization.

4 Identify problems and deal with them before they become severe and get in the way of fundraising. Ethical and moral issues in particular should be sorted out ahead of time. One of the most difficult may be deciding who you will – or will not – accept money from. I ran an agency that distributed farming information all over the world. For more than a decade, its major supporter was an international farm machinery company. That support stopped when the company left Canada, forcing us to expand our fundraising program. At a lengthy meeting, some board members drew up guidelines to cover the kinds of corporations from whom donations could ethically be accepted. After about four hours, they reached agreement. Then everyone realized that the farm machinery company that had been our major patron represented everything our organization had just agreed it would not touch, and we had been taking the money for ten years without a qualm. Finally, we agreed on a more flexible, sensible policy: before an approach was made to any corporation whose practices were questioned by a member of the board or staff, the board would have to give its approval. We also decided to worry about keeping "dirty" money only if and when it came. In fact, we never did get much corporate money but we did learn to be honest with ourselves before we began.

6 Reinforcing the board

Despite new members, a new mandate, training, and plenty of time, the board still may not be taking the lead in fundraising. Its members are always ready to urge staff members to raise money and they will ask volunteers to manage fundraising events. They may even have done the odd burst of fundraising themselves. But they are still not prepared to raise funds on a regular, systematic, and continuous basis. Most did not even approach the donors they did secure in previous years to ask them for a second donation this year.

At some point, it will become necessary to be realistic and stop pushing a board that is simply unwilling to raise funds. But you should know why it is unwilling. Are the members too spread out to be able to raise funds locally? Do they come from other voluntary organizations, so they are more concerned about raising money for their own interests than for your programs? Do they see their role only as providing technical advice? Have you not yet been able to find the right leaders? A good board chairman, possibly together with the manager, should talk to the members of the board individually – at least, to those members who are favourably disposed towards fundraising – and analyse the problem. Then suggest changes to make the organization's fundraising more effective. Perhaps, instead of asking for money, members could ask for in-kind donations. Perhaps they can enlist other people who will be more successful.

If the board is not doing the job, there are other ways to secure fundraising leadership. Several are discussed in the following pages. They do not, however, relieve the board of its responsibility for the financial health of the organization. The board cannot escape ultimate responsibility for the consequences of unsuccessful fundraising. The question is: Who will do the job best? If it is not the board, the following possibilities can be considered.

Informal help, outside of committees

You may be able to find someone who will give a great deal of help but does not want any sort of visible or official position – and may hate meetings. That happened to me. The most help I ever had when I was running an NGO was from the president of a company whom I met almost by chance. He had an emotional attachment to our work because he had done something similar while he was at university. He would not accept an invitation to serve on the board. But he arranged for a large debt we owed to be forgiven. The same man gave a lunch for other well-known people who had agreed to let us use their names in publicity and fundraising materials, thereby increasing the organization's credibility. Almost no one except the board knew of his efforts on our behalf, for his name never appeared anywhere in our materials.

The lesson of that experience is: Keep your eyes and ears open. Take support where you find it, and in the form the person wants to give it. Be flexible.

A patron's council

No matter what form the fundraising leadership takes, it can be reinforced by the support of people who are well known and respected, locally if not nationally. Many voluntary organizations appoint such people as "patrons," a largely honorary title. They may also be called counsellors, or honorary board members. If there are several, they may be formed into an advisory council, or given some other title that is more appropriate locally.

In appointing patrons, organizations usually approach one or two people whom they respect, and whose interests or work relate in some way to the organization's work, and ask them to allow the use of their names to increase the organization's credibility. Patrons need have no role in governance.

Patrons should be chosen carefully. It is unnecessary to seek the biggest names. Don't shoot for the moon in seeking patrons. Don't ask national figures or big name entertainers unless you know them personally. Start small. Take a few short steps. A long list of people leaves little room to add members later if other excellent candidates come to your attention. And you will have to live with the list for a long time. You can drop people if they become an embarrassment or no longer seem useful, but it is not desirable because you may lose them as friends.

Aim to enlist one or two people whom you respect and who will come to understand and appreciate the work you are doing. Look for people who are respected in the community and who belong to sectors in the community that you especially want to think well of you – sectors you may not have involved before, such as merchants, business people, leaders of religious communities.

Most people, when asked to be patrons, will assume you are going to ask them for money. You will want to tell them that you are not looking at this stage for people who will give you money. You will also need to reassure them that you do not intend to put demands on their time.

Treat patrons gently. Keep them informed about the organization's activities and plans. Invite them to events of special interest. You want them to speak well of you to their friends, but don't flood them with information or activities. Most will be too busy, or not interested enough, to read long documents. It is said that the richer people are, the smaller are their eyes. Many patrons may not even want to attend a social gathering.

Do ask patrons for advice from time to time. Everyone likes that. It can be useful to invite them to meet with the board of directors every year or two. That way they can keep up-to-date with the organization if they want to.

Counsellors or patrons may do more than was first expected. Once they have become friends, they can also be asked to invest in your organization.

Some organizations enlist patrons and then don't keep in touch with them or take enough advantage of the prestige they bring. I have done that. I did not put their names on our organization's letterhead, for instance, although I listed them in the newsletter and sometimes on letterhead used for fundraising mailings. Why not? I think I was too slow to recognize the good impression their names made. It took several comments to wake me up. Donors said, "I was impressed with what you said you do, but I had never heard of your organization. Then I saw that list of names. I thought, well, it must be all right if respected people like that think it is good." It's a good idea to include the names of patrons, and their positions if the position is better known than the name, in everything you produce. They are giving you their prestige.

You may call this special group an advisory board, in which case you are entitled to ask them for more assistance. The director of an Indonesian environmental NGO said, "advisory board members, mostly business people, open doors to influential people. The advisory board is also a reality test. I put projects to them, especially if the projects involve corporate partnerships. The advisory board networks well. We asked donors, whoever they are, to help with the advisory board."

A separate fundraising management group

A weak board that does not grasp its fundraising responsibilities can be strengthened or circumvented by forming a separate body to manage fundraising. This new group can be set up in either of two ways:

• A subcommittee of the board headed by a member of the board, with additional board members and other volunteers. All members of the subcommittee are active fundraisers. The subcommittee is part of the board: it has an official position, but is free of the other concerns and the inertia of the full board.

• A special task force set up by the board with a mandate to raise funds. The task force may report to the board, and have representation from the board, but operate relatively independently. Such a group may attract the people you need to do fundraising because it can work in a highly focused way, free of other concerns of the board. It may concentrate on a single program, perhaps a special event, for a limited amount of time. Or it may focus on a specific area such as corporate fundraising, in which case it might consist of a group of business people who have been enlisted specially for the project. Some experts feel a task force works best when it is not left to do all the fundraising, but is asked only to supplement what the board is already doing. Both arrangements make it possible for the organization to increase the number of people from the community with whom it is involved. Both relieve the board of some responsibilities and a good deal of work. Both are also relatively easy to organize: only few changes to the by-laws may be needed, if that.

The special groups are not without problems, however. Some members may be happy not to have board responsibilities; they just want to get on with the job of raising money. Others may think they are being treated as second-rate because they are not board members. For them, it will be more satisfying if the committee has a clear sense of mission – to benefit the community – and a set of attainable goals in money and time.

One further problem may arise. If the special fundraising group is successful, it may achieve a higher profile than the board, both inside and outside the organization. This can occur especially if the board has been lucky enough to recruit people who are better known in the local community than its own members. That does not happen every day, but it can happen. The board may then come to resent the attention its fundraisers are receiving. The manager will have to make greater than normal efforts to assure the board of its continuing importance.

A separate foundation

Many organizations set up a separate foundation to solicit and manage some or all of their donations and bequests and the income earned from the investment of this money. It exists solely to support the organization's work. A foundation of this kind is a legal entity, separate from the parent organization. It is governed by a separate board, likely made up of volunteers, possibly with one or more non-voting members of the staff. The board may also include representatives of the parent organization's board of directors. It is much more independent of the organization than a fundraising management group or committee. Setting up a foundation should be considered only by established, well-managed organizations.

Advantages

A foundation has several advantages:

- A separate foundation, registered as a charity, may be the only way an organization can accept some funds legally.
- A separate foundation leaves the parent organization free to serve the purpose for which it was created, without the distraction of fundraising. Fundraising can so dominate board meetings that no one has much time to talk about the program. At the same time, a foundation can devote itself entirely to the raising and management of funds without any responsibilities for running programs.
- The foundation can attract business people with a special interest in financial matters who might not find governing a voluntary organization as appealing.
- The foundation gives the parent organization an opportunity to broaden its support by bringing in a new group of people in addition to its governing board.
- Donors may feel their money will be handled more responsibly if it goes directly to a foundation, governed on financial principles, instead of the parent organization whose goals are altruistic. This will, of course, depend on the credibility of the foundation's board members.

• A foundation is able to concentrate on securing the long-term financial stability that results from an endowment, because it is protected from the ups and downs and resulting pressures of an organization's normal funding cycles.

• Funds held by a foundation are protected from board members who, if money gets tight, may decide to spend the reserved funds thereby threatening the organization's future security.

Disadvantages

There are, however, disadvantages in establishing a special fundraising foundation. It is wise to consider all other ways of solving board problems before setting up a foundation:

• The foundation may be subject to endless government regulations. That can be a headache, especially at the beginning.

• A foundation can be expensive to set up. There may be legal costs and government registration fees.

• Although there can be some overlapping membership, a new group of people must be found to govern the foundation. (It is common, and useful, however, to have the chairman and the treasurer of the parent board on the foundation board.) An organization may already have difficulty finding good members for its governing board.

• For an organization that is only beginning to raise funds, a separate foundation may prove an unnecessary complication. Foundations are most useful when they have a substantial amount of money to manage.

• Only major donors are likely to be persuaded to give by the existence of a separate foundation. Most donations will come as a result of the reputation of the organization and the power of the appeal to people's charitable instincts.

There are also concerns to be faced if a foundation is established:

• Unless special care is taken in choosing committed people, the foundation's directors may prove to be better at managing money than at raising it. If financial management and fundraising are expected of foundation board members, that must be made clear from the beginning.

• The structure of the combined organization may prove too large and cumbersome for a small agency.

• The costs of maintaining a separate foundation may outweigh the advantages.

• A foundation can be demanding to manage, requiring skills that no one in the organization has.

• The executive director of the parent organization may end up managing two entities instead of one. Even though foundations are intended to be managed independently, to be at arm's length from the parent organization that will benefit from the foundation's work, this does happen. Then conflicts of interest may arise. For example, how much of the foundation's money should go to the parent organization each year? Should some be retained as a reserve? How much should be retained for fundraising in the coming year? An executive director who manages the foundation as well as the parent organization can influence such decisions, which may in turn affect his or her own salary.

• Because they control the purse strings, the foundation board members may feel they have the ultimate responsibility for the money raised. They may want to control how the parent organization spends it.

• The foundation can grow remote from the parent organization. It can begin to forget that it exists only to serve the organization, not to have a life of its own.

• If they are asked to give to a foundation, donors may feel remote from the parent organization's service to the community.

Overlapping membership, clear, regular communications, and precise by-laws will overcome some of the problems. By-laws, for example, should specify that grants from the foundation can be made only to the parent organization. While a separate foundation is usually restricted to supporting only the parent organization, it is possible that some could expand their interests and influence, becoming donor agencies themselves. Such expansion would require significant changes in the by-laws and structure of both parent and offspring.

Consortia/clearing houses/coalitions
The board of an organization may turn over some of its fundraising activities to an agency that will then raise funds on its behalf through mailings and other kinds of solicitation such as payroll giving. The funds are then distributed to participating organizations. The GAYE scheme outlined in Book 3, Chapter 17 is an example.

Many voluntary organizations receive money from umbrella agencies. This topic is dealt with in Book 3, Chapter 22 on applying for grants. See also Chapter 10 in Book 1, on building alliances.

Outside experts
In many countries, only a few people have had extensive training in fundraising. And most who have had some training are already working for organizations with fundraising programs. However, some experienced fundraisers have decided to work for themselves and to act as consultants. They offer their services to several organizations, charging a fee based on the complexity of the work they must do and the amount of time it will require. (See Book 3, Chapter 21 about consultants and staff fundraisers.)

Some consultants live in the North but work with agencies in the South. Others are located in major cities in the South. Some consultants carry out short-term projects, such as staging a special fundraising event for an organization that does not have the resources itself, or advising on specific projects such as making a fundraising plan. They may help in setting up good records or starting a letter writing/direct mail campaign. Others work on projects over a long period of time, in effect becoming part-time members of the organization. The trouble is that, even if a few trained fundraising consultants are available locally, the non-profit organizations that need them most usually are the ones that can least afford to pay them.

The advantage of working with consultants, if they are trained and experienced, is that they can get a fundraising program running quickly, either by doing the work themselves or by showing an organization what it needs to launch a program. An outside consultant can often stimulate a board to raise funds when staff and a few board members have failed. A consultant can help the staff members and board members identify potential donors that are all around them – people who need only to be invited to contribute time and money.

Local (but not necessarily foreign) consultants are usually well aware of the climate in which the organization must operate, and especially of the social trends that will affect the chances of success. A good consultant will also know what the competition is doing, what techniques have been shown to be successful locally, and what techniques are not working.

However, consultants, like every other professional group, can be good, bad, or indifferent. Finding the right person takes time. Even the right person, once found, may be too busy to give the time needed. Consultants can also be expensive. Before hiring one, an organization should feel some confidence that, within a couple of years, donations will have risen to the point where it is possible to pay the consultant's fee and the fundraising costs and still have a significant amount left to improve the program.

ILLUSTRATION: CAROLE CABLE

"Agreed. This organization's primary objective in the coming year will be the recruitment of new board members."

Two final warnings: Using consultants may be an excellent interim measure, but if they do almost everything, the organization itself is not strengthened. Consultants can guide; only rarely can they make a board do what it simply does not want to do.

Another form of expertise is available in some cities, where small businesses will conduct fundraising events for a fee or a percentage of the revenue.

Celebrities

A major celebrity willing to help your organization can be a marvellous asset, attracting media attention and financial support. Such a person can also be a horrible burden, unreliable, and unreasonably demanding.

Most organizations don't know celebrities. Until an organization has invested in building its credibility and reputation, it will probably not be able to attract national celebrities to give their time.

Local celebrities, on the other hand, are effective in building local support. In my own town of 12,000 people there are artists and performers who always attract a crowd, even though no one has heard of them 50 kilometres away. Any local celebrity who will support your work could be an appropriate spokesperson for your cause. Look for celebrities who have a genuine, credible connection with the area of your concern. People like that should be asked, preferably by the chairman or another member of the or ganization who knows them, to support you publicly. They might appear or perform at special events, sign fundraising letters, talk about the organization in the media, or call on potential donors with volunteers. Ways to use celebrities for specific fundraising programs will be discussed in Chapter 23 in this book and in Book 3, Chapter 11.

7 Fighting fear of fundraising

I was having lunch with a group of women on International Women's Day a few years ago. One woman at my table was about to make a speech. Another said, "What people fear most in the whole world is having to stand up and talk in front of a group of people." I disagreed. I said most people are far more afraid of asking others – especially friends – for money. Everyone said, "Yes, that's true."

If your local fundraising is to succeed, the fear of fundraising must be brought out into the open. Board members and other volunteers on whom the organization depends for its survival must learn to deal with that fear.

There are, basically, four types of fundraising. Each uses volunteers in a different way. Each can cause a degree of fear. Not every volunteer needs to do every type of fundraising. With the right training and support each volunteer can find a niche:

1 *Promising an immediate, tangible benefit in exchange for money.* The organization may offer merchandise, services, or events. This may be, for example, hats, T-shirts, crafts, food, clothing, greeting cards for holidays (Chinese New Year, Eid, Christmas, Chanukah), tapes, compact discs, or videos. The services may include consulting, technical assistance, training, microcredit, or newsletter publishing. The events could be parties, concerts, or long distance runs.

The organization is not asking for donations from the community. Instead, it is looking for consumers. However, the purchase price or fee the consumer pays is always more than the cost to the organization, so participants are also making a contribution. If it is legally permissible, some of the price may be described as a donation for tax purposes.

This type of fundraising – marketing and income generation – causes little fear among volunteers, who act mostly as salespeople, extending the reach of the organization. We are all used to the exchange between merchandiser and consumer.

Where there is no culture of giving, there is no culture of asking. Civil society organizations may feel intimidated by the prospect or at a loss as to how to approach it.

DANIEL Q. KELLEY AND SUSAN GARCÍA-ROBLES, SUSTAINING CIVIL SOCIETY

We are too shy to ask for money. Staring people in the face will be good for us.

KOBUS PIENAAR, LEGAL RESOURCES CENTRE, SOUTH AFRICA

Is what you believe in bigger than what you are afraid of? We make up stories about donors to avoid asking: they don't like to be asked, they don't support the cause. What you feel is not what donors feel.

KIM KLEIN, CONSULTANT, UNITED STATES

2 *Asking for money without meeting face-to-face.* In this second category, the organization writes or telephones potential donors, places advertisements asking for donations, distributes donation boxes, and undertakes similar activities that do not involve face-to-face contact. These techniques can be used to reach a large group of potential donors and thus build a donor base.

Volunteers can be asked to suggest names of people and institutions to approach and ways to interest them. Volunteers will be needed to do clerical work, record donations, issue receipts, telephone, and collect donation boxes. They can also arrange in-kind donations that support a fundraising activity, such as free printing of letters and brochures or free space and time in the media.

This type of fundraising arouses little fear because the volunteers, staff, and board do not usually come into direct contact with donors. The further from home a donor is and the less direct the connection, the easier it is for people to ask for an investment in the organization.

3 *Asking organized groups.* Requests may be made to business corporations, foundations, service clubs, umbrella and intermediary civil society groups, labour unions, religious organizations, and local governments. The approach is often made in a brief written presentation. The donation is often a group decision and is usually corporate rather than personal.

Volunteers may help in the research needed to decide which groups will be the most receptive to an appeal. Then they can help prepare presentations, arrange introductions to decision-makers in the target group, and deliver or assist with presentations and follow-up.

This type of fundraising, especially when the target is a business corporation, may bring the first real shivers of fear. Some people are nervous about approaching a corporation or other organized group because they are unfamiliar with the ways corporations think and act. They want to do the right thing and make a convincing case but they're not sure they know how. On the other hand, the exchange is still relatively impersonal, between organizations rather than individuals, providing even a hesitant volunteer with a corporate shield.

4 *Making personal requests to individuals and small groups.* In this final category, requests are usually made face-to-face. Personal fundraising is the simplest, least expensive, and most efficient way to raise money. It may be a new role for volunteers in your organization. It works best when volunteers who have themselves already given generously approach people they know, asking them to do the same. But fear takes real hold when a person is asked to ask someone else for a donation.

Why is it so hard to ask people for money?

When fundraising is first mentioned, board members and other volunteers usually express enthusiasm about any efforts to improve the finances of the organization. Their reaction is often different when they realize they may have to raise money themselves – and give money themselves. They may respond in many ways. Underlying all the responses is fear of change, of doing something new, of failure or rejection. They are really saying, "This terrifies me," Fundraising leaders need to be prepared for this kind of reaction. Here are some responses to use.

Volunteer: "I believe in the cause. I said I would help. But I didn't say I would go out and ask people to give money. You didn't ask me to do that."

Response: "You will be asking people you already know to join you in investing in our community. You are not asking for charity. You are not begging."

Volunteer: "I don't know any rich people. This is a poor country/town/village/area. Nobody has any money to give to anything."

Responses: "You do know some people who care very much about improving their community. That is important. You believe in our organization. That is just as important as knowing rich people."

"Everyone here wants a better, more prosperous community. We are looking for small donations from many people."

"We hope everyone will give a little bit. We know from experience that support for organizations like ours comes, not from rich people, but from average people. They are willing to give a little if they and their community will be helped in the long run."

Volunteer: "I am too busy right now to call people about donations. Ask me again in six months."

Response: "Thank you for making this commitment. Perhaps, until you have more time, you will agree to make just three calls over the next six months."

Volunteer: "I'm here to give policy advice. The staff should do the fundraising."

Response: "There are certainly some programs the staff can run successfully, but long-term success comes from the efforts of people who freely give their time and money to our cause. That commitment is what impresses people and encourages their philanthropy."

Volunteer: "I can give you a few names of people who might donate. I don't want to ask them myself. That might affect our friendship. You will have to ask them yourself."

Response: "People prefer to answer requests from people they already know. You will be asking people to join you in investing in improving our community. Your commitment is what will impress people and encourage their philanthropy. However, if you are uncomfortable, then please give us the names of your friends and we will arrange for another volunteer to approach the people you suggest. You can trade lists with another volunteer and take turns opening doors."

Volunteer: "Anyway, we shouldn't have to find our own money. We should be getting money from the government."

Response: "We are already approaching the government, but it won't meet all our needs. The fact that our organization is seen to have a committed board and wide community support strengthens our case."

Volunteer: "And you certainly never asked me to agree to contribute myself."

Response: "If board members are not willing to put money on the line for a cause they serve and believe in, who else will? Once local fundraising becomes necessary, board giving is also necessary. No one should ask others

People would rather face down a psychopath than ask nice people who have money to give them some of it.

KIM KLEIN,
CONSULTANT,
UNITED STATES

for support unless he or she has first made a donation appropriate to what he or she can afford."

Volunteer: "Ahmed gives a lot of time to our organization. We cannot possibly ask him for money too. Isn't giving time enough?"

Response: "Giving time is enough if fundraising is not high on the agenda. We have no hesitation in asking people to give time to a good cause. But when it comes to asking for money, we panic. Yet we all have the same amount of time and, once we give it away, we never get it back. Money is renewable. It should be easier to ask for money."

This last dialogue introduces an important lesson. When raising money is a high priority, no one is more likely to help than the people who have already committed time to the organization. Yet too often they are not approached.

At a board meeting, a new member asked whether members of the board were asked to contribute. No one had approached him in the year he had been on the board. The chairman said that, while board members were not asked to contribute, all of them had done so. The chairman said there was no way he would ask board members to increase their contributions. He mentioned a board member, a prominent physician, whose enthusiasm and service to the organization were known to most of the community, and said: "I would not even think of approaching her to increase her support. Look what she is doing for us already."

Why would that organization ignore its most committed members and instead invest its time and energy in asking for support from people with whom it had only the tiniest connection, if any at all? The answer is simple. Because it was not truly committed to raising money.

Fundraisers are trained, not born

Jim Lord says in *The practice of the quest* that "fear of fundraising is all about fear of change. As with any activity, it gets easier and more enjoyable with experience, knowledge and a little bit of success. When we are told that someone enjoys fundraising or is good at it, what is usually meant is that the person has enough practice and success to build his or her comfort and confidence level."

From time to time, an organization will be lucky enough to find a person who knows naturally what to do and how to do it when the time comes to raise money. But such people are rare. It is best to assume that volunteers must be involved slowly, one step at a time, first in learning about the planning and policies that underlie fundraising and then in actually raising money themselves. Most people are reluctant to ask for money but, as will be discussed further below, there are ways to reassure them and appeal to their sense of commitment.

Fundraising usually has to be learned. Asking a friend for money should be no more difficult than asking for help in any small job. But we don't ask for money as often, so we need training. We need to learn, for example, that part of asking is listening. The worst salesman is one who is so involved in selling that he never pays attention to the audience's reaction. By letting potential donors talk, it's possible to find out their interests and what might convince them to support your organization.

It's best to begin by explaining the organization's plans and policies fully, carefully, and convincingly to potential canvassers – board members and other volunteers. As a next step, ask them to suggest the names of six possible donors each, or involve volunteers in fundraising events where they will not feel too exposed. Finally, turn them loose, full of new confidence, on personal solicitations.

Thirteen practical ways to overcome fear of fundraising

1 Recognize fear of fundraising right from the beginning. Don't pretend it does not exist. Talk about it and take steps to reduce it. (Overcoming fear in several specific fundraising strategies will be discussed further in Book 3.) Few people, after all, have been involved in the mechanics of fundraising. Like people in a theatre watching a play, they have never been backstage, let alone on stage – they may have been asked for money but have not been part of a fundraising task force.

2 Encourage early donations. Think carefully about who should be approached first. Identify the most likely donors. The chairman and executive director should lead the way by making their own gifts. If this attracts other volunteers and board donors to donate early on, so much the better. There is an old saying, "If you give early, you give twice." An early gift means more: it sets an example for others and encourages their generosity. Share good news as soon as you get it. Everyone will be encouraged by a few early successes.

Donors will be impressed if your organization has received financial support from all its board members. If the board and staff are not keen and committed financially, why should anyone else be?

3 Make your own commitment of money, along with a public commitment to the organization's goals and its fundraising program. Encourage reluctant volunteers to make their own donations. Nothing inspires confidence more than making one's own commitment. Giving is a good feeling. Unconsciously, one's whole attitude to the organization changes. People who make donations appropriate to their means feel proud, happy, and committed. They are more relaxed asking others to give once they have given themselves, because they know they will be asking them to do something that brings pleasure. Most of all, they are inviting by example. This is always far more effective than telling people what to do.

4 Keep fundraising closely tied to the program and purpose of the organization. It should not be given over to a few people who may feel isolated from the program of service to the community. Fundraising is not a secondary activity. Nor is it more important than the program. If either perception is allowed to develop, morale will suffer. In fact, fundraising and program cannot be separated. Without money, there would be no program. Demonstrate this integration by ensuring that the fundraising budget is part of the total budget.

Be sure staff members, board members, and other volunteers know as much as possible about both the program and the financial situation. Bring people together whenever possible. This will help to counter any fear among volunteers that they don't know enough about the organization to answer questions they may be asked. Few volunteers have the inside knowledge of an organization shared by those who work in the office or in the field every day. Even the most active volunteers are likely to know only one part of the operation. Also be sure everyone, especially its members, understands the role of the board in fundraising. It should be a board priority. If the board is not going to be active in fundraising, it must delegate that responsibility to another group of volunteers.

5 Encourage positive attitudes towards potential donors – especially corporations, foundations, and governments. It is easy for people involved in voluntary work to fall into the trap of questioning the motives and ethics of such organizations. Suspicion and cynicism are hard to conceal and will not endear you to people whose help you want.

6 Recognize that few people are natural born fundraisers. As with most of what we do in our lives, we need to learn how to ask for money. Provide the training board members and other volunteers need if they are to be comfortable with fundraising.

CARTOON: JOSEPH A. BROWN

"Shipwrecked or not, I never miss sending out my annual contributions."

Many people don't like to admit they need training. They always want to look as if they know exactly what to do about everything. You may want to use more acceptable words than "training" – perhaps "orientation," "setting up a task force," "planning a campaign," or "fundraising strategy." If you are lucky enough to have one or two volunteers with some experience in fundraising, you can ask them to do the training. Training is more palatable, sometimes, when it is given by a peer.

Help in training can be found in many places.

- Some resources are listed at the end of this book. Some are books that can be kept for reference in the office. Some pamphlets, brochures, and booklets might be ordered in quantity for distribution to volunteers, who won't likely want to take time to read books.
- Some international donors can provide simple materials with guidelines for the effective use of volunteer boards as fundraisers.
- Intermediary agencies and umbrella groups with whom you work may have similar guidelines or may be able to suggest local trainers who could help you.
- Local colleges and universities may have fundraisers or other professionals (psychologists, journalism professors) who can help train your volunteers.
- Fundraising associations or centres of philanthropy can provide materials and training.

7 Give new fundraising volunteers subtle coaching, combined with small Start by asking them to work on events, or to stuff envelopes for a mailing, or to sell advertising in a publication. Get them writing thank-you letters; people feel good about saying thank you.

8 Give people partners. Volunteers will do things together that they might fear doing alone. Assign an experienced volunteer to work with a new member. Or pair a volunteer with a staff member until the volunteer feels comfortable and can make the case forcefully and successfully. That will speed up the process of making the new person feel at home as well as confident. Even then, continue the training. There is much to learn.

9 Be patient. People resist change. Make your most pessimistic estimate of how long it will take to build and train a fundraising team. Then double or triple that time and you may come out about right.

10 Build some social time and some fun into the schedule, in addition to the necessary meetings. Give everybody involved in fundraising some time to get to know the organization and one another.

11 Give volunteers a taste of success. Jim Lord suggests volunteers visit donors to say thank you. That way they will understand how rewarding the donation was to the donor and, therefore, will find it easier to talk to people about what their desires are for the organization.

12 Deal with disagreement. People who take the trouble to disagree are to be treasured. They care. If a board has a broad membership, there are bound to be disagreements. If all the members agree, they are bored, disenchanted, or insufficiently challenged. Most destructive of all, they may be keeping their disagreements quiet at the meeting, only to air them afterwards and, sometimes, very publicly.

Fundraising is likely to cause a lot of arguments because everyone has an opinion on the subject. Board members may hesitate to venture strong opinions about the technical aspects of the work of an agency, but they will almost certainly have strong opinions about its fundraising because they are exposed to fundraising in one form or another all the time.

What has been said about the board is equally true about any group of volunteers.

13 Reinforce the goals of your organization regularly. Bring people who have or will benefit from your services to fundraising meetings and events. If the beneficiaries are far away, bring photos, audiotapes, and videos from the field. Make sure people at the centre are fully aware of what is happening where the organization does its real work.

Fighting fear by recognizing strengths

In Book 1 we talked about the strengths and weaknesses of non-profit organizations. Strengths will enhance the likelihood of success in fundraising. Failure to correct weaknesses will almost guarantee failure. Everyone connected to an organization can work to ensure that the foundation for fundraising is strong. That also reduces fear.

Volunteers who have confidence in the organization they are serving are more confident in asking for contributions. It is up to the organization – its manager, its staff members, and members of its board – to instil that confidence. They must convince fundraising volunteers that the organization deserves support. They can do so most effectively if the organization is strong. Strong organizations instil confidence for five reasons, each a strength.

1 They exist for the good of the community. The people who work in them know their contribution is essential and are proud of what they achieve. This is an organization's greatest asset in its work, and its greatest strength when it comes to fundraising.

2 They provide inspiration. They show what people with courage, initiative, and a desire to help can do, often in the face of great difficulties. They attract other people to help them.

3 They have credibility. Potential donors know good voluntary organizations are motivated by service, not profit. When they see a job that needs to be done, and that it will require an investment, they often prefer to see that job done by a voluntary organization. They are concerned that government may be corrupt or inefficient. Donors know that a voluntary organization committed to helping people will use most of the money to solve the problem at hand.

4 They grow in number and power every year because they use low-cost volunteer energy. Neither private enterprises nor governments use volunteers to the same extent, although they are learning quickly. Some private enterprises use interns, for example, and some publicly owned libraries use volunteers to check out books. Volunteers are one of the greatest strengths any organization can have. It is not only that they work without pay. Their enthusiasm and commitment to the job make them good ambassadors and the best fundraisers.

5 They are innovative and can adapt to changing conditions. They can constantly expand their bases of support by enlisting new volunteers and by meeting new kinds of needs, usually very quickly compared to governments. In this way, many organizations that began as small groups of villagers and city dwellers continue to grow after achieving their first goals. Adaptability and innovation are essential to successful fundraising.

ILLUSTRATION: CHRISTOPHER BURKE

"Did I just give, or did I give wisely? That is the question."

Ask yourself:
How many of these five strengths does your organization have?
What other strengths can you build on?

Recognizing possible causes of weakness

If you cannot honestly say your organization has most of the five strengths listed above, or equivalent strengths in other areas, there is obviously room for improvement. The stronger the organization, the weaker the fear of fundraising. To achieve improvement requires strong and imaginative leadership. Weaknesses in leadership may be harder to identify than in other areas, in no small measure because they require the assessment of people who have been key participants – senior staff members, members of the board, and the most active volunteers. Often it is necessary to assess one's own performance – the most difficult assessment of all. Recognition of weaknesses present a wondelful oppertunity to renew organization that may have just been drifting along.

The future of your organization depends on the quality of its leadership. Only strong leadership will bring about renewal and fundraising success. Even one or two people can change the whole direction of any organization. Some reasons leadership may need strengthening:

1 Voluntary organizations are usually built on the enterprise, vision, and dedication of a single person or a small group who saw a community problem and set out to solve it. When the first leaders depart, the organization may falter. The people who join later may lack the founders' commitment. Therefore they may be less successful in making a strong case for support.

2 Many organizations are started by amateurs. Often the same amateurs, or new ones, continue to run the organization for years after its founding. In the beginning they knew what needed to be done. But as the years pass and the organization grows, they begin to face problems for which they are unprepared. They lack the technical expertise and management skills that are essential for growth and financial stability. They feel threatened by people who know more than they do about such matters.

3 People in voluntary organizations often fear anyone outside their own closed circle. They think in terms of "we" and "they." In this case "we" are doing good through our commitment to our organization. "They," all the people we don't know well, are at best indifferent and at worst hostile.

Too often members of voluntary organizations generalize about what they see as the failings of these "others." Consciously or unconsciously, they think, "These people don't really understand us, so we don't need to listen." They may feel they have nothing to learn from "others" whose ideas seem less worthy than the organization's. Or they may close their minds to new ideas that could come from outside because they are afraid; if they did accept that way of thinking they would have to change, perhaps in ways they wouldn't like.

People in business and people with power are especially suspect. Too many people in voluntary organizations say: "Business people are only interested in money. They are just greedy capitalists. What will they want in return for helping us? Will they want to take us over?" They say: "Governments are all corrupt. They have no real interest in the welfare of our people as we do." "We serve the poor, so we also should be poor. Having money would be selling out." People who approach business or government organizations with these intolerant, smug attitudes get a cool reception, no matter how well they think they are hiding their prejudices.

4 Some know their organizations need to invest in the future even when money is tight. That belief frightens people who worry about even the tiniest expense, especially when money is short. People will argue about how many pencils should be used in an office. Or whether money should be spent to entertain someone who might give much more money than a meal would cost. They spend more time thinking of ways to save money than of ways to raise money or of ways to invest in order to grow. They prevent growth.

Conflicts between leaders with imagination and others who think small can paralyse an organization. The small thinkers resent money and time being spent on anything other than their own programs. They fear their little kingdoms will receive less money, that they will become less important. They cannot see that an investment of time and money now will pay off later.

5 Many people in voluntary organizations are so busy that it is hard for them to look beyond their daily problems. As a result they may not know nearly enough about what is happening outside their own community – or even within it. Yet the changes they are ignoring could shape their future. They say to themselves: "We are doing good work, we know that. The money will come. We just need to be patient." That may have been true in the past. But the climate has changed: traditional sources of funding are being reduced, and the competition has increased.

6 Some workers in voluntary organizations rely on resentment to keep themselves going. To each other they say: "We work until late at night, we are away from home for weeks at a time because we believe in what we do. No one else cares." Or they say: "People around here don't understand that what we are doing is important. If they weren't so ignorant and selfish they would give us what we need."

People who think like this believe their commitment to their cause is so worthy and pure that money should just appear. When it doesn't, they almost take delight in feeling unappreciated and misunderstood. They tell themselves it's not their fault they can't achieve anything. It's someone else's fault. When approaching people outside the organization, what do they say? Chances are, it sounds like: "You wouldn't like to give us money, would you?"

7 Voluntary organizations are governed by boards of volunteer members. These volunteers are often dedicated. Nevertheless, as discussed earlier, very few boards do a good job. They have a hard time understanding how voluntary organizations try to achieve two conflicting goals – to grow and serve more people and at the same time to keep their special spirit and purpose. Boards may think a volunteer organization can be managed like a business. Some disagree with the organization's managers, who are more concerned with service than with the bottom line of a financial statement. Some are not involved in many important decisions and do not always receive enough information to know what is happening in the office or the field. Often, board members don't read the information they are given. If the management is competent, the board may trust the managers far too much, especially on financial matters. Boards can also make bad decisions, especially about hiring senior people.

Boards also often lack the competence to set policy on the technical matters that are part of an organization's work. How many people on the board of the World Wide Fund for Nature know in detail all the pros and cons of cutting old growth forests? How many people on the board of WaterLink, can we imagine, would know about the mechanisms of a hand pump or the construction of roof storage tanks?

8 Management may be weak. In fundraising, many problems arise, not from the quality of the activities – which may be excellent – but from the inability of the manager to get them started. One excuse follows another. The chairman is out of town, the brochure was damaged by water, it is the wrong time of year. Excuses do not produce money. Fundraising, after all, is not essentially all that complicated. You just have to ask effectively for an investment in your organization and say thank you when you receive it.

9 Managers can be worn out by the pressures of struggling to find the funds to ensure the organization's survival, while at the same time being expected to give daily leadership. Their expectations and ambitions shrink. They may no longer believe their community values their service enough to support it. They don't promote new fundraising ideas. They end up merely going through the motions of management, uncertain whether they can reach their goals. They lack the energy for fundraising; when they ask for money, they are likely to be half-hearted. They don't really expect a donation, and as a result they don't get one.

Ask yourself:

Does your organization have any of these weaknesses?
Does your organization have weaknesses that have not been mentioned?
How can they be overcome?

If your organization has any of these weaknesses, they will reduce your ability to raise funds. Try to reduce the weaknesses and maximize your fundraising potential. Strong leadership is the first essential ingredient in building confidence in any area of activity. It is crucial to overcoming fear of fundraising.

8 The role of volunteers

The fundraising plan is in place. It has been approved by the board. Board members have been raising some money from friends and colleagues. Several board members have agreed to take the lead in launching a volunteer fundraising program. Six prominent people have lent their names in support of your fundraising program. But more is needed. That means having more volunteers out in the community talking to potential donors. The board wants to recruit what we will call a fundraising task force – a small group of people who will actually do the asking. Thinking of volunteer fundraisers as a task force says "focus," "action," "urgency." Don't form a "committee." That word says "deliberation," "meetings," "relaxation." Encourage people to start talking whenever they get together and at board meetings about possible volunteers. "That is just the sort of person we need out raising funds."

Organizations that have had bad experiences with volunteers in the past might think about giving a volunteer program another try. Those who have had no experience with volunteers should think about investing some time in enlisting volunteers to help with fundraising. You have to ask. Do it. You have nothing to lose. You do not need to start with a large group. Five or six volunteers should be sufficient. Several may already be serving on the board of directors. The theory is that these few committed volunteers will attract the other volunteers needed to form the Task Force.

It's true, of course, that staff working alone will raise money. In the short term, they may even be very successful, but their ability to reach into the community is limited. Staff members are few and busy already. Over the long haul and just about everywhere, experience has shown that volunteers supported by staff will raise a lot more money than staff alone. Volunteers are essential: People give because they choose to give. And they give most to people like themselves who have also chosen to give, rather than to people who are paid to raise money.

Volunteers also donate more generously to the organization they are helping than do people who are not volunteers. The kind of commitment

Groups are destroyed by having one or two people do all the fundraising. You must have a group of volunteers who will get involved in fundraising.

KIM KLEIN, CONSULTANT, UNITED STATES

It is difficult to have volunteers when you have paid staff. Volunteers can feel they are raising money for your salary. It is important to show them where your salary comes from and what your job is. They should understand that the staff is paid from projects, not from fundraising. The volunteers expect staff to do the fundraising. We must be clear about our roles.

KATALIN CZIPPAN, GÖNCÖL FOUNDATION, HUNGARY

that can be achieved can be seen in a Mexican program called MIRA. In English, the full name of the program is "Look out for others." Citizens who join MIRA are asked to show a commitment to a social cause by giving both time and money, at least one hour a week and 1 per cent of their income. Most of them do.

Do you see the potential for raising money in your community but lack the resources or contacts within your organization to take advantage of the opportunities? Then you are ready to make the investment required to use volunteers successfully in fundraising.

The four kinds of local fundraising

As we have seen in the preceding chapter, there are basically four kinds of local fundraising. Volunteers are essential to the success of all of them. The four kinds are:

1 *Sale of merchandise, services, or events.* In this type of fundraising, the donor is a consumer. To be effective, goods and services must be available continuously and events must be repeated every year for several years. Only then will they become part of the community's annual cycle, something people think of automatically and look forward to.

Volunteers may organize and assist at fundraising events such as dinners and bazaars, or sell advertising in programs for events. These activities are also useful for promoting the organization, bringing supporters together, and raising limited funds.

2 *Broad-scale, individual solicitation asking for small donations.* This category includes letters mailed to a large number of potential small donors, telephone campaigns, advertisements with requests for donations, and donation boxes. These marketing techniques are important for building a large group of donors.

Volunteers are an excellent source of ideas, and are essential for clerical support such as recording donations and issuing receipts, making telephone calls, canvassing, conducting flag days, and collecting donation boxes. They can also help arrange in-kind donations such as the free provision of printing and free space and time in the media.

3 *Solicitation of organizations.* The approach – whether it is to a corporation, foundation, service club, umbrella or intermediary group, labour union, or religious group – is usually made in a brief written presentation, often followed by a visit. More than one person within the organization is likely to be involved in any decision to give money; a committee may be involved, or a board.

Volunteers can help with research to decide which organizations will be the most receptive, and in preparing presentations. They may be able to introduce you to the people who make the decisions, and deliver or assist with the presentations and the follow-up.

4 *Solicitation of small groups and individuals who can make substantial donations.* This kind of support is usually asked for face-to-face. Personal fundraising is the simplest, most efficient way to raise money, but it may be a new role for volunteers in your organization. It works best when volun-

teers who have themselves already given generously approach people they know, asking them to do the same.

This chapter covers some general principles of working with all kinds of fundraising volunteers, both those who ask personally for donations and those who support the fundraising program behind the scenes. In Book 3 we will see how volunteers can best be used in specific kinds of fundraising programs.

Fundraising volunteers come in many styles

As you set up a volunteer program, think about the kinds of people and the mix of attitudes, skills, and experience your fundraising program will require. The key to success is to get people doing what needs to be done and what they do best.

There are several varieties of volunteers, who can be described by the way they respond to a request for help.

1 *"Tell me what to do and I'll do it."* Some volunteers work to support fundraising in much the same way as other volunteers work in the core program. They may assist regularly and frequently, perhaps by helping at a fundraising event or giving a few hours each week to sell in a shop, by distributing and gathering donation boxes from stores and banks, or by doing the extra clerical work that new fundraising programs can entail. While they may be asked to use new skills – to use computers, for example – their work can be planned in the same way as the work of core staff.

Some may not want a lot of responsibility. They will be quite content to do routine jobs that don't demand much skill or effort. Others may be happy to take on detailed work that must be done with great care. Many volunteers simply want to do the job assigned and become impatient with a lot of talk. They enjoy being followers and don't want to lead. My favourite volunteer came to the office every week. He spent the day typing and sending out receipts for donations. He had no interest in attending staff meetings, but he cared deeply about the organization and he did the receipts perfectly. Because he lived alone, he also enjoyed social times with the staff members and having the Thai food we often brought into the office for lunch.

2 *"Let's have a meeting and talk about what we should do."* Many volunteers love meetings. They are happy to give time to policy discussions, to planning, to organizing. That is fine if they think clearly, speak briefly and to the point, make genuine contributions to the discussion, and like decisions to be made quickly. If instead they love to hear themselves talk, they will stretch out discussions; the result will be frequent, endless meetings. Even that can be manageable provided you have time and don't involve others who are impatient with too much talk. And provided the talkative volunteers make a significant contribution that compensates for the time they spend speaking.

3 *"I have often done that kind of work. I can help solve that problem."* These people could be described as old hands. They are the foundation on which success is built. They have the experience to perform a task themselves or help other, less experienced people learn to do it. They may or

may not like meetings. They may prefer to help out when needed rather than fit into a routine, and to get the job done without caring about drawing attention to themselves.

Many business people who give professional help to organizations fit into this category. Their help may come with the blessing of the person's employer and be given during office hours, or it may be given on the employee's own time. Retired professionals of many kinds can be especially helpful.

4 *"I can organize that event. And I guarantee it will attract more people and raise more money than last year."* And it probably will, if the promise is made by someone who has proved through experience to be trustworthy. Once such people have been persuaded to take on a job, a manager can turn them loose and relax. These good performers may not like committees either, unless they form their own.

They may give a great deal of time to organizing activities that have a tangible benefit to the donor. The benefit may simply be enjoyment – a concert, a long-distance run, or a picnic. Many organizations have been using volunteers to raise money in this way for a long time. The activities may require detailed, intensive planning and a major commitment of time by the volunteers involved. The volunteers are likely to operate somewhat independently of the organization's staff.

5 *"I'll talk to some of my friends. I know they will invest in your organization if I ask them."* Volunteers of this type may work with an organization's board or committee members, but they may prefer to spend their time talking to donors rather than sitting at meetings.

They may be part of a campaign to solicit funds once or twice a year or, sometimes, year round. Working closely with the board or fundraising management group, they actually go out and ask for financial support. This role for volunteers is new in many places and is always controversial. It challenges volunteers in ways they may never have encountered before. Meeting these challenges has been dealt with in the preceding chapter on fear of fundraising.

You will surely find more types of volunteers. It s rarely possible to know a person's strengths and weaknesses before they have been around the organization for a while. But, from the beginning, you should have in the back of your mind the types of volunteers you want. You would certainly not be happy to find you had assembled a group of volunteers that wanted only to have meetings or were prepared only to do clerical work.

What are the characteristics of good fundraising volunteers?

It is easy, in making a list of the qualities of a good volunteer, to describe a person so perfect he or she could never exist. More reasonably, you might hope for fundraising volunteers who:

- share your vision of what the organization can achieve
- believe strongly in the service your organization provides today
- recognize that private support is essential
- are willing to give their own financial support, however modest

- have many of the skills you need to get the job done
- have a friendly, outgoing personality
- have an optimistic view of life
- are not easily discouraged
- enjoy learning new skills
- make only promises that can be kept and keep these promises
- can arrange some free time. The best volunteers I know are busy people who have learned how to schedule their time carefully.

You may have noticed that one characteristic is not on the list. Knowing prominent people is certainly helpful, but it should not be required. Reliability and dedication are more important than contacts. Of course, prominence is relative. For many small community organizations, it is more important to have a volunteer who knows the mayor or the largest shop owner than it is to have one who knows the governor or the head of the biggest industry in the state. And while knowing important people can be valuable, it is the strength of a volunteer's commitment to the organization that will produce results from that acquaintance. In any case, every volunteer will know dozens, even hundreds, of people who can help.

Try to get a good balance of men and women among fundraising volunteers. In the past, men have been the board members and women the volunteers. That is no longer true.

Recognize. Reward. Thank.

Feeling useful, working for a cause that is bigger than yourself, is rewarding in itself. But it is not enough, especially in the difficult and often thankless task of fundraising. Here are some further suggestions about ways to keep fundraising volunteers happy and motivated.

1 Volunteers wear out if they feel too much pressure – if they never hear or do anything but fundraising, fundraising, fundraising. Give volunteer fundraisers time to get to know one another and enjoy each other's company. Don't forget about having fun.

In 1997 a group of women launched a movement called Womenpower. Its purpose is to get more women elected to the Philippine national government. Senator Leticia Shahani, the sister of the then president, Fidel Ramos, was the special guest at one of the launchings – a meeting of 300 women north of Manila. Each of the women present was asked to go home and get small donations from dozens of other women to finance this movement. Senator Shahani suggested that the women should not be serious all the time – there should also be time for fun. After the meeting, everyone watched a performance by a group of dance students from a university. Everyone went away feeling that, although most of the meeting was extremely serious, they had also had a good time.

2 Arrange dinners, lunches, picnics, or other social events volunteers will enjoy. Be sure such events are not paid for from any money the volunteers are raising. Arrange outside sponsorship, or charge for admission.

3 Find ways to reward those who bring in financial support, especially at the beginning when it is easy to get discouraged. Perhaps an event was

much more successful this year than it was last year because a new volunteer took charge. The chairman thanked him profusely at the event. What else could he do? Perhaps write a letter to the man's employer with his permission? Thank him in the newsletter or the annual report of the organization? Present him with an inscribed plaque or certificate commemorating the event or with some other suitable memento? In fundraising, the results are clear. They can be quantified. If four people are each asking a number of individuals for donations, it may become obvious that one has been particularly successful. One person may consistently bring larger donations than anyone else, but is sometimes turned down. Another may not bring in as much money but gets at least a small donation from everyone she approaches. Both have succeeded. Reward successful volunteers with promotion, if they want to be promoted. One of them, who proves also to be a good organizer, could eventually become head of the fundraising committee. Later, the same person could be elected to the board. In this way the board would be strengthened and diversified. No one can argue with the record of a successful volunteer.

9 Planning an effective communications program: introduction

Successful fundraising requires credibility. And credibility is like a bridge. A voluntary organization cannot start to build a bridge the day the river rises. Like a bridge, credibility must be built in advance. You cannot wait to build it until you lose some overseas funding, or when you need corporate support, or when your organization is criticized.

Book 1 showed the importance of building credibility and many ways of doing it. The second half of this book talks about how you can use effective communication to build your credibility, to communicate effectively with people whose opinion you value, from a simple message on a poster to a site on the World Wide Web. It also describes ways you can get feedback about the success of your communications projects. Effective communication is essential to gain the financial support you want. It will help you ensure that you are trusted and respected – but only if your organization is worthy of trust and respect, and if people know enough about your organization. "Serving the community is the best way to increase credibility," according to Manuel Arango, founder of the Mexican Center for Philanthropy. However, he adds, "Visibility can accelerate the downfall of an organization if it does not have clear goals and effective delivery." Public confidence cannot be built overnight. It must be built over time, by a continuous program to raise public awareness of the services your organization offers and their value to society. This program should start long before actual fundraising begins.

Building a good reputation takes:
- long-term planning
- continuing attention
- the involvement of everyone in the organization
- a bit of money
- actual achievements
   and
- a clear commitment to the values of the organization

It is easy to forget the last requirement. People can get so excited about seeking publicity or raising funds that, along the way, the basic philosophy of the organization becomes fuzzy, if not compromised. An agency work-

Hungarians can now donate one per cent of their income tax payment to almost any NGO that has been operating at least three years, has no public debts, and does not serve political purposes. The biggest interest was in the organizations that have good public relations and good media leverage. What the NGOs learned was that they had to communicate better.

MARIANNA TÖRÖK, NONPROFIT INFORMATION AND TRAINING CENTRE, HUNGARY

ing for a clean environment might want to attract a large audience to a garden show. If it drops stacks of leaflets where they can blow around and litter the streets, is the organization truly committed to its own cause? What about an organization that exists to end poverty and towards that goal holds extravagant fundraising events?

Building the bridge of credibility requires attention to the traffic in both directions. Credibility comes not just from what goes out. It also comes from responding to what comes from outside. You must listen as well as talk. You need to keep in touch with the changes that affect your work and your world. Keep current with news and public affairs. Read magazines and newspapers; look at television and videos. Gather feedback about your organization's work and its communications activities. The knowledge you gain will help make it credible in the wider community.

A good communications program extends to all areas of an organization's activities. Too often, "poor communications" or "inadequate public relations" are the result of bad management or bad systems – for example, when requests for information go unanswered or telephone calls are not returned.

Communications programs require the full understanding, support, and participation of staff members and volunteers. Don't assume this will be given. Sometimes staff members resent money being spent on fundraising programs. That resentment will likely diminish when programs are seen to be successful. There may be even less readiness to accept an investment in public relations or friendmaking. These programs are essential but, to some people, any payoff seems difficult or impossible to measure, and far too long term. Once credibility is established by these means, the same tools can be used to obtain the resources you need.

The following chapters discuss various media. They are only introductions to techniques that are increasingly being carried out by professionals. Think of what follows as a beginning. Try to learn more from some of the many books on specific media. Ask experts for advice. Study what other people are doing and adapt to your needs what you find successful.

10 Competing for attention

Plants in a rain forest compete for light. Animals compete for food. People compete for money. We all compete every day for the time and attention of our families, our friends, and other people whose opinions or emotions we want to influence. The most difficult competition is for the attention of people who don't think they need to be interested in what we say and do. It is not enough for us to be convinced that our cause is worthy and that people should pay attention. We have to get them to want to pay attention.

For example, organizations often decide to publish a newsletter because they feel people need to know what the organization is doing. These organizations are fooling themselves. People don't need to know very much. People generally feel they need information only about their health, their family, their physical security, their financial situation. They are not watching the mail for a newsletter to tell them how to help their community by supporting your organization. They are not walking around town looking to see what new poster you have put up this week. Nor are they running to the radio to hear news of your latest successful project. You have to make them *want* to learn more about your work. The only way to do that is to make the information so interesting and attractive that people will want to pay attention.

People everywhere make up their minds in two or three seconds whether or not to look or listen. There is very little time to catch their attention. Articles in a newsletter or newspaper compete with other articles. Publications compete with other publications. They compete as well with radio, television, videos, films, and other forms of information and entertainment. And all these media compete with other demands on their intended audience: telephone calls, correspondence, meetings, social events, and sports, not to speak of family, friends, noise, sickness, and the need to sleep.

How does an organization compete successfully for attention?

People who attract favourable attention to their organization have, for a start, a worthy cause. What else do they have? They connect easily with other people because they have taken the trouble to find out what will interest and excite them. They talk persuasively about their work. They know the basics of effective communication. As well, they have a strong sense of competition. They are determined to capture and keep people's interest. That means always having a target audience in mind. It means understanding and empathizing with that audience. Successful competitors for attention know that first impressions are most important. If the message is not immediately appealing, the intended audience is apt to go on to something else.

These organizations know also that once attention is captured, it can be easily lost. An audience will listen to a speaker for the first few minutes. If they are not interested then, people may leave. More likely, they will just stop listening and think about other, competing matters. In the same way, readers may pay attention to the beginning of an article, but stop reading as soon as they lose interest. Very few people feel they must finish everything they start reading.

Successful competitors know they must keep the audience's attention. They know the rules to capture and keep attention. These rules are always the same, whether an audience is sitting together in a village square or school room, attending a service club meeting, reading a magazine or newspaper, listening to the radio, or watching television. They are:

1 Analyse the intended audience, to learn what will interest its members. Keep the interests of the audience in mind throughout each speech, article, broadcast, or broad communications program. Keep asking yourself: "Will this interest the people I am trying to reach?"

2 Plan a special presentation for each audience, tailored to its interests. Even if the same material is used on several occasions, it may need to be introduced differently for different audiences.

3 Begin with a striking title and opening. Get attention immediately.

4 Talk and write about people and achievements, using examples, illustrations, and anecdotes.

5 Speak like a person with feelings, a person who can empathize with members of the community. Talk in a personal way. Don't sound like a bureaucrat. Convey excitement.

6 Demonstrate how the information you are giving will help the intended audience and its community. Talk about benefits, benefits, benefits.

7 If possible, use more than one medium: combine talking with writing and pictures; combine print with pictures.

8 Emphasize all the good things you are doing. People prefer to support success, not failure.

9 Never forget that the audience has a short attention span. Fight constantly for its attention.

10 End with a positive summary – often a call for action.

These general rules can be applied in different ways in speaking, audio-visual presentations, printed publications, and on the Internet. Some successful techniques in each of these media will be discussed in more detail in the following chapters. Follow these simple rules to develop other successful techniques for capturing and keeping attention.

11 Planning to communicate

This chapter provides 11 general rules for effective communications for fundraising. These make clear that a successful communications program is a two-way street; information must be gathered as well as distributed. It will become equally clear that an effective communications program does not start or run by itself. Even a small program takes time and thought. Plan to spend several hours each week.

1 Do research

Information is power. Think of the middleman who buys fish on the beach from the fisherman. He knows the price of fish in the market. The fisherfolk probably don't know the price. They know only what the middleman will pay. Who has the power? Who has the greater freedom?

A voluntary organization cannot afford to be ill informed. It needs systems to tell it what will happen in its areas of concern tomorrow, and for the next five years. It needs to anticipate troubles and opportunities and plan for them. That job usually falls on the executive director, but all the active participants in an organization should be aware of what is going on outside. They must act as bridges between the organization and the public, explaining each to the other.

Useful information is everywhere nowadays. Some will come to you without your doing anything. Other, more valuable information comes only with hard work. Is your organization aggressively looking for the information it needs to provide the best possible service? For example, you need to plan for changing circumstances in the community you intend to serve. Do you know what these changes are likely to be? You also need to be up-to-date on the interests and requirements of your financial supporters. Do you look at these only occasionally, when you remember? Or do you look in a systematic way?

What tools can you use?

Listen to the radio, read newspapers, look at videos, watch television if it is available. As you listen and read, ask yourself questions like these:

- Has the government changed its policies about supporting organizations like ours?
- Are new politicians gaining influence nationally or locally? What can we learn about them and their ideas? How may they affect our work?
- Are there major political changes, such as elections, that could affect our funding or the needs of the people we serve?

- Are there major economic changes such as currency devaluation, high inflation, or declining exports that could affect the amount of money people have to spend or the lives of the people we serve?

Subscribe to local and national magazines; read books for background information and analysis. Ask:

- What are the social trends in my country and the rest of the world that could affect my work? Is support for protecting the environment increasing, for example? How do these changes affect my organization?
- What are the economic trends locally and globally? How will they affect the lives of the people we serve? What new programs may be needed? What programs may need to be expanded or altered in response to these trends?

Phone, visit, or write embassies and foundations for information and help. Ask them:

- What programs do you support?
- Could you please send us more information about your programs and how we might apply for support?
- Can you tell us the names of potential donors – individuals, granting bodies, and businesses, that might support our organization's work?

Use reference material in libraries, colleges, embassies. Use phone books, directories of businesses and business people, foundations, and other possible lists of donors.

- What lists of prospective donors, both local and international, can we find?
- What can I find out about prospective donors that will help me approach them successfully?

Talk to people. Visit municipal offices, the legislature, appropriate government departments, service clubs, the Chamber of Commerce.

- What political changes are happening?
- How will they affect us?
- Who should we be telling about our work?
- Are there new people we should meet?
- Are there new grants available?

Visit local businesses to find out their interests and to tell your story.

- How can our organization help your business improve our community? What can we do together?

Visit colleagues in your own and other voluntary organizations to find out what they are doing and thinking about.

- What trends are they seeing in support for their work?
- What changes are they seeing or anticipating in their communities?
- What should we be hoping for that we have not yet planned for?
- Are there new ways we can work together?

Speed up your communications if you can afford it. Don't wait weeks for an answer to a letter. Use the telephone or cell phone. Send faxes. Use e-mail to send and receive messages, ideas, news. If you do not have an Internet connection, find a local group that can send and receive mail for you.

Get on the World Wide Web if you can afford it. Otherwise find a Web user. You will be able to read useful material from around the world. This may help answer questions you have about issues in your organization, and the experiences of organizations around the world can help in your work.

No organization, no matter how isolated, can afford to say it does not know where to look for grants. It may be difficult to find the right person who speaks the right language to make a telephone call to an embassy, foundation, corporation, or library. It may require learning new skills such as typing, to use a typewriter or a computer. It may be necessary to travel to a telephone and there may be endless delays in making calls. It may require finding the money to travel to a city. You may need to take risks, to make mistakes, to find dead ends where you thought valuable help or information would emerge. And there may be a cost. But the returns may more than compensate for the cost. As your knowledge increases, so your credibility will increase.

The benefits of reading, listening, and research

Example 1: I saw an advertisement in the paper by a company that sells organic foods. I phoned and found out who the local director is and I wrote her a letter saying I would like to meet with her to tell her about our work. Now we have an adviser from the company who comes every two weeks to help our farmers. The president of the company also has arranged a donation from her head office.

Example 2: I heard on a farm broadcast about the new world trade regulations. They scared me. People here raise cattle and sell the milk. But I read that now milk powder from other countries is going to be cheaper than the milk we produce. We may not be able to sell our milk. We should help farmers learn other ways to make a living. We have started research into other possible crops, using the Internet.

Example 3: The head of a health clinic in the next town said he had asked the manager of his bank if he could put boxes on the counters so people could leave donations. He told me how it worked. But I wanted to know more before I talked to our local bank manager. What should the boxes look like? What should they be made of – plastic, metal, wood? How often do the boxes need to be checked? How do we ensure that money is not stolen? I knew I wanted to be the first person in our town to ask so I had to act quickly. I went to the library but there was no information there. So I asked a friend in an office to send an e-mail to a foundation in England that has supported us. It sent some information from a magazine. Then I spoke to our bank manager, who agreed to our plan. It has worked out well. We now have boxes in six banks and we get donations nearly every day.

2 Choose the message

An organization needs to explain to the public what it is doing and how it helps people. It should be able to express this in one or two short sentences – some people say "in not more than twelve words." If you can't compose a simple message, one theme that anyone can understand, more thinking is needed. Your mission statement may serve this purpose but it may need refining and simplifying.

Say, as simply and specifically as possible, what you plan to do. That is better than a statement of what you want to do or a statement of policy. People may not understand or approve general statements. They are more likely to respond to a concrete explanation of how their support will be of benefit.

Don't say: *The Women's Volunteer Organization is committed to helping local women increase their income.*

Instead, say: *Thirty more women will help support their families next year. With loans from the Women's Volunteer Organization, thirty village women will start businesses next year and add to their family's income.*

It is also important to have ready-to-use examples of what you are doing: *For the first time Maria Gonzales has earned enough money to feed her family and have money left over. Last year she was able to arrange a small loan to buy the supplies she needed to produce and sell the bread her neighbours have praised for years. She got the loan from the Women's Volunteer Organization. Marie is only one of fifty women starting small businesses who have been supported by the organization since it was founded just two years ago.*

Best of all, try to find a slogan that will capture attention and be remembered. Think of a radio commercial, or an advertisement on a billboard. These messages are simple; they are repeated over and over and over. They talk about the benefits to the purchaser. Soap commercials don't talk about the chemical composition of detergent. They talk about how a particular detergent will get your clothes clean. Your message should always stress the benefits of your work to the community or the country. You will repeat it over and over, perhaps for several years. It is a good idea to put it in every publication and on a large sign on the wall in your office so that everyone has it in mind every day. For that to be possible – and effective – the message must be short and memorable. One sentence will be better than two, five words better than twelve: *Small loans to fight poverty.*

3 Choose your target audiences

A voluntary organization may have many publics. It takes years and a lot of money to change public opinion. Don't try. Too many organizations, when asked who they want to influence, will say "the public" or "the media." Unless organizations have huge sums of money to spend on marketing over at least three years, they cannot do it. But they can try to influence several of the audiences who are important to their future.

Concentrate your resources on reaching only the audiences that can do your organization the most good or the most harm, or both. Make a list according to your priorities. Even if the list is long, put all your efforts into influencing only the most important audiences. Don't waste time and effort trying to persuade people who are most unlikely to support your work. Use your resources where they are the most effective. In reaching larger audiences, we must make a conscious effort to understand the people we want to influence and to learn their interests and experiences. Then we can anticipate their possible responses and tailor our message to meet them. Ask:

Who are the people we want to reach?
Do they understand the goals of our organization?
Do they approve of them?
How would we like each audience to respond to each of our efforts?

My belief is that the people closest to you need the most attention. Staff members who speak well of their organization are its best ambassadors. Disaffected employees cause irreparable harm. Your neighbours are also important. They may not know much about your organization at the moment but, should there be some trouble, they could cause a good deal of harm. A small agency should concentrate on people in its own community and people in the region who can affect its stability and its work. The decisions of local politicians can affect it in many ways, but the actions of politicians or businesses in the national arena may have little impact. On the other hand, a large agency will have to be concerned about local, state or provincial, and national, even international groups. There are many other groups to rate in terms of good and harm – volunteers, other voluntary organizations, granting agencies, students, current donors, local media, etc.

Ask yourself what you can write down about each audience you want to address.

4 Know the audiences

Ask yourself what you can write down about each audience you want to address. This question is far more important than it may seem. If you don't know your audiences, you won't know how to approach them. Your time and your money will be spent for nothing.

- Where do they work?
- Where do they live?
- Where is the best place to reach them?
- How old are they? (You will talk to high school students one way, to a group of retired teachers another way.)
- Are they mostly men or mostly women? How should we adjust our message for each group?
- How much education have they had? (For people with little education, your most effective printed communication might be a poster with only two or three words. For people who finished high school or college, a short letter might be just right.)
- How do they see the world? Are their interests purely local? Are they happy with life as it is or do they want political or economic change?
- Who or what is likely to motivate them to give? The church? A popular performer? A description of local needs? Everybody gives to someone. Who do they give to now?

5 Set targets

For every communications program and every audience, plan the result you want. Set targets with specific numbers. Perhaps you want more volunteers. You decide that an open house would bring people to your project. Some might become new volunteers. How many volunteers would you need to enlist to consider the event a success? How many people should you invite? Who should you invite? Obviously, you will invite potential volunteers. Will you invite the media? Only if you want publicity for your efforts to recruit volunteers.

6 Choose the best media to meet the objectives and reach each audience

Words spoken to another person face-to-face are the least expensive, simplest, most effective – and most neglected – way to communicate. Why? Because in personal contact you have more than words. You also have gesture, expression, and body movement, which together are more powerful than the words themselves. However, the number of people who can be reached is limited. In contrast, print can reach many people. The printed word is the easiest to control: you can plan everything you want to say beforehand. The printed word is also very visible. But it is often used badly and is therefore ignored. Images, photographs, illustrations are difficult to use well and can be expensive, but they can have a wonderful emotional impact. Television is the most powerful medium available today but is expensive to use, and broadcast television is often state-controlled.

Selecting the medium depends on the response you want from each audience. For each target audience you will need to choose the medium most appropriate for your needs:

* *spoken word:* radio, meetings, open houses, special events and celebrations, public speaking, word of mouth

The spoken word is a simple, effective way to communicate: people decide what to think by listening and talking to other people more than by any other means. It is also the most neglected when planning a communications program. Most of us feel nervous about putting ourselves in situations we cannot control. We fear saying the wrong thing or making a bad impression. We may also feel we cannot reach enough people by personal contact. Nevertheless, the effort is worthwhile.

* *images:* motion pictures, slides, television, film clips, displays, exhibits. These techniques are the most complex and expensive, but they are also more powerful than words. They are valuable reinforcements to print.

* *printed word:* magazines, pamphlets, booklets, manuals, books, letters, bulletins, newsletters, printed speeches, bulletin boards, posters, advertising, annual reports. Print gives control, is relatively inexpensive, and can reach large numbers of people. But print is easy to ignore. Lots of people rarely read anything. Others cannot read. With print, moreover, there may be no direct opportunity to respond.

7 Write down everything you plan

Write down the main messages you want to deliver, who you will deliver them to, the media you will use to deliver the messages, the schedule, what the program will cost.

Most people think they can do more than is really possible. The advantage of writing everything down, no matter how briefly, is that you will be able to see exactly what is involved in the communications program you have planned. You will bring together in one place all the programs you would like to carry out – speeches, brochures, newsletters, exhibits, and so on. You will then be able to decide whether you have the time to do it all and the money to pay for it.

8 Decide on a budget and a timetable

The rule with producing communications materials, like most of life, is that all the steps will take longer and cost more than you hope.

• Allow twice as long as your most pessimistic assessment to get anything planned, written, produced, and distributed. A dozen or more people can be involved in even the simplest publication, from the person who saw the need in the first place to the writer, the person who approves the material, the printer, and the clerk at the post office. If the work is done too quickly, mistakes happen. A misspelled word or a wrong number may mean the publication goes in the trash. Even worse, the error may go unnoticed in the rush. If the publication is distributed, your money may be wasted and your credibility damaged.

In budgeting, it is easy to estimate and track costs if people outside the organization are paid to do the work. But often most of the work is done by staff members or by volunteers who need supervision by staff. In such cases, organizations rarely bother to keep track of how much time is spent, not just in completing the publication, but in talking about and tinkering with it. It is a good idea to keep track of the time spent on each publication. If people are allowed to make endless changes, time is wasted. The cost of a publication in terms of time can be out of proportion to its benefit. A method for putting a cost on staff time is explained in Chapter 1.

The steps in producing any communications materials are much the same. As an example, the process that might be followed in preparing a brochure with photographs and drawings is outlined below.

• Be sure to include enough time for thinking about the publication and then for writing and revision. Make a time chart that includes as many as possible of the following steps and a date when it will be completed.

Planning time, to determine:
   audience
   purpose
   content
   quantity

when required
budget
method of distribution

Writing/illustrations

first draft
approval of first draft
second draft
design prepared
design approved
taking photographs
rough sketches of drawings
final sketches of drawings
approval of second draft
final version
typesetting
preparation of final material

Printing

ordering envelopes if necessary
printing brochure
delivery
checking printing

Distribution

addressing and stuffing envelopes
delivery to post office
other distribution

Once you have dates, prepare a time chart similar to the one for advertising books in Book 3, Chapter 4. Some steps can be done at the same time. For example, photographs can be taken while the text is being revised. Use the time chart to make sure the different stages mesh together for efficiency.

Many of the steps involve money as well as time. If outside, paid contractors – a designer, a writer – do some of the work, their fees should be included in the budget unless you have the good fortune to arrange a donation. Some jobs such as stuffing envelopes may be done by staff or volunteers, which means only time needs to be watched. Even so, allow for snacks and other minor expenses involved in using volunteers.

If you can afford a designer, be sure you work with one whose pricing you can trust to be fair. If you have not had experience with a designer, ask two to give a price for the project and other work for your organization, so you get to know their work and their charges. You will also want to ask two or three printers to tell you how much they will charge to do the job. Printing is a highly competitive business. The budget should include these costs:

Writing/illustrations

> writing several drafts
> design preparation
> arranging illustrations
> taking photographs

Printing

> preparation for printer
> trips to printer
> printing
> envelopes

Distribution

> stuffing envelopes
> delivery to post office
> postage
> other distribution

While you want your publicity, indeed all your communications, to be effective, be careful not to overdo public relations. You don't want to be getting so much publicity or putting out so many lavish brochures that people think you are spending money on appearance instead of on programs, or that you have all kinds of money and don't need more.

9 Get the plan approved

Formal approval of a communications program may not sound necessary, but it is essential for good management and for keeping the confidence of your board of directors. Much of what a manager does in an organization is invisible even to the board. But a communications program is visible. A manager suddenly becomes vulnerable. Many people think they are experts in communications. They feel entitled to comment on every item that appears in the media – every brochure, every issue of the newsletter. They will tell you what to do, criticize what you have done, and probably expect immediate change.

Give your communications plan to your board for their information or their approval. Talk about it thoroughly. That way there will be no surprises when new publications appear or you start looking for opportunities to address business people.

10 Create and distribute the materials

This will be covered in the next few chapters.

11 Monitor and evaluate the results

It is essential to keep learning. Watch all the time to see what works and what doesn't. This activity circles back to step 1. Without all these steps the organization has no idea what it should be doing or why. Without evaluation, it's possible to do some things right by luck and judgement, but it's equally possible that time is wasted and money thrown away.

Ask:

How do we want each audience to respond to each of our efforts?
Do we make clear in every communication what response we hope for?
Did the number of people responding meet our targets? If not, why not?
Were the responses as positive as we had expected? If not, why not?
What lessons did we learn? What can we do better next time?

Monitoring and evaluation are discussed further in several of the chapters that follow.

12 Seventeen paths to effective communication

This chapter presents 17 rules for effective communication. They are true for any medium – speech, print, illustrations, radio, television. In print they can be applied to everything from posters and advertisements to newsletters and books. If you follow them, there is a good chance that your message will reach its intended audience, will be understood, and will generate the response you wish.

The basis for these rules is very simple. Every message links a sender (you) and a receiver (the audience, whether one person or thousands). The sender has something to say. It may be information or entertainment, as is common in the popular press. It may be advice that will benefit the receiver. In fundraising, the message is usually that people in the community need a service and that action must be taken to meet that need.

In any message, the sender has two principal objectives. The first is to capture the attention of the receiver, and then keep it. The second is to be sure the message is so clear that the receiver will understand it and then act upon it. (That may sound simple but it is not. There are many ways to muddy a message. Bad spelling and grammar are two ways. Others are less obvious.) The rules that follow will help you to achieve these two objectives.

1 Think of the audience

Picture a typical listener or reader. Perhaps she is a new member of your local government to whom you want to introduce your organization. Perhaps she is a new board member. Perhaps she is a potential donor. Once you have a person in mind, speak or write as if you were trying to convince that one person. Ask yourself: Will she understand this? Does she need more explanation? Will she be interested? Am I using words she will know? Am I giving too much detail? If you don't like the answers, revise your message to meet the interests of the person you are writing for.

The most important question to ask is: Am I talking to her about benefits she will appreciate? You will need to persuade her that the programs of your organization will benefit her. This usually means rethinking entirely the way that you have described your work in the past. You have likely simply described your organization, its mission, its activities. Now you will want to put everything in terms of how these activities improve the life and the community of a typical member of your audience.

It is always easier to write for one person. It is much more difficult to write something for a group of people who have different personalities and different lives. Don't try. In writing, have a single typical person in mind. In the same way, if you are giving a speech, focus on a person who is typical of the group. Choose someone in the audience who seems friendly as well as typical and watch how he or she responds to what you are saying.

2 Write about people
People are interested in people. They can identify with people more easily than with things or with abstractions. Effective writing and speaking bring ideas down to the level of the individual.

3 Use examples
Examples bring the message to life. They bring the discussion to the level of the individual. Even the most complex issues can be explained by examples. For instance, the world is running short of forests as people cut down trees for fuel and timber.

4 Be positive and straightforward
Speak positively. Don't say, "If it were not for the work of WaterLink, two hundred people in our village would not be alive today." Instead, say, "WaterLink has saved two hundred lives in the past three years."

You are trying to convince people that your organization provides a worthwhile service. Don't make claims you can't prove. But don't sound uncertain when you are sure that something is true.

Don't say: "At the time of writing, evidence suggests that dirty water is one of the main causes of sickness in the villages."

Instead, write: "It is clear that dirty water is one of the main causes of sickness in our villages."

A writer explained the size of the danger with two vivid statistics: In Lusaka, the capital of Zambia, the price of a bag of charcoal has increased fivefold in a year. In less than two years, the woodlands surrounding the city may vanish.

5 Add details to make sure the reader understands
When you write or speak, you want every person in the audience to understand exactly what it is you are trying to say. Be sure to define any technical term that may be unfamiliar to your audience.

If I write, "We want to provide water to the villagers," you know my intention. But you will have a much better understanding if I write, "We want to drill wells to provide clean, safe water to the villagers so that they will be healthier. There will be enough water for them to grow more vegetables." Which version is more convincing?

6 Assume readers and listeners don't know what you are talking about
Keep asking yourself: "Will my audience understand this? Does the typical member of it have the necessary knowledge? Have I written enough explanation?" Readers and listeners who don't understand quickly stop paying attention.

A speaker will likely know if the audience does not understand what is being said. People will ask questions, or leave, or go to sleep. If that happens, the speaker can revise the message, start explaining, answer questions.

It is more difficult with print to tell in advance whether a typical reader will understand. When you finish writing, it's a good idea to give the text to two or three people who know nothing about your organization. Ask them to question everything they don't find clear. If they can understand what you have written, then anyone else who reads your plan will be likely to understand.

7 Avoid jargon

Ask yourself whether the typical member of your audience will be comfortable with the jargon used in your particular field. The answer is probably not. After all, jargon is not designed for clear communication. Jargon tries to make its writer sound important. It is intended to lay a smokescreen of difficulty to keep people from thinking too hard about what has been written. It consists of long words that sound impressive when simpler ones exist. It uses several words when one would do the job. It uses long, complex sentences when shorter sentences would be easier to read.

Often, despite knowing already that such language is designed to obscure the facts, we must use it anyway because donors expect it. It makes them feel important. But, for most of the world, this kind of language prevents clear communication.

Crucial to the attainment of rural development are four requisites: (1) redistribution of rural assets, particularly land; (2) timely and adequate provision of support services to assist producers in making these redistributed resources productive; (3) a strong, dynamic and militant rural movement among marginalized rural sectors than can advocate for reforms, claim/take needed programs and policies from government, implement self-reliant or self-sustaining development programs, and exercise participatory, pro-people and responsive governance; and (4) rural enterprises with strong linkages to agriculture and the local economy, which not only assures accessible inputs and markets for producers but also generates off-farm employment for the majority unemployed and underemployed in the countryside.

That one sentence has more than one hundred and ten words. What does it mean? What does claim-take mean? Perhaps the paragraph should be rewritten as follows:

For rural development to be successful, we need:
- *people who have the land and resources they are entitled to*
- *enough support services at the right time for farmers to be productive*
- *strong organizations of poor farmers who will be able to set up, manage and sustain their own development programs*
- *rural businesses, strongly linked to agriculture and the local economy, that will serve two purposes: (a) provide fertilizer and other needs and markets for farm products and (b) create jobs off the farm for the unemployed and underemployed, the majority of rural people*

This version has 93 words. Using the fewest possible words is important. Using short words is also important. The revised version is easier to read because there are fewer long words and because each point has been separated as a distinct unit that can be absorbed easily.

8 Keep sentences short (and paragraphs too)

Use a sentence to tell one idea. If you have two ideas, use two sentences. Reading is like eating. So is listening. You know that if you take too big a bite of food, you will have trouble chewing it. A sentence is like a bite of information. If there is too much in a sentence, it is hard to understand.

9 Look for short, simple words

Short, simple words are easier to understand than long words. They take less time to read. And they don't complicate the message. The example shows some English words that are often used and the simpler words that can replace them. In English, watch out for words that end in "ize," "ise," or "tion." Look always for a simpler word.

Remember that you may be writing in a language that is your second language for readers who must use their second or third language to read what you have written.

Don't use	Use
assist	help
initiate	begin
utilize	use
during the course of	during
for the purpose of	to
in order to	to
in view of the fact that	because
up to the present time	now
with a small amount of effort	easily

10 Remove unnecessary words

It is easy to use more words than necessary. But extra words slow down the reader or listener. They may also confuse the message. An effective written document is as streamlined as a jet plane. The example shows some ways you can save words and help your readers.

11 Avoid initials

Your audiences won't be happy if they encounter initials that mean something to you but not to them. Use the full names of organizations or the full technical terms. How many people know UNHCR is the United Nations High Commissioner for Refugees? If you do use initials, make sure you explain what they mean. Most writers use the full name the first time, followed by the initials – e.g., "United Nations Development Programme (UNDP)." You do not need to include initials if you do not mention the organization again.

12 Define words the reader or listener may not know

Use words that typical members of your audience will know from their own experience. Definitions fail if they are written in words as hard to understand as the original term. It does not help to say: "Snow is crystals of ice formed from the vapour of water in the air." (That is a definition in a dictionary.) You have a clear picture if I write: "Snow falls in tiny crystals like diamonds in the air. It piles up like a dry, cold, white powder."

13 Use point form to simplify and give emphasis

There are many examples of point form in this booklet. In speech, say how many points you will make and number them as you proceed.

14 Use gender-free language

Are you talking to everybody you want to talk to? In English and some other languages, it is common to use a masculine pronoun, adjective, or noun when you mean both men and women. "Every voter should take his form to the polling booth." That practice ignores half the world's population, its women. Be conscious of the need to use gender-free language all the time. There are many ways to do this. One is to write in the plural. That is perhaps the easiest solution:

No: The average person would help if he knew what was needed.

Yes: Most people would help if they knew what was needed.

Another solution is to change the offending word:

No: All men are created equal.

Yes: All persons are created equal.

15 Explain statistics

Keep statistics simple. Cut out any that are unnecessary. Relate them to what is important to the reader. Put them in terms the reader can understand. Statistics should be set in perspective. A short article reported that "India has a buffalo population of more than 62 million. That is about half the world's total. Buffalo produce more than half India's milk." People cannot easily understand a number as large as 62 million. The last two sentences set the first in context. They give it meaning.

16 Try to make your writing sound as close as possible to the way you talk

Spoken language is simple and straightforward. If a sentence is interesting and easy to understand when you say it out loud, it will be interesting and easy to understand in writing. When I am having trouble writing something simply, I ask myself: "How would I say this to a friend?" That usually solves the problem.

As of now, most of the recently established committees require additional personnel to perform ongoing assignments that are critical to the success of the organization. As well, there are one or two additional committees still to be established which will require staff.

These words are from a newsletter I receive. Can you imagine using them when talking to a friend? You would more likely say:

Most of the new committees need more members. We need them to take on long-term assignments. That is critical to our success. We will also form one or two more committees. We also need more staff to work with the committees we plan to form.

This rule applies not only to written materials but also to formal speeches that are written in advance. Too often they are stiff and unnatural, uninteresting and unconvincing. My husband, who has written many books and articles, talks to himself all the time when he is writing. That is one way he tests his work.

17 Use direct quotes

Quotations bring the audience directly into contact with the person who is involved in the work being reported. Quotations are convincing. They involve people. (They must, however, sound like the person being quoted.

They should not sound like the writer of the whole piece.) This example sums up most of these principles – writing about people, quoting directly, and sounding like the speaker, not the writer:

When Zhou Guihou, a south China rice grower, started raising fish in paddy fields he found he had struck riches. Fish breeding earned him 12,500 yuan in three years. This is a good sum of money, considering that an average young state farm worker can earn only 540 to 600 yuan a year. "Raising fish in paddy fields can make a big profit," Zhou said.

The writer used simple, direct words, chose a person as an example, explained statistics in a way the reader can understand, and made the main point with a quotation.

13 Personal contact: making the most of the spoken word

The most effective way to gain support is through personal contact – face to face, eye to eye. It is easy to ignore a printed document. It is much more difficult to ignore a person. Moreover, no printed document can convey the concern and enthusiasm of a dedicated and knowledgeable speaker. Nor can a printed document respond to the questions and interest of an audience.

For all these reasons, it is valuable to find occasions to speak about your organization. It may be to large groups of people who belong to a club or association of their own. It may be to a small committee that decides how an association or corporation will divide its charitable gifts. It may be to a single person who is the executive director of a foundation, the head of a government agency, or a potential donor. With larger groups, you may simply be trying to raise the profile of your organization in the community and hoping to interest people in the work. With smaller groups and individuals, you may be asking for specific support for a specific purpose.

In every case, there are certain rules that can increase your chance of success in making a personal presentation. This chapter deals with the most important of them.

Preparing for the talk

Effective public speaking takes practice, practice, practice. It also takes preparation. Here are some questions to ask every time you are going to make a speech or make a case for support. If you are invited to address a group of people, ask the questions of the person who issued the invitation. If you asked to make the presentation to a small group of possible donors, you may have to answer the questions from your own knowledge or research. Know the answers ahead of time.

You should not take any more than 15 minutes for your initial presentation.

1 *How long am I expected to talk?* If you are invited to speak to a group, you will probably be told how much time you have. In talking to a committee or an individual, plan to talk for about 15 minutes. (If you are invited to speak for longer, then consider using a visual aid, such as slides. See the next two chapters.) If you are speaking to potential donors, you should not take any more than 15 minutes for your initial presentation, and 10 minutes would be even better. In such cases, don't give a monologue. Conduct a conversation. If you were not able to learn their interests ahead of time, take time to ask about their interests before you talk about your organization. Make time for questions during and after the presentation.

If the time to speak is limited, regardless of the size of the group, don't take longer. That is not only inconsiderate; it is likely to offend the listeners. Stop when your time has run out. If people in the audience want to know more, they will ask you to continue or they will ask questions.

Very few people are able to talk within the time they are given. There is only one way to be sure that you will not speak longer than you are asked to. That is to practise your speech, saying it out loud as if you were in front of an audience. Find out how many minutes it takes. If it is too long, plan to cut something out. If it is far too short, which is unlikely, add new ideas. In English, most people speak about 150 words a minute. A double-space A4 page holds about 300 typed English words.

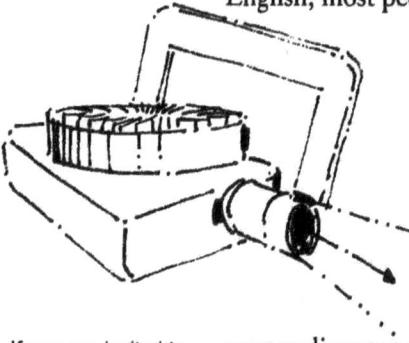

Practising in this way will make you aware of other possible problems in the speech. You may find that some words that are suitable in a written text are difficult to say. You may find that some sentences are too long to say comfortably. If you practise your speech in front of a friend or relative who is not closely involved with your organization, you may learn that some things in the speech are unclear and need more explanation.

If you are invited to speak for longer than 15 minutes, then consider using a visual aid, such as slides.

2 *Who will be in the audience?* Are the members of your audience mostly wealthy, middle class, or poor people? What level of education have they had? You may want to use different words when talking to business people than you would use when taking to government people. No matter who you talk to, use words they will understand.

What are the people in the audience interested in? Are they part of an environmental group? Are their interests largely political? What are they likely to know about the subject? Will the organization be new to them? Or are they all old friends?

If there are likely to be reporters at the event or if you are saying something you would like publicized, have copies of your remarks to give out at the end of the meeting. That will improve your chances of being quoted and quoted accurately. Even if there are no reporters present, don't say anything you would not want reported. There is no such thing as speaking "off the record" at any meeting.

Think too about the physical problems. Will the hall be large? Will there be a microphone? Will there be loud air conditioning? If the room is hot or crowded, will people get sleepy quickly, especially if they have just eaten?

3 *What do I want to accomplish by giving this speech?* What do you want the listeners to do when you have finished? Do you want them to give money, to write a letter to a politician, to tell their friends about your work? Be sure you are clear about a single purpose. Organize your speech to achieve that goal. Be sure to tell the members of your audience what you hope they will do after hearing you. Spell it out.

Eventually, you may want to ask a service club for a donation to your program. Get advice from a member of the club's executive body about the best way to do this. Some clubs prefer that a person asking for a donation not do so during a speech to a meeting. They prefer that a request be made in writing before the meeting. Or, it may be best to follow up the talk with a request for a donation.

4 *What is the audience likely to think about me and my organization?* Are they coming to the meeting with pre-set images? In the first book, I listed a number of prejudices some people have about the members of voluntary organizations. Do any apply to yours? Even if they do not, might your audience think of your organization as:

- a group of activists out to embarrass government or business?
- critical of government or business policy?
- having leftist or even Communist tendencies?
- not answerable to anyone?
- having sloppy management and financial practices?
- unable to prove value?
- well funded from overseas and so not needing more support?

If necessary, you will want to address these perceptions. Find ways to correct them if they are wrong. This is best done with true stories, anecdotes, and specific examples. A simple, even irate, denial is not convincing.

The impression you make

In forming an opinion about you and what you are saying, people do not rely most on what they are hearing. Research has shown repeatedly that they rely most on what they see, on the visual impression you make.

A year or two ago I went to an evening of speeches. It was a formal occasion. The people in the audience were mostly well-dressed professionals. Two of the speakers on the platform were slim, well groomed, and dressed in tailored clothes. The third was very overweight, had long messy hair, and wore overalls. She was such a powerful speaker that after a while her words became more important than her appearance. Even so, she had to battle a certain amount of disapproval. And very few of us can speak so effectively. It is best not to take chances.

Dress the same way as the people you want to impress. If you are going to talk to business people, carry a briefcase, not a backpack or knapsack. Casual dress, especially among men, is part of the non-profit culture in many countries. It may not, however, be part of the business culture or the government culture. If your audience will be wearing ties and jackets, dress accordingly.

Think about several other physical questions. How close do people sit or stand to each other in your society? If you are talking to a group, will they expect you to stand on a platform talking down to them like an authority figure? Or will they be more comfortable if you are sitting or standing at the same level as they are sitting?

What gesture of greeting is right for each situation? How does social rank or wealth affect the style of greeting? If the people you are going to talk to are from another culture, what greeting will they expect? Should it be formal or informal? If their language is different from yours, would it be appropriate at least to greet them in their language, even if you cannot continue in it?

You want to convey your own enthusiasm for what you do. Do it with the tone of your voice and with your body movements – your gestures, the way you sit or walk, your facial expressions. Don't be too informal; that may appear disrespectful. On the other hand, unless it is expected in your culture, don't stand stiffly like a puppet the whole time you are speaking. But be careful: too many gestures can be distracting, and can even make an audience laugh.

People rely on the way you speak to make up their minds about what you are saying. If you hesitate too often or talk too quietly or slowly, you are less likely to be persuasive. If you seldom smile, your voice will flatten. Smiling actually animates the voice.

Be a good listener as well as a good speaker. Give people lots of opportunity to respond to what you have said. Use facial expression and gesture to demonstrate your interest in what other people are saying. If you lean back in your chair, if you tap your fingers or shake your leg nervously or look at what is on the walls, the person who is responding to you will think you are not interested. So will others in the room. You may have offended a potential donor by appearing rude.

That is why it is important to rehearse and rehearse until language, gesture, and tone are consistent. And best of all, rehearse in front of people who are not familiar with your work. Find people who will suggest, criticize, and comment until you sound sincere and confident.

Giving the speech
Occasionally it is appropriate to read your speech from a prepared text. This is likely to be the case if you are speaking on a formal occasion to a large audience and have been given a strictly limited amount of time. If you must read it, be sure to practise your speech so you can make it sound as if you are speaking from your heart, not reading words from a piece of paper. Remember that spoken language is more informal than written language. Make certain your speech is written in language that will sound like your own speaking voice – not as if you are reading from a printed text. You may need to edit your speech, once everything else is complete, to make the language sound conversational.

For smaller groups, don't plan to read your material. Nothing puts people to sleep faster. If you need to, memorize your opening sentences and perhaps the final few sentences. For the rest, memorize only the ideas you want to get across. Don't memorize the exact words. If necessary, make a few notes – the headings of the subjects you plan to cover. The notes should fit on a single small sheet of paper.

Make eye contact with your audience. That is, look at their eyes, as if you were talking to a single person. If you stare at your notes or above your listeners' heads, they will feel you are not interested in them, and they will lose interest in you. They may even think you are embarrassed by something you are saying or, even worse, that you are avoiding contact with them because you have something to hide. Maintaining eye contact keeps your listeners focused on you, and keeps you focused on your listeners. Sometimes it helps to pick out one or two people in the audience who look friendly and interested, and spend some of the time in eye contact with them.

Capturing and holding attention

If you are speaking to a public gathering or a meeting of a club, the first problem is to attract an audience. The title of a speech is even more important than the headline of an article in a magazine or newspaper. The headline is followed immediately by the story, and as long as it has even a little interest a reader is likely to make the small movement of the eye needed to read the first paragraph. The title of a speech must attract people to make the effort to get to the place where the speech will be given.

I hope you find the second of each pair in the example more appealing. If you do, it is because each title relates in some way to you, to your health or your economic and social well-being.

Once people are sitting in front of you, they have made a commitment of time and attention – at least for a few minutes. It is usually more important then to make the audience feel relaxed and interested in you, the speaker – to make a personal connection between them and you. This can be done in various ways. One of the best methods is to begin your talk by describing an experience you have had that some or all your listeners will also have had. Perhaps you have done the same kind of work. Perhaps you have gone to the same school. Perhaps you belong to the same social organizations. If you can show that you have something in common with your listeners, you will form a bond with them and they will listen more attentively.

Which speech would you be more likely to attend?
The regeneration of our rural areas or *Six paths to a more prosperous community*

Future directions in public health care
or *How you can lead a healthier life*

The impact of current environmental protection activities
or *Can we clean up our canals?*

For the first few minutes, an audience is likely to listen to what you say. Holding the audience's attention after that is more difficult. If you can, change the tone of your speech from time to time. Illustrate the points you want to make with examples and anecdotes about people. No matter how important and serious the subject is, try to introduce a little humour. Don't be afraid to laugh at yourself a bit, but don't make fun of the listeners or their friends. Talk about people and things, not about abstract ideas. Use some of the visual aids described in this chapter.

What you say

It is said that less than 10 per cent of an audience's impression of a speaker is formed from the actual words that are said. But powerful words stay in an audience's mind. So choose your words carefully, and be positive. People like to support success, not failure. Talk about your successes.

You may be asked or expected to describe your organization to many different kinds of audiences. Each audience will require a different style of presentation. What you say will depend on the interests and social make-up of your audience, and on your purpose in speaking. But always, regardless of the nature of the audience, speak from the heart, not just the head. Talk about the experience of several people – individual adults and children with names – and how your organization has affected each of them. Then connect that experience to your audience:

• to a business audience:

WaterLink contributes to the local economy. Last year, we gave jobs to ten unemployed people. This year they are shopping in your shops and using your services.

• to a potential donor:

We share your goal. Your investment in WaterLink will help bring healthier lives to people in our community.

• to a group of health workers:

WaterLink's work in providing clean water means that fewer children are missing school because of illness this year than last year.

It is usually safe to assume that most members of an audience have almost no knowledge of the work of your organization and its social importance. Be certain to explain everything clearly. At the same time, be careful not to sound like a teacher giving a lesson. You must walk a difficult road between saying too little and saying too much. If you are unsure how much you need to explain, watch the faces of people in the audience. If they look puzzled, you will know you have to say more. If they look bored, you are saying too much.

Be sure to introduce yourself if there is any possibility that someone may not know who you are. Do so even if your role is minor. How often have you had a person stand up in front of you to introduce or thank a speaker without telling you his or her own name and position?

Before you start talking, think carefully about who is listening and choose the right words and the right style. It is fine to talk about the "product" of your organization or about the "bottom line" to a businessperson, but it is more appropriate to talk about the "result" and the "financial situation" when you are talking to a general audience or to someone in the non-profit field.

Follow the 17 rules for effective communication in Chapter 12. Use words to which your listeners are accustomed. Use examples and words from their experience. If you are talking to architects and engineers, talk about your work (even if does not involve any construction) as building bridges between people or increasing efficiency in operations. If you are talking to doctors, talk about ways your work (even if there is no medical component) makes people healthier or cures social ills.

Avoid jargon. Don't baffle listeners with sets of initials that have no meaning to them. Be specific. Describe what you are really doing. Avoid phrases like "The Kenya Farmers' Community Development Club empowers people to undertake capacity building for sustainable development," and "GEMS will work to improve the quality of life for families in the region and to promote the personal empowerment of rural households, especially women." Say instead "I work with the Kenya Farmers' Community Development Club. We help poor small farmers buy seeds, farm implements, fertilizer, farm machines. We help them pay their children's school fees," and "GEMS new silkworm project will help support village banks among these women. They will be able to borrow small amounts of money to start small businesses. Then they will to able to earn money. There are many kinds of business they can begin. For example, they can start rice milling, fish farming, food processing, book binding, or clothing production."

Don't offer information in too much detail. That confuses listeners. Don't say, for example, *48.5 per cent of households in the village have children in school.* Instead, you can say: *Almost half the households in the village have children in school.* Which statement do you understand more easily?

You can speak conversationally, using simple words, most easily if you yourself are relaxed. But you can be relaxed only if you have mastered your subject and know all the facts about your organization and its concerns. When you are the master of the subject, you will automatically find simple ways to explain the facts. You will need only the briefest of notes to ensure that you cover all the topics in the order you think will be most convincing. You will be able to concentrate on using the right material, and the right tone, to convey what you think is important to your audience.

When to stop talking

One of the most difficult things in trying to be persuasive is knowing when to stop.

If you are speaking to a large group, you probably have prepared everything you plan to say, building up to a powerful conclusion. You will not want to give up that ending. And you should not – as long as you are holding the audience's attention. If you see people looking around the room, or at their watches, or getting up to leave, it is time to change your plan. Summarize the rest of your speech and get to your conclusion as quickly as possible. Don't stop speaking without stating the conclusion if you can help it.

When you are asking only one person or a small group for support, it may be more difficult to know when to stop. You do not want to stop until your listeners have had a good chance to decide what action they will take, but it is a good idea to be aware when that happens – especially if you have been successful. When I have made my point, I too often go on making my sales pitch anyway. I don't know why people do this. Perhaps we become too involved in making the presentation we have spent ages rehearsing, and don't really hear the other person agreeing with us. Or perhaps we cannot believe our good fortune.

Once you stop, ask for questions. From the questions, you will learn whether you have communicated your ideas effectively. It may be necessary to explain some points in greater detail, or to repeat something of importance. Be patient when that happens. Don't say, *But I explained that earlier!* even if that is what you are thinking. Don't even suggest such an idea in the tone of your voice.

Listen attentively to the questions. If your mind is on what you are going to say next, you may not hear the question correctly. Or you may start talking before the other person has finished. Misunderstanding and confusion may result.

Ask your own questions in response. Feed back to the person what he or she just said so that you are clear about the information you are being given. *Am I right that what interests you most is our work in cleaning up the river? Why is that?*

While you don't want to overstay your welcome or talk too long, be sure you have said what you want to say. If you are asking for something, be sure you have actually made the request and had a response, even if it is only a preliminary response. We will talk more about this in Book 3 under asking for donations.

"Quick! Is there a philanthropist in the audience?"

Finding opportunities to talk to groups of people

Look for opportunities to talk to groups of people in your community who may be influential or who are potential donors. Use the opportunity to talk about the achievements of your organization, the benefits that have come from its work, and the importance of your plans for the future. Don't think of these as fundraising events. They are long-term investments in public education, raising awareness of your organization and establishing its credibility. Take with you copies of your general brochures to reinforce your message. The brochures should include a form for people to use if they wish to donate money as a result of your talk.

Phone or write to groups in your area offering to talk about current issues you and your staff know a lot about, or asking for a chance to talk about your organization. Find out when these groups set their speakers' schedule for the next year so that you can approach them at the right time. Suggest several titles for talks that might get their attention. Suggest a month that would be good for you. That might help pin them down.

Here are some suggestions of groups to approach:
- service clubs, e.g., Rotary and Lions Clubs
- business organizations, e.g., Chamber of Commerce
- professional groups – engineers, doctors, lawyers, etc.
- women's groups
- political organizations
- religious bodies, e.g. churches, temples, synagogues, mosques
- academic associations
- school staff and/or students
- youth groups

Here are some other ways to make personal contact with people:
- If there are government offices or businesses nearby, offer to come to talk to the employees at lunch time or after work. Take whatever materials you have – a display, brochures.
- Whenever possible, take along several of the people who have benefited from your services, who can tell their stories.

- Offer to do presentations about your organization or some aspects of your work at meetings of development agencies.
- To meet corporate people, take a table at a trade show or industrial fair. Go to conferences and conventions of business people. Mingle. Introduce yourself. Ask questions. Be visible. Make an impression. Keep going back each chance you get.
- Try to join any associations where business people gather, such as the ones listed above.
- Join social clubs of the people you want to get to know.
- Put up a display about your organization in churches, municipal offices, office buildings, markets – anywhere crowds gather.
- Invite all these groups to visit your office or your projects as a special event in their schedule.

Not all these possibilities will repay the effort of making contact and appearing in person. Some may take more time and effort than they are worth. I used to think it was good to accept all speaking engagements. I changed my mind after I spent two hours writing a speech, drove for an hour to the church that had invited me, talked to twenty-five polite people, had coffee with them, and drove an hour home. All this for a thank-you note and a small donation. Perhaps these twenty-five people spoke well of my organization, but I realized that this was not the best use of six hours of my time. However, one never knows. Some of those twenty-five people might eventually encourage the church or another organization to make a large gift. Don't be too quick to turn down invitations.

Don't miss an opportunity to speak just because the group does not share your goals. It is not easy to speak to an audience that at best may be unsympathetic and at worst antagonistic. But taking up the challenge gives you a chance to address directly any negative images these people have of you and your organization. These may be the people most important to convince of your credibility. In this case it is especially important to be sure you understand the thinking of your audience before you speak. It is equally important to recognize their viewpoint in your remarks and explain how working with you might meet some of their goals. Don't argue with them. Don't expect them to change their minds entirely or quickly. Try to bridge misunderstandings.

Reinforcing your words visually
It is not always easy for an audience to listen to a speaker, unless the speech is extraordinarily powerful. You can help the reader focus on your message by reinforcing your words with images. People will be able to follow the organization of your talk if you write an outline for them as you go along. They will remember it better also.

Some information can be presented much better with a drawing, or a graph, or a written set of figures, than by any number of spoken words. It is very hard to grasp some statistical information in words. If you say that over five years the yield of maize has increased 20 per cent, the audience will understand. But if you want to show how that increase was achieved year-by-year, and relate the increased yield to increased application of fertilizer, it is best to draw a graph. No one will be able to follow you if you say, "In year 1, when only a small amount of fertilizer was used there was an increase of 1 per cent; in Year 2, the amount of fertilizer was doubled and the increase in yield was 5 per cent ...." and so on. Your listeners will be so confused by all the figures that they will simply stop trying to absorb them. And once you lose an audience's attention, is hard to get it back. On the other hand, they will understand immediately if you draw a graph showing the rising use of fertilizer and an even greater rate of increase in the yield.

Most people in your audience will be used to a speaker writing on a blackboard, from their days at school. For that reason alone, you may wish to use something more attractive than a blackboard. There are several options. Using any of them takes some practice, however. You must plan in advance what you want to write down. You don't want to have to stop to think in front of an audience, or have to erase or scratch out words because you made a mistake. If you do not show confidence in your writing, you will not build credibility in your listeners.

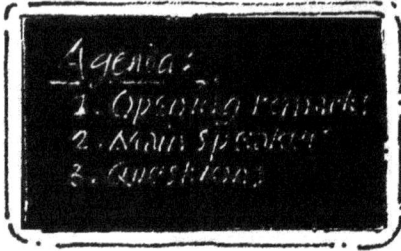

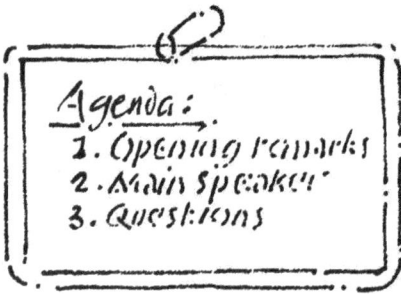

Blackboards/chalkboards/whiteboards

Writing and drawing on a board has worked well for centuries. It is a simple, cheap way to get information across to a small audience, but is not always appropriate for formal presentations. The people in the audience may feel they have gone back to school. That may make them uncomfortable. And when you write on a board you have your back to the audience. If you want to keep its attention, you have to be able to write and talk at the same time. That is difficult.

Blackboards in particular are difficult to use because writing with chalk is slow and the boards quickly become dusty and messy. A whiteboard is easier to use. It is a piece of smooth white plastic on which you can write with coloured felt marker pens. The writing can be erased easily and cleanly – if you use pens made for this purpose. Otherwise it may be impossible to erase.

If possible, write some of the material on the board before you start talking. The great advantage of boards is that what you write can easily be erased and changed. As a result, you can draw people into suggesting what you will write, and how to revise what gets written. Blackboards and whiteboards can be used therefore in discussions in which the audience is actively involved in defining and solving a problem.

A speaker can begin, for example, by asking members of the audience to tell her the problems they think are most serious in the community. Then she can ask them to suggest ways these problems can be solved. As each problem and solution is given, she writes it on the board making two lists. Then she demonstrates how her organization is working to help the com-

Blackboards (top) are difficult to use because writing with chalk is slow and the boards quickly become dusty and messy. A whiteboard (above) is easier to use. It is a piece of smooth white plastic on which you can write with coloured felt marker pens.

munity in these areas. This kind of presentation takes confidence and practice. Inevitably some problems will be outside the work of your organization, and some suggestions may be difficult to write in a few words or in a way that fits your needs. But when this method is used properly, it is extremely effective. Instead of your telling the audience that your work is important, the audience convinces itself of that fact.

Magnetic and felt boards

Special boards exist on which you can stick letters, symbols, or whatever you need for a presentation. The two main kinds are magnetic and felt. They are good for small presentations to small audiences. For magnetic boards you may not be able to obtain a huge variety of letters or shapes since each piece has to have a small magnet on its back. You might find them inflexible. With felt boards, you can cut endless shapes, since the pieces adhere easily to the board. Felt boards are not suited to sophisticated audiences who may think such tools are best used only with children. However, they are easy to use and to move around and inexpensive to buy.

Big pad of cheap paper (flip chart)

A flip chart consists of a number of large sheets of paper and a stand or easel that will hold them firmly in place, allowing you to turn over each page as you fill it up. If there is no stand, you can attach the sheets to a blackboard or a wall with tape. Use broad felt marking pens to write on the paper.

Flip charts are flexible, easy, and cheap. They are good for leading and summarizing a discussion. By asking people to write on the charts, you can involve them in the discussion and draw out their ideas. If your meeting involves several sessions, the sheets from each session can be taped on the walls of the room as a permanent record of what has been said. You can also write out a presentation ahead of time, so you don't have to turn your back to the audience.

A flip chart consists of a number of large sheets of paper and a stand or easel that will hold them firmly in place, allowing you to turn over each page as you fill it up.

Use big, clearly written letters so that a person at the back of the room can read the words easily. Try not to write more than a dozen words on a page if the audience is large. If your handwriting is illegible, ask someone else to do the writing.

Two tricks will make your presentation easier:

• If you are preparing pages ahead of time, add some little tabs to the edge of each sheet and write the subject of the sheet on them. That will make it possible for you to find what you want the audience to see if you have to go back and forth. You won't have to search through many pages to find the one you are looking for.

• Write little notes to yourself on the flip charts at the side of the paper where you will stand. Use a faint pencil. These notes will remind you of what you wanted to say. No one in the audience will know you are checking to see if you have covered everything.

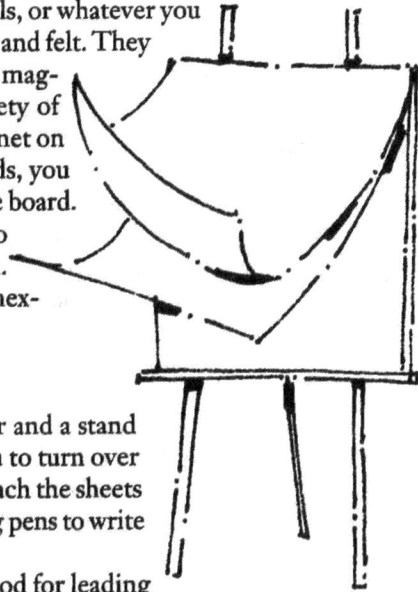

Flip charts are quick to use because you don't have to erase anything; you just turn the page. But, as with boards, you may have your back to the audience much of the time, unless you have prepared the pages in advance. You will find it hard to keep the attention of more than about 30 people.

Overhead projectors

An overhead projector is a flat box with a glass top and a powerful light inside. Above the box there is an angled mirror that projects the light onto a screen. An overhead projection sheet is a piece of clear plastic, the size of a normal sheet of paper, on which there is writing or drawing. The sheet is placed on the glass, and the image is projected onto the screen. Documents can be magnified by almost any amount, depending on the distance of the projector from the screen and the size of the screen.

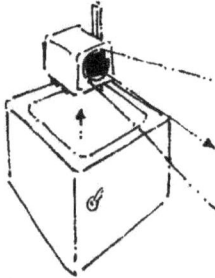

Overhead projection has several advantages over the other methods described for reinforcing speech with writing. First, it is possible to prepare the plastic sheets in advance. Second, the machine is arranged so that the speaker stands between it and the screen, always facing the audience even while talking or pointing to material on the sheet. And when the speaker faces the audience, the sheet on the machine looks exactly the way the image of it appears on the screen. This makes it easy to write or draw on the sheet, using special coloured pens, while talking and facing the audience. The overhead projector is an excellent way to show simple graphics and print. The equipment is relatively inexpensive – cheaper than, say, a slide projector. It may be possible to rent an overhead projector or to borrow one from another organization.

Preparing overhead projection sheets in advance is simple. You can write them out using the special pens. Or you can start with pages of writing, printing, or drawing and copy those images on to the sheet of plastic using a standard photocopier. (But make sure first that your copier will handle the sheets.) No professional help is needed. If you have a laser printer, you may be able to print onto the plastic sheet directly from the computer, as if the sheet were made of paper.

Overhead projectors do require a darkened room, however. And the larger the image, the more need there will be for darkness, because the light from the projector will be spread over a greater distance.

Despite its advantages, the overhead projector is difficult to use well. It requires rehearsal and experience. It is possible, for example, to put the sheets on the projector upside down, back to front, or in the wrong order. And it is human nature when using one to turn away from the audience and start reading from the screen, thus losing much of the advantage of this technology. That is never necessary. It is possible, for example, to point to important words on the sheet with a pencil; the shadow of the pencil will be projected onto the screen. In doing so, however, be careful not to block out anything you want the audience to read at that moment. A further danger is that you can become so involved in writing and erasing and adjusting the sheets that you lose contact with the audience. Remember that the projector is a tool to improve contact with the audience, not something that can be allowed to get in the way.

An overhead projector is a flat box with a glass top and a powerful light inside. Above the box there is an angled mirror that projects the light onto a screen.

You may not want the audience to see everything on the sheet at once. There is an advantage to exposing only one subject at a time. In that case, you can hide part of the image on the plastic sheet by laying a piece of ordinary paper on top of it. The paper will block the light passing through the sheet and nothing will be projected. Move the paper down each time you want the audience to see another line.

To be effective, also:

• Be sure everyone can read the image on the screen. Use large, bold type. Don't have two many words on one sheet. Test the readability of your sheets beforehand by projecting them and standing at the back of the room to read them.

• Put tabs on the edges of the sheets with notes to yourself about what you want to say.

• Turn the projector off while you are changing pages.

• Turn it on only when the page is positioned correctly.

Computer presentations

Many computers give you the opportunity to prepare a presentation that can be displayed on a large screen before a sizeable audience. Microsoft PowerPoint is an example. Like a traditional slide show the person using the computer can handle the flow of the material with a click of the mouse, or can give the job over to someone else while still doing the talking. Such programs provide tools to create presentations, organize and format material, illustrate points with your own images or clip art, and even broadcast your presentaions over the Web. This is done much more easily on a computer than it is by making slide shows. However, where I live, PowerPoint presentations are used mostly by business people in business settings. These programs may be expensive. They require skill in designing and setting up, and a great deal of skill and practice in making the presentation.

This section has been concerned with displaying words. Images, especially photographs, films, and videos, are even more effective in reinforcing the spoken word. They are discussed in the next two chapters, because many are equally important for effective communication in print.

14 Using images

There is an old saying that one picture is worth a thousand words. In fact, a picture may be worth considerably more than that. Illustrations can explain the gravity of a problem or draw forth an emotional response with a power that is impossible for most of us to achieve in any number of words. They attract attention. They give information quickly. People who can't be bothered reading a few hundred words will look at a picture and – if it is effective – may learn a great deal from it about your organization and its work.

For these reasons you will want to try to use illustrations in your fundraising efforts and in other materials used to build credibility. But using illustrations effectively is not simply a matter of taking a photograph and inserting it in a brochure or newsletter. There are basic rules for using illustrations, just as there are rules for using words. This chapter deals with the most important ones.

One picture is worth a thousand words.

Choosing the most appropriate type of illustration

Four kinds of illustration are useful in explaining the work of your organization and the need for its services. Each one is particularly well suited to convey a certain kind of information.

Photographs show exactly what the camera sees. They are also relatively cheap and easy to produce. Many photographs can be taken in the time it takes an artist to make one drawing – if in fact you can find an illustrator. Good quality photographs are hard to come by and hard to take, but are usually worth the effort. Photographs reproduce actual events; they have credibility. They are well suited for newsletters and slide shows. Videotapes and films are a form of photography with special impact because they have sound and motion.

Drawings control the viewer's perceptions and emotions because they show only essential details. They omit unnecessary details that may distract the viewer. A good drawing is far more powerful than a poor photograph. A drawing can also show how something works, or explain the various steps in a process.

Maps can show the extent of a problem or where your organization has projects.

Graphs are useful for showing changes and trends – for example, an increase in the number of people benefiting from your services.

All four types of illustration may be used in a single document. For example, an organization concerned with the provision of safe drinking water might use:

- photographs of women drawing water at a polluted river and of other women pumping clean water from a storage tank
- a cross-section drawing of a roof storage tank, showing how safe water is brought from deep down in the ground
- a map showing all the villages where the organization has helped people install eavestrough (rain gutters) on their houses
- a graph showing the increase, year by year, in the number of people getting clean water as a result of the organization's work and the decrease in diarrhoeal diseases in that population

Choosing good photographs

You may be taking photographs yourself, or you may be working with a photographer. In either case, it is important to keep certain rules in mind. These also apply when you are using photographs that already exist. Remember that a bad photograph does not convey a message – except, perhaps, that you were too lazy to, or could not, find a better one.

Photographs first must meet certain technical requirements.

- They must be in focus. The image should be sharp, not fuzzy.
- They must be properly exposed. They should not be too light or too dark.
- There should be contrast between the main subject and the background. The most important details should stand out clearly.
- The photograph must be in good condition. Has it been folded or damaged in some way? Is it dirty? Are there pencil or pen marks on it? Has anyone written on the back with a ballpoint pen or hard pencil, making marks that show on the front? Any defects will show up if the photograph is reproduced.

Good photographs also meet certain conditions of content.

- The photograph should present one clear piece of information – its message. It may say, for example: This is a person casting a vote *or* This is an example of successful alley cropping *or* This is the insect that causes dengue fever *or* Here is the president of our country visiting one of our projects. Whatever the message is, it should be obvious. It should not require more than a few words of explanation in addition to the image.
- The best pictures not only have a message; they tell a story by showing people *doing* things. Pictures of people looking at the camera are boring. The people in them usually look nervous or tense or uninterested. They will look more relaxed if they are busy at some activity. Pictures of action are always more interesting than pictures without activity.
- Some kinds of photographs are used so often that they no longer attract attention. When is the last time you looked with any interest at a picture of twenty-five people sitting in rows in the official photograph of a con-

From top to bottom: too fuzzy, too dark, too light, and just right.

ference? How many times have you been interested in a photograph of a person who is staring into the camera as if posing for a police identification photo, or standing at a microphone talking to an audience, or shaking hands with a colleague, or presenting a plaque? These kinds of photos are impersonal. They do not convey much information except that one more conference was held or one more person was speaking or received an award. They do not attract readers or create emotion.

• The image that conveys the message should fill most of the photograph. Many people taking photographs stand too far away from the subject of the picture. Then the person or the thing that is most important becomes very small, and the message is hard to detect in all the background. Make sure that what is important fills most of the picture. If you are working with a photographer, get him or her to move up close to the subject.

• Remember that photographs printed in publications are rarely large. This means a photographer should not crowd too much detail into any one picture. For example, try not to have more than three or four people in any one photograph. If you have more, their faces will be so small when the picture is printed that it will be difficult to make out their features.

• Examine the background. Avoid cluttered backgrounds that will distract the viewer from the important image. Make sure that background and main subject don't come together so that, for example, a tree seems to be growing out of a person's head.

• Make sure the picture has a pleasing composition. There should be a strong, single centre of interest. There should be balance in the parts of the picture.

• Use photographs that are positive in their message. Show a health worker on the job. Or two photographs, one showing how things were in the past, the other showing how much they have improved.

• Avoid showing poor or unhealthy people. That exposes them in unpleasant ways. It is often an invasion of privacy. Even if they know they are being photographed, they may not be in a position to complain. Some people call photographs of this kind "development pornography." It's better to use drawings.

• Ask the people who have been photographed for permission to use their pictures in your talks or publications, if their faces are going to be recognizable. If possible, obtain their written and signed permission before you take the photographs.

• It is possible to reprint a photograph that has already been published, but often the results are unsatisfactory. If you look closely at a published photograph, you will see that it is made up of many dots. When the published photograph is reproduced, more little dots may be added during printing. If these do not match the old ones perfectly, the result is a very ugly plaid or check pattern over the whole photograph. Use original photographs whenever possible.

Taking good photographs

You may be taking photographs yourself or asking other people to take them for you. You will want a pictorial record of your work. You may also want photographs for your publications, to use in displays, or to put in slide shows. Think about the advice above and the specific points below as you take photographs.

• Stand close to the subject. No matter how you intend to use the pictures, this one rule is more important than all the others. It is also the most often ignored. How many times have you seen a photographer standing ten metres away from the person who is the subject? How many photos have you seen of tiny people in front of a monument? Did the photographer intend to take a picture of the people, or of the monument? If you are taking a picture of one person, stand not more than two to four metres away. Be sure the person or people fill the viewfinder on the camera. Don't feel you need to include the whole person. The legs of a standing person are rarely interesting. Concentrate on face and hands.

If you are photographing people working in a field or you want to show how well rows of plants are growing, getting close is even more important. If you are not careful, most of the picture will be of sky and field: the crop will be too small to be identified. From a distance, all people and many crops look much the same.

Other rules will help ensure interesting photographs that will attract the eye of anyone looking at them in print, in an album, or on a screen.

• When photographing groups of people, make sure each face can be seen clearly. When the photograph is reproduced for a publication, no face should be much smaller than the nail on your little finger. Being able to recognize people does not matter, of course, if your intent is to show crowds.

• There should be little empty space. If you are taking pictures of several people together, make them move close to one another. Even a small space between people will look larger in the photo than it does in life.

• Try to have the picture tell a story or give information.

• Keep people busy. If they are busy doing something, they are likely to be more relaxed. Photos of people standing still and looking straight at the camera are boring.

• Watch the background. Avoid clutter.

• Try to photograph people on a cloudy day. Clouds remove harsh shadows and people don't have to squint. If the sun is bright, move people into open shade under a tree to get them out of the direct sun.

• It is best to have the sun behind you or to one side. If you take photographs towards the sun, you will lose detail because your subject will not be lit properly.

• When photographing people with dark skin, use a flash. When using a flash, don't stand closer than 1.2 metres or your photo will be overexposed.

• Take several pictures of each subject from different angles and viewpoints. That will give you some choice when you are ready to use the photographs.

Using drawings, maps, and graphs effectively
You may be using an existing drawing, painting, map, or graph. If so, you

must be aware of certain technical concerns. Or you may be commissioning an illustration from an artist or mapmaker. In that case, the person who is creating the illustration needs to understand these concerns. Here are some of the most important:

- Illustrations are usually reduced in size for printing. That is, in their final form they are smaller than the original image. Remember that when an illustration is reduced in size, everything in it shrinks. Lettering that was easy to read in the original may become too small to read without a magnifying glass. Lines that are narrow in the original may almost disappear. It is a good idea when ordering an illustration to tell the artist to make it 1.5 times the size that it is going to appear in print. (That is, if you want a drawing in the publication to be 7 cm x 10 cm, have the artist draw it 10.5 cm x 15 cm.) Unless it is very big and bold, don't reduce an illustration to less than half its original size.
- Simple illustrations should be black and white. Additional colours can be added, but each extra colour adds to the cost of printing.
- Drawings, maps, and graphs must be clean and in good physical condition, just like photographs.
- Artists are not always perfect. Make sure the drawing says what you want it to say. Check that any words in it are spelled correctly. To save money and time, ask to see a rough sketch before the artist prepares the final drawing.
- Keep illustrations simple. Omit all unnecessary details. Let the main message stand out.
- In maps, make sure that every place of importance appears on the map. Any place mentioned in accompanying text should appear. Unimportant places and other details – perhaps railroads, for example – that are not mentioned should not appear on the map (unless they are important, such as provincial or national capitals).
- Do not try to pack too much information into a single graph. If a graph shows trends in lines, don't put more than four or five different lines in a single graph if you can avoid it. With more than six lines, it is very difficult to tell them apart. Make sure the lines can easily be distinguished from one another. Avoid three-dimensional graphs; these are easy to produce on a computer and look pretty, but tend to distort the information.

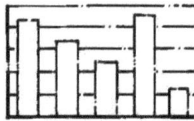

Maps, drawings, charts: keep it simple

Working with photographers and artists

Perhaps you have staff members or volunteers who are skilled in taking photographs and in creating drawings, maps, and graphs. Perhaps you will need to hire people who do this work professionally. In either case, it is most important that the person who is planning to use the illustrations talk to the person who is going to create them. In particular, the following matters should be discussed:

- how the illustration will be used – on a poster, in a newsletter, in a slide show, in a fundraising brochure, etc.
- the purpose of the illustration
- exactly what it should show. (It is a good idea to go with the photog-

rapher who is taking the picture and make sure everything is correct. For illustrations, it is a good idea to give the artist an example of what is wanted, either an actual object or a rough sketch.)

- how many colours are to be used
- for drawings, maps, and graphs, the size it will be when it is printed and the amount of reduction permitted
- when the illustration is needed
- how much money the work will cost

Further advice

This chapter only introduces a subject that can be extremely technical. Ask experts in your community – printers, photographers, artists – for more information. There may also be books on the subject in your local library.

15 Combining voice and image: effective audiovisual presentations

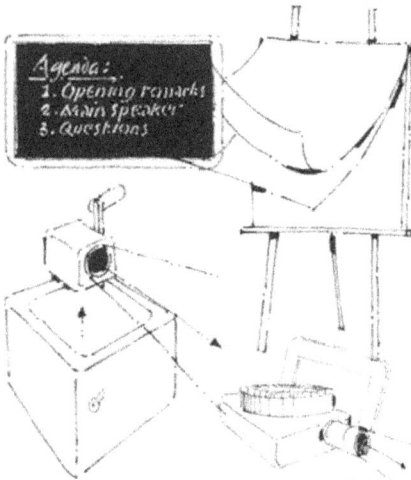

You can add images and sound to your personal presentations in several ways. You may use an overhead projector that uses plastic sheets as discussed in Chapter 13, or another kind of projector that magnifies paper images on a screen. A simpler medium is a scrapbook, or some more formal presentation book, containing photographs, letters, graphs, maps, and informative text. And any speech can be improved by using blackboards, felt boards, magnetic boards, or a big pad of cheap paper in a flip chart – the simple visual aids to reinforce the spoken word discussed in Chapter 13.

This chapter covers the more complex technologies of photographic transparencies (slides), moving picture films, and videotapes – media that are particularly effective in creating emotion as well as giving information. By combining speech and images, you can present information quickly and in a way that makes it easier to remember. Such audiovisual techniques have greater impact because:

- We remember what we see more easily than what we hear.
- Pictures communicate emotions better than words.
- Tables and graphs communicate facts about numbers more clearly than words.
- Illustrations add variety – a change of pace – that keeps the audience interested.
- You can communicate more information in a given time by presenting some of the information visually.

If you add music, or the voices of the people in the photographs, the presentation will have even greater impact. When you use words in audiovisual presentations, use the rules in Chapter 12.

If your illustrations are not of high quality, or if you cannot handle audiovisual materials easily, don't use them. It is better to rely on your ability to talk persuasively than to fumble with a technology that you have not yet mastered. If you are unfamiliar with audiovisual techniques and equipment, or are unsure about your ability to use them, you may be able to obtain advice and help from a local shop or business or from a college, university, or school.

The most important thing about audiovisual materials is not technical. It is to have your materials ready to use all the time. When someone asks to see your slide show, you don't want to have to say that it will take several hours to put it together. Or, when someone important to you visits your office, that you left your presentation book at home.

Getting started

The location

The location for your presentation is very important. In large part, it will be determined by the size of the audience. If possible, match the size of the room with the audience you expect to attract. Don't use a large room unless you expect to be able to fill it. There is nothing worse than a room that is three-quarters empty. It is discouraging for the speaker, and suggests a lack of interest in the subject. It is better to have the room too crowded than too empty.

For small groups, try to obtain the use of a small room and arrange the seats informally. You will want to encourage interaction with the audience before and after the slide show. You don't want to remind your listeners of a classroom.

Check the location several hours before the meeting if possible, to ensure there will be no problems when you actually get up to speak. Try to allow enough time for the organizers to make any necessary changes.

Here are some things to look for.

• If you will be meeting during the day, can the room be darkened for films or slides?

• If the meeting will be outdoors, will people be able to see the projected images? (In daylight, videotapes are more effective than films or slides.)

• Either indoors or outdoors, is there likely to be a lot of background noise? (I have had more than one talk almost ruined by the noise of road traffic, or of construction in the same building or nearby. A big meeting next door can also be a problem.)

• Is there adequate power to run the equipment you will be using? Are there electrical outlets where you will need them? Will you need an extension cord? Does the building have an emergency power supply in case of a power failure? (It is always wise to carry an extension cord of your own, and a spare bulb for the projector.)

• Are there enough chairs for everyone?

• Will everyone in the room be able to see clearly the images you will be using? (How often have you been forced to look at slides or flip charts or blackboards filled with writing too small for you to read from where you are sitting?)

• Are the speakers for the sound system placed so that everyone can hear easily?

Check the location again just before you make your presentation to ensure everything is working properly.

The audience

Think carefully about the people who will form your audience. You will want to plan your presentation to meet their needs and interests. The medium you use (slides, videotape, flip charts, etc.) should fit them as well as the response you want to obtain. Don't ignore dances, puppetry, theatre performances. They can be successful if local people find them attractive and if they illustrate your messages. The skill lies in blending your message with the entertainment.

• What will they find appealing? If they are young people, you may want to prepare a fast-paced presentation with strong music. If they are older, or have had little education, you may want to tell your story more slowly and use larger than normal lettering in the images. A small group of professionals may be annoyed by an audiovisual presentation designed for a large group; for them overhead projection sheets or a flip chart might be most suitable.

• What kind of audience participation do you want? Do you want people to be active – to give you ideas you will write on a board, or even to draw diagrams or pictures on a flip chart themselves? Or do you want them to relax and absorb impressions? Should you use a medium best suited to presenting facts (overhead or slide projections of text and graphs) or should you use a medium designed to evoke an emotional response (still or moving photographs)?

• What do you want your listeners to do as a result of your presentation? Plan specific action and make clear to the audience what you hope for. Do you want them to support your organization after the talk by speaking about it to friends? Do you want them to give their time and money to your cause? Do you want to arouse their interest in a social problem your organization is concerned about? Do you want them to give your organization money?

Planning the presentation
It is possible, but never wise, to give a speech without much preparation. It is impossible to make an audiovisual presentation without a great deal of preparation. Even if you are using only a blackboard or flip chart, you must be quite certain what you are going to write. You don't want to have to start erasing or scratching out words in front of an audience.

These are some of the questions to consider in planning an audiovisual presentation.

• How much time will you have? Keep presentations as short as you can without making people feel rushed. Twenty minutes is a good time to think about. If you need more then 30 minutes, you may need to give the audience a five-minute break in the middle. Shut down the projector and give people a chance to ask questions. But don't let them leave their seats if you want to keep things moving quickly. If people start walking around, the break will take a lot longer than five minutes: you will have lost the continuity in your talk and may have lost the full attention of the audience.

• Unless the presentation is pre-prepared (a film or video) set aside twice the amount of time you think you could possibly need to get the presentation ready. Build in rehearsal time. Have one rehearsal well ahead in case some part needs improving with new slides. Rehearse again just before the actual presentation. Even if you are giving a talk for the tenth time and know you don't need more rehearsal, check the slides or overhead projection sheets to make sure they are in the right order. Make sure slides are in the projector tray facing the correct way and right side up. If you have not used an overhead projector before, practise with it.

• Keep presentations simple. Break up complex information into small components. Again, information is like food. People can swallow only so much at one time, and small bites are more digestible. Present one idea in one image at a time.

• Make the words and illustrations big enough so that everyone will be able to see them clearly.

• If you are using slides or a computer-generated presentation, rehearse so many times that you never lose track of where you are and what you want to say.

• Memorize what you are showing so that you don't keep looking at the screen. When you look at the screen, you turn your back on the audience.

Making the presentation

Remember all the rules for effective personal presentations given in Chapter 13. In addition:

• Be sure your voice can be heard clearly, especially if the room has noisy air conditioning.

Be sure your voice can be heard clearly.

• If you want to give an impression rather than convey facts, show the visual material first, with little or no introduction, so that it has maximum impact on its own. After a few seconds, explain the significance of the slide. Or wait until the last slide is shown and give your commentary at the end.

• Never ever read out the exact words from the screen. If many members of the audience are illiterate, it is better to use pictures alone. Other audiences should be able to read the words for themselves. They will just be bored or irritated if you make them wait while you read the words. Instead, think of what is on the screen as only a list of subject headings. It is then up to you to talk more about each subject. That will keep the audience interested. The text that is projected is simply a guide for them to what you are talking about and where you are heading.

• If you want to convey facts, tell people what they are going to see, show the visual material with some commentary, and then give further explanations at the end if they are necessary. The repetition will help the audience absorb the information.

• If you are giving a talk that includes slides, work out carefully in advance how you will know when, during your talk, to move to the next slide. Mark the places on your script. Rehearse. It takes practice to run the show smoothly.

• Take your time. Allow people enough time to understand what the projected image shows.

• Allow time for audience feedback. Encourage questions and comments.

Using slides

Slides may be used to present purely factual information, mostly in words or possibly graphs. But there are less expensive, simpler ways to present this kind of information. Several are described in Chapter 14.

Slides are most effective when used to convey information that will arouse the emotions of the audience. The pictures, magnified on a large screen or white sheet in a darkened room, have a powerful impact. The best presentations are a carefully planned blending of sight and sound – artwork, words, and photography, voice and music. They work best with groups of up to about 50 people. The trend is to use videos rather than slides, but I don't think any video ever approaches the impact of good slides unless it is very high quality and shown on an enormous screen.

Even the simplest shows take care, a significant investment of time, and some money. Photographs must be taken; if some slides are to contain words, the text must be prepared and photographed – tasks that require special skills and a better-than-average camera. (The text can be prepared on a computer, using a special slide presentation program, but that requires extra equipment and skills.) You will also need a projector and, if there is to be a sound accompaniment, a tape recorder. Most of the expensive equipment can be rented or borrowed, but the time that must be put into making the slides can be considerable.

This means slide shows are worth doing only if the slides are likely to be used many times. It is not necessary to give exactly the same show every time, however. You may want to use the slides in different ways for different audiences.

Slides have an impact because the projected pictures are large and colourful, in strong contrast to the darkened room in which they are shown. Because the room is dark, there are no distractions and the audience's attention is focused on the screen. The size of the picture adds special power. When you are setting up a room for a slide show, make sure it is as dark as possible. Then move the projector and screen around until you have the projection as large as it can possibly be, preferably filling the whole screen.

Organizing the slides

Preparing the script for a slide show is very much like organizing any piece of writing. The first step is to decide on the purpose of the show and the audience you hope will see it. Start by writing down, in any order you like, all the facts, messages, ideas that you want to include. Once you have done that, rearrange them in a logical order that will tell your story. Always keep in mind what you want to happen as a result of your presentation. You may not use everything you write down but, by writing a script, you will be able to decide what pictures need to be taken and the order in which they will be shown.

It's a good idea to plan the slides with what the professionals call a "story board." Lay out small cards or pieces of paper on a table. Based on your

outline, write a description of each slide that you need on a card, one slide to a card. Try arranging the cards in different orders for various effects. Think of showing not more than six slides per minute. Plan fewer slides if there are to be many words spoken as you show each slide. If you go too fast, the audience will stop paying attention.

When you have the pictures, you must add details to your speech that will make the story interesting and make the pictures meaningful.

For example, you may be planning to talk about relieving poverty in a rural community. During your talk, you may begin by showing a picture of a woman selling vegetables in a market. That gives you a chance to talk about how much that person earns from her family farm and what that can buy for her family. Then you can go on to describe what it costs to raise the vegetables, the difficulties of making a living in the community, and the measures that can be taken to help the people. You can then show some of the steps that have been taken and the results. This is a good way to explain what you are doing – working from specific individuals (the market women) to the more general problem, and back again to specific examples of achievement.

A good way to organize a slide show is to think of each major point you want to make as a chapter in a book. You may want some spoken words to introduce each chapter or some taped music to create the right atmosphere. Each chapter may require several slides and supporting material. In some of these chapters you may want to go from the general to the specific – beginning with a broad picture and gradually moving closer. Imagine, for example, that you want to show the benefits of a new agricultural technique your organization helped local farmers to learn. You might first show a village and its surrounding fields from a distance. Then come closer: show a group of farmers working in one field. Come closer still. Show a picture of one farmer demonstrating the technique. Show another of a farmer displaying a sample of the improved crop to other farmers. Then show a graph that traces the increase in yields in this village. Or maybe you want to show how a factory is polluting the water supply. You might show a broad view of the river valley. Then show the factory from a distance as you describe the situation. Gradually move closer and closer until you are showing the polluted water actually flowing into the river. Show people who are trying to improve the situation and, if you have been successful, show the clean water entering the river. You may conclude with another picture of the valley as you describe your hopes for the future and move on to the next set of slides.

While the slides are being shown, you will be talking – about the people in the pictures and what they are doing, and about the significance of what the audience is seeing. If you can't easily produce a graph of the increased agricultural yield, be sure to explain how much larger the crop is now. With the pictures of the factory, explain the procedures that were followed to clean up the pollution. Also, talk about the effect of the cleanup on the health of the community (clean water has reduced disease by such and such a percentage). Let the audience hear your own enthusiasm as you

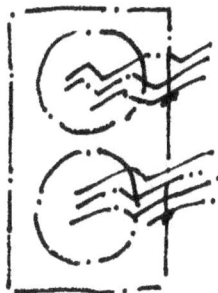

The best presentations are a carefully planned blending of sight and sound – artwork, words, and photography, voice and music.

describe these achievements.

Often short slide shows must be put together from slides you already have. Look at them carefully, weeding out those that are poor quality or do not fit the story you want to tell. The best way to do this is to use a special slide sorter or – if you don't have one – a piece of glass with a light underneath it. Lay the slides out on the glass. With the light underneath, you will be able to see each slide clearly and move slides around until you have a presentation that flows smoothly. You may have to adjust the story to fit the materials you have. If you want to protect the slides from dust and dirt, use a story board instead.

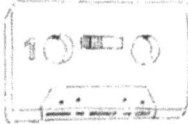

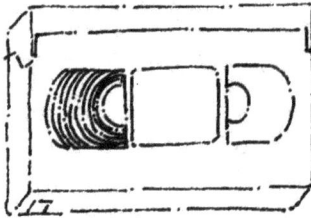

When you have all the slides you need and have organized them for the presentation, number the slides. On the script you will use when showing the slides, write the number at the point where you want to show each picture.

It is a good idea to keep a list by number of what is shown in each slide in case any get lost or damaged. It is also a good idea to make at least one copy of each slide. Store the master set of slides in a safe place. Moisture, sunlight, and fungus can ruin slides, so keep them dry, clean, and stored in a dark, cool place. Make sure the slides you are using are free of dust, hairs, and other dirt that will show when they are projected.

Organizing a computer presentation demands the same planning and organizing, e.g. moving from the general to the particular, coordinating the words to the images on the screen.

Using audiotapes

Tapes of voices or music can add impact to almost any audiovisual presentation. You can even use tapes of voices during a speech without pictures. Tapes are easy to make if you have the right equipment.

Be selective about what you use. You might, for example, use a tape of people telling about their good experiences with your organization. In that case you may be tempted to include comments from a large number of people. Don't. Keep the tape short – several minutes only – because people will not concentrate for much longer. Make sure every word is important. If the sound is not clear, or if there is background noise, the tapes should not be used. The fastest way to lose an audience is to make it listen to tapes that cannot be understood.

Music can be played throughout a slide show if there is no commentary and if you want to create a mood, not convey information. You may be able to use purchased tapes that create the right atmosphere. But music works best interspersed with spoken words. If you have the time and the equipment, you can record both music and spoken words so the tape can run without interruption throughout the show. In that case, introduce the show in person. The tape can be set up to signal with a little beeping noise when it is time for the person running the projector to go to the next slide. With the right equipment, you can even insert a signal in the audiotape that will make the slides change automatically.

Films and videotapes

Short films and videotapes can add impact to illustrate and reinforce your message. Films in particular can be shown to a large group. A college, library, or other resource centre may have suitable films to borrow or rent. Be sure the equipment you use works perfectly.

Making good quality films and videotapes for your own organization is expensive and demanding. It is rarely done well by amateurs. Most amateur videos are horrible to watch – the camera wobbles, it focuses on one subject too long, or it moves too quickly. You need professional help and a good deal of money to get a good result; you may need to find a sponsor for the project. If you are going to try to make a worthwhile video without professional help, follow the instructions that come with the video camera and find a person who can teach you at least some of the skills you need.

Videos can be shown only where there is electrical power, a television set, and a videocassette player. Usually the screen is too small to have the same impact as large film, computer, or slide projections. Videos are therefore best suited to giving instruction or information to a small audience.

Presentation books

By far the simplest visual support for your presentation is a book of photographs, clippings, letters, and other materials that you have kept about your work. Books like this can be shown to two or three people at a time, but no more.

It is more difficult to make an effective presentation with this kind of scrapbook than might appear. Don't put too many items on a page. You must avoid sounding like a proud parent showing pictures of the new baby. After you have made the same presentation several times, you will have trouble sounding spontaneous about each page. Try occasionally to question the people you are talking to about what they are seeing. Give them a chance to comment or ask questions. This will help making the presentation sound fresh. Use presentation books to give an impression, not to convey a lot of facts.

16 Making the most of print

With print, you can control what is said about your organization: you are saying it, not someone else. Print materials also give you flexibility. You can use the form that best suits the message, the purpose, and the audience – a brochure, a poster, a newsletter. You can use photographs and illustrations for information or emotional impact. Your print publication can reach hundreds, even thousands of people, at low cost. And, unlike television or radio, your print message does not disappear immediately. It can have a much longer life. But effective use of print is not simple. It requires:
- planning, analysis, and appraisal
- an attractive design to catch the reader's eye
- well-written text that presents your message clearly, interestingly, and convincingly

First steps: planning, analysis, and appraisal
For all publications, small or large, the same questions need to be answered. The first three should be asked before anything is written. The others should be asked before anything is published.

1 *What do I want to say?* Be absolutely certain about the answer. It should be possible to give it in a single specific sentence – for example, "We want to tell people what we will accomplish next year so they will think well of us." "We are telling mothers how to cook vegetables to get the most food value."

The first step in clear communication is to know precisely what is to be communicated. The second is to stick to it. Sometimes publications have two or three purposes that cannot easily be combined. Sometimes people start off writing with one purpose in mind, but become so fascinated with part of their material that the purpose changes. If the publication loses its focus, readers may be left wondering what to make of what they hold in their hands.

2 *Who exactly are the intended readers?* Be clear. A publication for one group of readers may not be suitable for others. Before you produce any printed material decide the target audience and plan the material with their needs and interests in mind. One leaflet explaining your services, for example, could be targeted only to the people in rural villages who could benefit from them. It would be in the local language and speak in the way that the local people talk among themselves. It would be written differently from one addressed to policy-makers or a third version meant to explain your

services to overseas funders.

Often, however, you will be short of money; you may want to try to aim one publication at a large, mixed audience. This will never be as effective as publications tailored to specific audiences but may be unavoidable. Even then it is important to define the audience before you start, to help in making the publication understandable and attractive to all those you hope to reach.

3 *How much information do I need to communicate?* It is dangerous to assume that the intended readers know a fact just because the writer knows it. If there is any doubt, it is usually better to tell too much than too little.

Here are questions to ask about the content of anything prepared for publication. If you are the writer, ask them of yourself as you write. If someone else is writing, check the manuscript before it is set in type.

- Does this give readers all the information they need? Will they have enough background to be convinced, and to respond in the way we want them to?
- Does this give readers more information than they really need? Too much information stops interest. Too little prevents communication. Provide just the right amount – enough information to interest, instruct, or convince readers, not so much as to discourage, bore, or repel them.
- Does this give readers more information than they can absorb easily at one time? How big are the bites? Keep them easy to chew and absorb.
- Is this longer than necessary? Often we get material we would like to read, plan to read, but don't have time to read at the moment; so we set it to one side. Short documents are more likely to be read.

4 *How can I write the text so that it is likely to interest its intended readers?* Effective publications attract readers by looking interesting and being interesting. They explain why their contents are important and how they benefit the reader. Other material may not be read.

5 *How will I reach the intended audience?* Plan to use forms you know your intended readers are comfortable with and find attractive. That may mean a one-page formal summary for a policy-maker; it may mean a comic book format for health publications aimed at a poorly educated readership. (There is nothing unsuitable about comic books, if they might appeal to the intended readers.)

6 *Will the intended readers be comfortable with the style of the presentation?* Writers must be certain that their words are right for the intended readers. The vocabulary must be suitable for their level of education and the words should be ones they normally use. The examples should relate to their experience. Readers should not have to stop and ask, "What does that mean?"

Illustrations also must be understandable. Sometimes pictures do not communicate clearly. For example, a booklet in West Africa told people how to store clean drinking water. One picture showed people gathered around a jar holding drinking water. They looked happy because it was obviously good to drink. Some readers understood this message. Others thought the people were standing around drinking tea.

7 *Publications are expensive. How can I get maximum benefit from each one?* Take full advantage of every publication you produce. Distribute as many

copies as you can afford to print, to as many people as you can afford to reach. Your audience may be wider than you first think. When you issue a publication, make certain all the staff and volunteers have it and take copies to give to friends and family. Give it to board members. Send it to all donors as part of any other mailing. Use a new publication, even a new descriptive brochure, as a way of opening doors to politicians and media people. Put it in displays in community centres, schools, local government and business offices. And don't forget your own office and project locations.

     8 *How can these questions be tested?* There is only one way to answer these questions, and that is to test them by asking the intended readers or similar people. A three-year plan could be looked at by one or two board members before it is presented to the whole board. A booklet for fisherfolk should be tested by showing it to people who fish, either in draft or in its first edition; then it can be improved, and the findings can be used to improve other publications aimed at such people.

     Everything you publish should tell readers how to respond to you. Make it easy for them to get in touch. Always include the name and address of the executive director or a staff member directly involved in a particular project. Ask for feedback. Offer tours, further information, program assistance, help with problems.

     Publications should not be issued and forgotten. Each new publication gives a chance to learn more about the process of communication and how to make it more effective. If response is poor, it is particularly important to know why, so mistakes will not be repeated. If response is good, it is equally important to know why, so that successful techniques can be used again.

Eye-catching appearance

All materials should reflect the real organization, or at most, the next stage of growth to which you aspire. Otherwise, people will sense or will learn that you are promising something you cannot deliver. Be honest.

     The self-examination you have already conducted (Book 1, Chapters 4, 5, 6) will tell you how your organization is seen by other people. You may be happy with the picture people have of you. For example, they may see you as an effective, small, informal organization without much money but with strong rural roots and close relationships with those you serve. If you think that image serves you well, then everything you produce about your organization should paint that picture.

     It is just as hard to look simple and yet appealing on a small budget as it is to look sophisticated and appealing on a large budget. Simple publications take just as much care and thought, if not more, than expensive publications. In either case, you should get some advice from a graphic designer if there is one nearby and you can afford a fee. A graphic designer is trained to look at your organization as a whole and to plan your publications to project the image you want. People should immediately recognize that your publications come from your organization. The publications need not all look the same but they should have a family resemblance.

Graphic designers can arrange for printing but they are not printers. On the other hand, printers like to give advice about how a publication should look, but most have no training in design. You may have to settle for a printer if you are in a small community but a printer is not a substitute for a trained designer.

Professional help from a designer can range from an hour's discussion and advice to improve what you have already planned to taking responsibility for all such materials down to the smallest detail. A graphic designer can get cost estimates for printing and supervise the production, making sure the material is ready when you need it. Whichever course you choose, the goal is to give visual interest and a unified, appropriate look to all your materials.

If using a designer is impossible, can you go to a library and look at books about design? If that too is difficult, the best thing is to look around you at what other organizations are doing that you like. Steal their ideas, not their specific designs.

A computer can do some of the job for you. Even the most basic word processing program will allow you to print a document in two columns. Since short lines are easier to read than long lines, two columns can give you a big advantage.

Many computers have simple graphic design software as part of basic programs. You may find a variety of standard formats for letterheads, for brochures, and for newsletters, for example. Give them a try. If you want to go further, think about getting a program, such as PageMaker, that is specifically for producing publications. Without training, the program may be difficult to use, so be sure to give the person who will use the program both training and time to practise. The results should justify the time spent. Good design does not need to be expensive. It is often cheaper than bad design because a good graphic designer knows how to save money on printing.

Some guidelines for effective design in print

• Allow for plenty of white space on each page. If the pages look crowded with words, people will feel tired before they even start to read. Lots of white space makes a page look easy to read. Short paragraphs also make for easy reading.

• Make the letters big enough for people with elderly eyes to read easily. Check on your computer or typewriter. 12 point type is a better size than 10 point. The difference is clear on the next page, isn't it?

• DON'T USE ALL CAPITAL LETTERS. They are hard to read even in headlines.

• Choose a typeface that is easy to read and looks ordinary. Computers have many typefaces and many are ugly. Some are unusual and may look beautiful when you see only a line or two, but are hard to read in long passages. Choose a typeface that readers will accept as familiar. Remember that the purpose of your publications is to convince people. Anything that impedes reading or looks unconventional may interfere with that goal.

Two typefaces that are easy to read and often available on computers are shown in the example. In both of these typefaces, the little hooks at the ends of the letters (called "serifs") tie the words together and guide the reader's eye along the line.

• For variety, you can use a type like Geneva but only for headlines. Because it has no serifs, this typeface is difficult to read in long passages.

• *You can use type like this but only for one or two lines, perhaps under a photograph or to set off examples, or for emphasis. This is called italic type. Because it is compressed, it is hard to read.*

• **You can use bold face type like this for headings.** Again, it is more difficult to read in long passages than normal type. Do not use it for emphasis. *Use italic type instead.*

12 point type is easy to read.

• Avoid long lines, which are also hard to read. Ideally, no line should be longer than 52 letters.

10 point type can be too small for some people.

For material that is to be read quickly, like a brochure, the lines should be even shorter – say, 39 letters. If lines are long, allow a little extra space between the lines. That will make is easier for the reader's eye to move from the end of one line to the beginning of the next.

ALL CAPITAL LETTERS ARE HARD TO READ EVEN IN HEADLINES.

• Put important material at the top of the page, less important material at the bottom.

• Use illustrations. Good illustrations are worth many words. They can communicate more directly and more clearly than words. Often they are the first thing read.

This typeface is called
Palatino.

• Make sure the material you send to the printer is clean and easy to read. If the material is typed on a typewriter, be sure the ribbon is new and that the metal letters that strike the paper are clean. If the original is poorly typed or has many hand-written changes, typesetting will be slower and more expensive. When using a computer and printer, be sure the ink in the printer is producing a clear, black image. Today, many printers will accept manuscripts on a computer disc and use the disc to prepare text for printing. This produces the cleanest image of all.

This typeface,
Times New Roman,
is always good too for the body of the text.

Geneva
can be used for headlines.

Finding the money for publications

No matter how economical a publication is, it still costs money. Sometimes a little extra money makes a big difference. It might allow you to buy slightly better paper or to use photographs to make a publication more effective. It is worth looking for financial help for any major publication. Think about whether:

• an advertising agency, a graphic designer, a design firm, or design students might donate time to help plan your publications
• a printer might donate printing
• local businesses might pay or help pay for design, printing, and distribution of your publications

Businesses usually have some money set aside each year for public relations, advertising, or, possibly, charitable donations. They want to support something that will give them recognition. While the cost of producing an annual report or a brochure may be high for you, it may not be high to a local business that can do it when it has time free. It is possible

that a printer might do your printing free, charging only for paper and ink, or at a reduced price. It never hurts to ask. Local art or design students might consider helping you as a class or individual project. Journalism students might help with the writing. But it is important not to expect that work done for free or at discount will be done quickly. Allow plenty of time for donated work to be done.

Remember to thank these supporters in the publication and to get copies to them with a thank-you the moment they are printed. A business may be especially cooperative if its advertisement or an acknowledgement of its generosity appears on hundreds of copies that will be distributed all over the community. The group that supported your publication might also want to distribute copies as part of its own public relations program.

We will talk more about these sorts of support in Book 3, in the chapters about corporate fundraising.

Capturing and keeping the reader's attention

Attractive, readable publications are produced by people who have a strong sense of competition. They are determined to capture and keep the reader's attention. They know the reader's first impression is most important. If a text is not immediately interesting, readers are apt to go on to something else. Attention can be captured by:
- an interesting title
- an effective opening paragraph
- an interesting or unusual design
- a powerful or attractive illustration

Design, illustrations, and title can all call attention to the facts in the story, but it is dangerous to depend entirely on them. Editors should make sure points of interest appear in the opening paragraphs. Here are some proven guidelines for capturing the reader's attention. They apply especially to newsletters, articles, press releases, and similar material, but are also valuable in writing brochures and annual reports.

1 *Appeal to the reader's self-interest.* People want to know how to:
- keep healthy and fit
- make more money
- understand the world and the people around them
- enjoy life more

A publication that appeals to any of these basic interests is likely to be read – as long as people can see from the very beginning how it will help them. If direct benefits cannot be shown, appeal to the reader's curiosity. Most people are curious about other people. Many are curious about the world around them. Many enjoy solving problems.

2 *Appeal to the reader's other interests.* Readers generally are more interested in facts, people, or events if they are:
- large in impact, size, or significance. A typhoon is more dramatic than a rainstorm.
- nearby or familiar. The typhoon is more interesting if it passes within

a few hundred miles than if it is far away; a lottery winner is more interesting if she lives nearby and not in a distant city.

• recent. Both the typhoon and the lottery seem more interesting if they happened yesterday than if they happened a month ago. We have been conditioned by the news media to attach special importance to new developments and recent events. Anything that happened four or five months ago – no matter how important – may seem out of date.

• unusual. The typhoon will be more interesting if it was totally unexpected; the lottery winner will be more interesting if that was the biggest prize on record. People are fascinated by the unusual – the biggest or smallest, best or worst, first or last, fastest or slowest.

3 *Write good titles.* Here are 13 rules for writing effective titles - for booklets, pamphlets, folders, magazine and newsletter articles, and any other kind of general publication.

• Read the text thoroughly and make sure you understand it.

• Search for the most important idea. Pick out key words.

• Use the key words to state the principal message in a few words.

• Ask: "Will this principal message interest the reader? Is there some way I can make it more interesting?" Try to find a wording that will show how the material can help the reader. One way to do this is to start the title: "How to ...." or "Ten ways to ...."

• Try for variety. There are as many kinds of titles as there are of openings. If an article begins with an unusual opening, however, the title should not normally duplicate it. Two questions, for example – one in the title and one in the opening – would be likely to annoy, not interest, the reader, who expects information, not puzzles.

• Continue revising. The rules of readability apply in titles twice as much as in ordinary text. Especially:

• use active verbs

• be positive

• find strong nouns

• avoid the verb "to be"

• use short, simple words

• avoid repetition

• cut words that aren't working

• Titles don't need verbs. But the most powerful ones do have verbs and make a complete statement. The present tense gives extra vigour.

• Check that the title is correct. In trying to capture interest, editors sometimes promise more than is in the text. Be sure readers will not be disappointed. Protect your credibility.

• Be sure the meaning is clear. Some people will read only the title. Because there are only a few words to work with, it is especially important to guard against ambiguity.

• Look for wording that is clear but unusual – an alliteration, a simple rhyme, or even a touch of mystery.

• Make sure the heading has the same feeling or flavour as the story. Heading and story should not read as if they came from two different writers.

• Think how the title will look. It should fill the available space comfortably. Some white space makes a heading more readable; too much looks ugly. Use capitals rarely: think of a headline as a sentence. If the title has more than one line, group the words so they break into lines neatly. Lines should be roughly the same length. Don't settle for titles that look like this:

Natural enemies control rice

insect pests

The first line should have been broken after the third word.

• Be prepared to work hard on every title. Good ones are not easy to write.

My favourite title was in a newsletter published by the International Centre of Insect Physiology and Ecology (ICIPE) in Nairobi, Kenya. It was: "The fatal attraction of buffalo urine." The article described a trap for tsetse flies, which cause sleeping sickness.

4 *Make the opening work.* The first words are crucial. They deserve considerable time and effort. If they fail to attract, the reader may be lost to the competition. Several examples of effective openings appear at the end of this chapter.

5 *Discard openings that do not work.* Good openings are hard to write. Authors in a hurry sometimes slip into routine kinds of beginnings that rarely attract uncommitted readers. Three common problems are:

• reports of conferences that begin with the fact the conference was held, where it was held, the dates it was held, and its theme. This usually takes five or six lines. Only after that, if they are lucky, will readers learn what was discussed, recommended, or decided. By that time they may have gone on to something else.

• descriptions of an organization that begin with its history, its place in a larger organization, its location, and its general goals. That information is for bureaucrats. Most readers will be more interested in what the organization has achieved, what it is doing now, what it will do, and how that will help them. Those facts should come first.

• statements so general that they could lead into almost any report in the same field. The story usually can start perfectly well if those openings are dropped. Here is an example:

Agriculture is our greatest industry and will remain so for many years to come. Any practice that increases agricultural production is therefore vital to the national economy. [The article goes on to discuss ploughing practices].

A more interesting start might be: *Ploughing is no longer standard practice ....*

6 *Make sure the opening is supported by the facts.* In trying to attract readers, it is possible to distort the message or exaggerate it. A modest advance may become a "breakthrough;" a conference may become "historic;" a plan may be made to sound like reality. In the competition for the reader's attention, never forget the facts.

Here are some of the ways articles can begin, with examples from newsletters and magazines.

• *Information.* This is a straightforward report of the subject answering three or more of the questions: who? what? why? where? when? how? It assumes the reader is interested and wants information quickly. A reader who stops after the first paragraph will already know the most important facts. Editors should, however, guard against packing too many facts into a single sentence, as in the following example.

Farmers in the 35 Topisi and Makoro extension areas have formed groups of 40 to 50 people to fight ticks, which have menaced their livestock for years despite all precautions taken by the government.

• *Picture.* This draws a scene for the reader, an illustration in words. Make sure the picture is clear, and that it is quickly tied to the main message. Here is a long opening, but an effective one.

Issifou is squatting on the ground under the big shade tree in the family courtyard in the large village of Dogondoutchi, in southern Niger. A couple of paces away his sisters are dehulling millet with a pestle. Spread around him are a hammer, shears, pliers, an anvil, and a thick strip of steel which must once have been a truck spring. Next to these tools of his craft is his raw material – empty cans.

In less than two hours, using the shears, the hammer, and the pliers, he makes a watering can. He only needs to solder it in a couple of spots before it can be sold to people in the village. He will sell it for 2500 CFA francs, about one eighth of the price of the same item in the capital, Niamey, 400 kilometres away. It is an essential tool for growing vegetables in the dry season.

Dogondoutchi is one of four centres of operations of a project for training artisans and supporting their enterprises.

• *Anecdote.* Everyone enjoys a story. Editors should make sure the story is short and is firmly related to the principal theme.

The politicians in Ankara had never seen anything like it. In the late 1970s, a petition with 60,000 names came before the National Assembly – more signatures than any other petition in the history of the Turkish republic. And what was surprising, in this land of male domination, was that all 60,000 signatories were women. What drove so many women to action? Their desperate need for child day-care centres.

• *Question.* This kind of opening appeals to the reader's curiosity and pleasure in answering questions correctly. These are the same qualities that make quiz games so popular. This type should not be used too often, however. If every story opens with a question, the device becomes boring. Used occasionally, questions can be extremely effective.

So you think you have problems with aphids on your houseplants? Consider this: Farmers near ICIPE's Mbita Point Station, hard by the shores of Lake Victoria in western Kenya, often complain about hippos lumbering ashore at night and ponderously munching their way through the field crops. How would you like to devise a management strategy for a king-sized pest with the temperament and appetite of a hippo?

• *Quotation.* Direct speech draws the reader directly into the report. But the quotation must be unusual or forceful. A bland quotation makes a bland opening. Here an article about dust and its danger to health begins with a verbal explosion.

"You want to see dust, do you? I'll show you dust!" exclaimed the National Guard officer. "Come home with me, look at my linen, my bed, my fridge! There's dust all over the place!"

The air in the mining town of Redeyef, in the south of Tunisia, is so dusty that one can't really see the sky, only a vague glimmering through the grey clouds.

• *Background.* This provides a context within which the reader can assess the significance of the developments reported. It should not be used too often, or readers will want to shout: "Get to the point!" Background openings should be short, so that the reader gets to the main message quickly. Here is one that provides the context in a single paragraph, then tackles the main message in the next.

Egyptian street vendors are famous for fried falafel, a nutritious snack prepared with fava beans. In Syria, shorbat ads – lentil soup – is a winter favourite. And in parts of North Africa and the Middle East, millions snack on hummos, a chickpea-sesame dip.

These and an array of other Middle Eastern dishes are made from legumes, dietary staples generally containing two to four times the protein of cereals, and hence known as the poor man's meat. Legumes are often a cash crop for the small-scale farmer, and they also supply straw for animal feed. The "big three" legumes – fava beans, lentils, and chickpeas – account for about two-thirds of food legumes produced in the Middle East and North Africa.

• *Contrast and surprise.* A contrast combines opposites; surprise plays on our delight with the unexpected. Both are difficult to use well and are only occasionally suitable. When they can be used, they can be effective. Make sure that in the first there is a real difference, and that the second is truly surprising.

Although Sri Lanka is endowed with substantial marine animal life in the deep seas surrounding the island, the tropical climate makes it difficult to keep the catch fresh. Ice is a necessity.

17 The printed materials of business

An organization's printed materials need not all look the same but they should look like members of the same family. People should be able to see instantly that a business card, a piece of writing paper, a newsletter, a slide presentation all come from the same organization. There are many ways to do this. A good symbol that appears on everything is one of the most effective. Think of the panda of the World Wide Fund for Nature, the Red Cross/Red Crescent, or McDonald's golden arches.

Symbols

You may be a small organization working directly with community groups. You will want to produce simple materials, likely using only black ink and white or possibly coloured paper. You may not want a fancy symbol, if you need a symbol at all. Typing in the name of your organization in big letters at the top of a page, or even handwriting it carefully, may convey exactly the impression you want to give.

On the other hand, you may want people to think of you as a well-established, highly professional, sophisticated organization. In this case, you may want to make greater use of colour, and may print your materials on more expensive paper. You may want your materials to simply display an attractive symbol. Or you may want to stay in between, so that you look well established but not too wealthy.

Whether you are large or small, if you use a symbol, choose it carefully: it tells the public who and what you are. A symbol says in a second what your organization is all about in a way no words can ever do. It can stay in people's minds for years, even after it is no longer in use. If you are using a symbol now, or are considering the design of a new symbol, ask:

Does it reflect the spirit of the organization now?
Does it convey a positive image of your organization?
Is it simple, so it conveys an immediate message?
Does it reflect the spirit of the organization as you see it in the future? Once you have a symbol, you will want people to recognize it. For that to happen you must live with it for a long time.
Does it dignify the people who are served by your organization?
Will it look good printed small or large?
Will it look equally good in colour and in black-and-white? Much of the time the symbol will be photocopied or faxed, so it should look good in black and white. In fact, you can never go wrong using black and white.

A logo that could be used by WaterLink is shown on the business card below.

When an organization is thinking about a symbol, someone always suggests a contest. This is seldom a good idea. Contestants rarely produce symbols that do the jobs described above. Contests also can take up a lot of time. At the end, they can leave unhappy losers, to say nothing of unhappy staff who may have to live for a long time with a symbol that does not serve the organization well.

Business cards

Business cards are a useful marketing tool, easy to use and inexpensive. But they are effective only if you don't leave them in the office or at home. They have two roles. One is to identify the person; the other is to identify the organization. When planning cards think of the emphasis you want to give.

WATERLink

Samuel Ojai
Executive director

Central Building,
#1234
P.O. Box 0000
Limgagi, Country 000
Tel.: (00) 000 000
Fax: (00) 000 000
E-mail:
sojai@malnet.mi

• No matter how small your organization is, it pays to have a business card even if it is as simple as a rubber stamp on a small piece of paper.

• If you have several jobs in different organizations it may be preferable to have separate cards for each job rather than to clutter one card with too much information.

• If is not clear from your name whether you are a man or a woman, give some indication (Mrs., Ms, Mr.). Otherwise people may hesitate to contact you because they won't know how to address you. This is important when writing to people overseas who may be unfamiliar with names in your country.

• Include the country where your organization has its headquarters. If you are using your local language on the card, give your title and the address in a language a person far away is likely to know, possibly English. Even if you think you are small and local, you never know where your material will end up.

Concern India Foundation supports a wide range of projects for the underprivileged in the fields of education, health, environment and community development.

• Include your e-mail address and your Web site if you have them.

• Use the back of the card (see examples). The cost of printing the card will increase only a little: the impact of the card will increase a lot. You could give your name, address and other information in a second language if that is appropriate; in some countries, this is common practice. You could use it to give your charitable registration number. Or you could use it to describe your organization, its mission, or its services. Put that

Education. Food. Shelter. Health. CRY [Child Relief and You] tries to restore these basic rights to deprived children in rural, tribal and urban India.
CRY does this by routing your contribution of time, skills and money to voluntary agencies working to give underprivileged children a better future.

message on the back of all business cards printed for staff members, not just your own. When you have put a message on the back, be sure to point it out when you give a card to someone. Two examples are shown from intermediary NGOs in India that have used the back of the card to describe

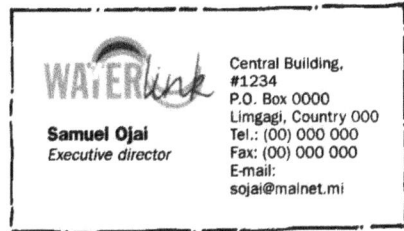

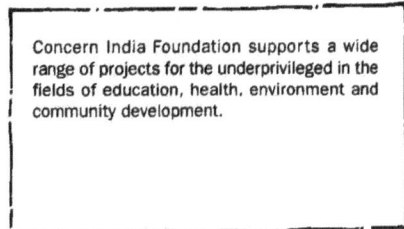

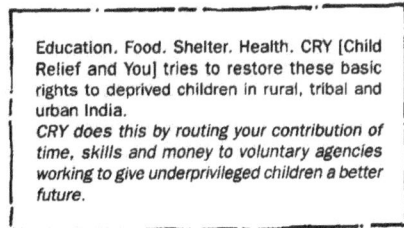

their work. In months of interviewing NGOS, these are the only two cards I was given, out of dozens, that had a message on the back.

Letterhead/stationery and envelopes

Often the first impression people have of your organization comes from your business stationery. That impression may stick with them. You need to be sure the design of your stationery is appropriate for your organization. Keep it simple. Don't have too many words on the page. Keep it clean. Use a design similar to your business cards. Use the same symbol. State clearly how and where people can reach your organization. If your organization has more than one address, make it obvious which one should be used. If your mail should be addressed to a box number, make that more prominent than the street address. I almost always address a letter to a street address before I notice there is a box number.

Make it clear how the writer of the letter should be addressed in a reply. The signature of the person sending the letter should be legible and look attractive. Often the signature is the first impression a person will have of the writer. The signature should be followed by the name and title of the person in typewriting or clear printing. If is not clear if the person is a man or a woman, add some designation. How often do you see a signature like the one below?

Executive director

You have no idea what the person's name is unless it is printed on the letterhead. Another letter may be signed:

Samuel Ojai
Managing director
Services for the Poor

"Nothing wrong with that," you might think. But the letter is on the letterhead of WaterLink. "What is going on?" You may ask, "Who is this person?" "Is Services for the Poor a department of WaterLink? Is it a separate organization? If so, what is the connection between the two? Where do I send my reply?" You may be so confused that you never answer the letter. Many people have several jobs and several employers. If there is any possibility of confusion, the writer should explain relationships in the body of the letter.

Always include in your letterhead and in all your other materials any charitable registration, bank account, or other number that would increase people's confidence in giving you their support.

Should you include a line or two at the bottom of the page listing your major donors? Should you list your board members and perhaps special advisers, with their permission? Should a one-line mission statement appear at the bottom of the letterhead? One of these elements is enough. The question is which is needed most.

Always include in your address the country where your organization is located. And put the address, not just in the necessary local languages, but also in a language that a person far away is likely to know. The envelopes of the National Amnesty and Redemption Organization (International) has its address in Hindi and English. That is good. But the English version says the international administrative office is in Bharat. (The organization has branch offices in six countries.) How many people who might want to contact this organization from overseas would know that Bharat is the Hindu name for India?

In using business stationery, follow the conventions for business correspondence in your country. This includes using correct business titles, forms of greeting, and endings of letters. For instance, do you sign off with "yours truly," "yours very truly," "cordially"?

If you have a computer with a reasonably good printer, you can save the cost of printing letterhead by installing the formatted information for the letterhead in your computer and calling it up each time you want to send a letter. This also saves changing the paper in your printer each time you change from letterhead to regular paper and back again.

It is not necessary to have printed envelopes if you want to keep things simple. Printed return address labels can be pasted on the envelopes. Or your computer printer may be able to print the return address on envelopes. If you do have envelopes printed, think about putting information on the flap or on the back of the envelope. The short CRY message, for example, could be used on the outside as well as at the bottom of the letterhead. A few words will not add much to the cost of printing, and they give you a chance to place your message where it cannot be missed.

A short message can also go on the front of the envelope, if that is permitted by postal regulations. Use the same line in all other print or promotion material and in your e-mail signature if you have e-mail.

Include a special symbol if you are using recycled or partly recycled paper.

Paper: 50% recycled, 20% post-consumer fibre

Over 55% recycled, including 25% post-consumer fibre

THE ASSOCIATION OF THE PHYSICALLY HANDICAPPED

THE ASSOCIATION OF PEOPLE WITH DISABILITY

Good change

18 Powerful posters

Come together!

Event
Date
Place
Purpose

Further information:

WATERlink

The message should be brief, direct, simple, and large so that it can be absorbed quickly.

A powerful poster can present a positive image of your organization. But posters require the same care and thought as more complex printed materials. Either in words or illustration, a good poster has an element of surprise that catches the attention of passers by.

The simplest, most effective posters encourage some sort of action. A poster that does not suggest any action may look attractive but may be a waste of an organization's money. Inspirational or "image" posters are for people with large budgets.

Why produce a poster? Because you want people to:
- attend an event – "Come to clean up the river day"
- use a service – "Free health clinic services"
- do something immediately – "Don't forget to vote"
- change their behaviour – "Stop smoking," Fight drugs."
- adopt a new technique – "Grow vegetables without chemicals"

People often look at a poster for only a fraction of a second before deciding whether they are interested in the message. That means the message should be brief, direct, simple, and large so that it can be absorbed quickly. In the first four examples, people need pause only for a few seconds to read the short message and take in the details they need to take the suggested action.

The fifth example involves a more complicated message. It may call for many words. The poster may be a wall paper – a newspaper on a wall. The publisher will expect people to stop for several minutes to read the words. If that kind of poster is put up where people normally sit or stand around, it may be read in full. Otherwise it may be ignored.

A poster:
- can be produced quickly
- can be produced cheaply; black and white is enough if the design is bold; one colour will add impact
- commands attention; a person may miss a newspaper or television announcement, but a good poster usually catches the eye
- presents its message over and over every day
- reaches both large and small, specialized and general audiences

- can be replaced easily and quickly when it is time for a new message
- reinforces other messages in a communication program

Planning a poster

As the first step in planning a poster, write down its purpose. Define the call to action – what you want the readers to do. Find a short, interesting and unforgettable way to say it. Think of Nike's "Just do it." You may want an additional brief message supporting or explaining the call to action. Use no more than four or five words in the main message, and as few as possible in the secondary message.

Decide if you want the message of the poster to be absorbed in seconds or in minutes. Don't fall in between the two, using too many words for people to read in seconds and too few to give them the information they need.

Write down what you know about the people you want to see the poster: their educational level and age, where they live, work, and shop. This information will help you decide where to put the posters and how many you need.

Design
- Make sure your type and illustration can be read easily from 2 metres (6 feet) away. Even a wall paper must have a short title in large type to catch attention. And be sure the rest of the words are at least 18 point type for easy reading (see example).
- Leave lots of empty space. A crowded poster is unattractive.
- Use a simple typeface (see Chapter 16).
- Use a simple illustration that attracts the eye and reinforces the message. Make it big.
- Use a picture of something familiar, or something commonly associated with your message. To many people, a red light announces danger, an open hand symbolizes charity. But this may not be true in all countries.
- If you use a photograph, choose a dramatic close-up of people. Avoid scenery.
- If possible, make the poster colourful. If you are limited to black-and-white, make sure there are strong blocks of black for maximum contrast with the white paper and the poster's surroundings. If you can afford only one colour of ink, consider using coloured paper. Don't use dark colours with black ink. Make sure there is good contrast between the printed words and the paper.

Words
- Use few words, unless you are sure your readers will spend time standing around near the poster.

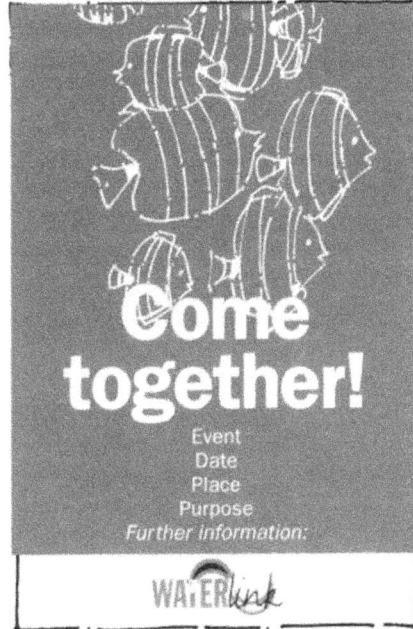

Come together!

Event
Date
Place
Purpose
Further information:

WATER*link*

Be sure the rest of the words are at least 18 point type for easy reading:

This is 18 point type

- Keep the words simple.
- Keep punctuation to a minimum.
- Always include the name of your organization and how you can be contacted. Include the names of any sponsors.
- If the poster is promoting an event, give the date, time, place, cost, special guests, contact name, address, and a phone number if there is one.
- If you use an illustration, put the words on a plain background. Don't put them on the picture, where they will be hard to read.

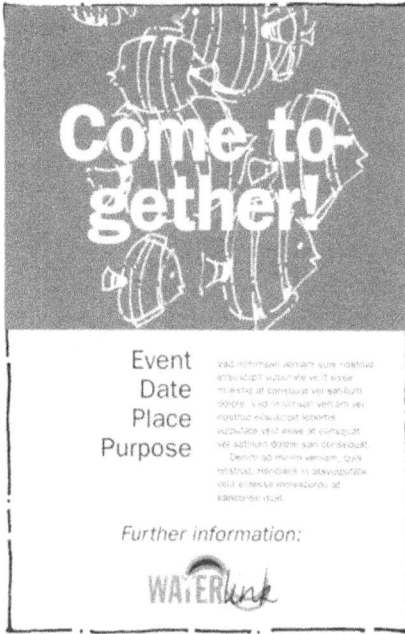

Putting words and pictures together
- Make a sketch of your proposed layout.
- Cut pieces of coloured paper the size and shape of the blocks of text and illustration. Move them about on a piece of paper the size of the poster until you have an attractive arrangement.
- Make sure the reader's eye will move easily from one element to another.
- Keep the design simple.

Placing posters for maximum impact
Choose the locations for posters carefully and in advance. A poster is usually mounted in many different places where the intended audience will see it repeatedly. The message is more likely to be absorbed if it is seen many times. Posters should be the right size for their locations. If too small, they will not be noticed. If too large, they may be seen as unnecessarily expensive. Posters should be placed:
- at eye level
- where there is clear space
- where the light is good
- where many people pass or wait
- where material is changed often enough that people are encouraged to look at it frequently

Posters can lose their impact if they are left in the same place so long that people ignore them. They should be changed every few weeks. If they fade or are damaged, they do not project a good image.

Gathering feedback
Ask your friends and colleagues if they are ready to act on the message of the poster. Get their impressions. Watch poster locations to see if people are noticing the poster. If they are not, plan what you can do to improve impact in the future.

19 The basics of brochures

You will likely need one general brochure (sometimes called a pamphlet, folder, or leaflet) to introduce your organization and add to its credibility. People all over the world expect to be given a brochure when they visit an organization of any size, meet a staff member, or request information. Someone who needs the services the organization provides may also expect to find a brochure in a library, resource centre, or government office. You can rely on brochures to open conversations and doors.

A brochure is a publication that fits on a single sheet of paper. Frequently the paper is an A4 (letter-sized) sheet folded twice, but it may be larger or smaller, and may be folded three or four times. The folds may be parallel or at right angles to one another.

A general brochure may carry many different kinds of messages. For example, a brochure may:
- urge readers to join an organization
- tell readers about an organization they are visiting
- advise prospective beneficiaries of services available to them
- demonstrate achievements
- highlight one part of a large program

In every case, a brochure can make a big impression in a small amount of time – only a few seconds. A good brochure can be all that is necessary to

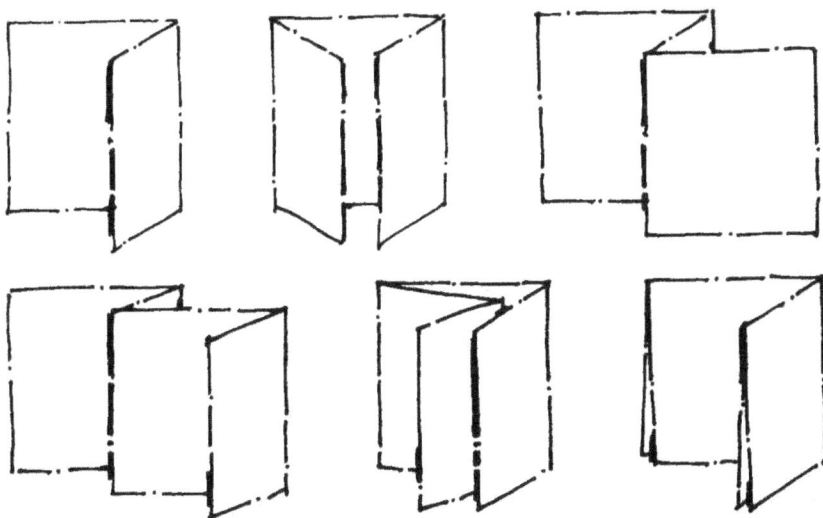

Brochures come in many sizes and shapes. They can also be folded in different ways. Shown here are from left to right, top to bottom: single fold, gate fold, concertina fold, continuous fold, parallel fold, and French fold. The variations are endless.

get people interested in your organization. But many brochures look so dull that they are ignored. They don't make any impression at all, not even a negative one.

Brochures present special problems in planning, writing, and design. Most people try to include too much information. A reader does not need to know everything about your organization. Try to present only the flavour of what you do. It may not be necessary to give a lot of detail.

A brochure must be attractive. If it isn't, the words likely won't be read. But the words are equally important.

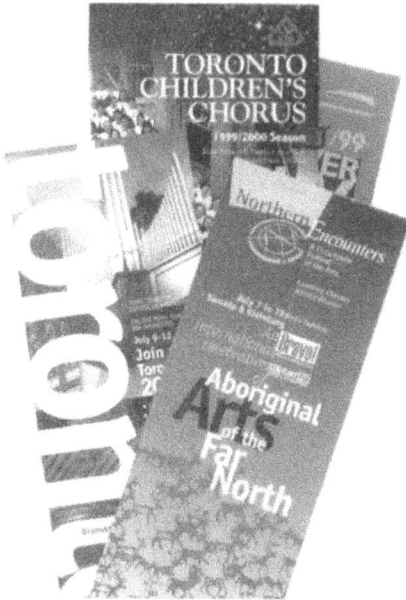

Qualities

An effective brochure is:
- personal: directed to one reader
- focused: limited to one clear message
- attractive: designed to capture the reader's attention
- simple: easy to understand at a single reading
- concise: free of waste words or irrelevant ideas
- instructive: clear in stating what action the reader should take

Planning a brochure

The front panel

The cover of any publication has only one purpose – to persuade people to read what is inside.
- Make the front of the brochure attractive and inviting.
- Ask always whether the words and design will make readers want to open the folder.

> The cover of any publication has only one purpose – to persuade people to read what is inside.

- Promise on the outside only what the inside actually delivers. For example, a full colour cover may suggest a large, sophisticated organization, not the small peasants' organization described inside.
- Show how the information in the brochure can help the reader. People won't take the time to read the whole message unless they can see some benefit to themselves.
- Attract the reader's attention. Write a title that gives the main message briefly. Direct it at the reader. ("How WaterLink helps you," "Ten ways to better health," and so on).
- If you want the reader to do something specific, make that clear right away. Put your main message right on the cover ("Give this little girl safe water").
- Use an attractive photograph or illustration, preferably showing people doing something. Best of all, if you can, is to show your workers helping people. If the brochure is about your organization, remember that an organization is its people, not its buildings. A building on the cover of a brochure gives the impression that the organization is cold and impersonal. Too often the building looks empty.

- Make sure any illustrations are of high quality.
- Follow the guidelines (Chapter 14) for using illustrations effectively.

First inside panel
- Start by showing how your organization helps people – especially (if possible) how it helps or can help the reader. This means talking about present and future benefits to the community and, above all, to the reader.
- Remember that you are talking to only one person – the person who is holding the brochure. You are not addressing a crowd. Be personal. Don't be afraid to say "you."

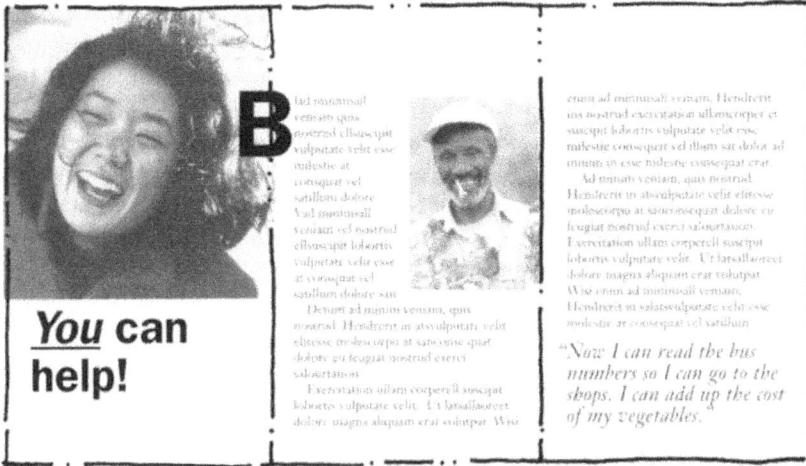

Remember that you are talking to only one person – the person who is holding the brochure. You are not addressing a crowd. Be personal. Don't be afraid to say "you."

- Begin with the present. Continue with what the organization wants to do in the future. Give a brief mission statement, not more than two short sentences.
- Don't begin with history, when the organization was established, or its place in the government hierarchy, or its buildings, or its formal objectives. These facts don't interest most people. If they are necessary, they can be stated later, preferably towards the end.
- Talk about individual people. People like to read about people.
- Explain what the organization is doing, what it has achieved, and what it offers – and do this as simply as possible. Avoid jargon.
- Urge the reader to take some kind of action – to visit the organization, tell friends about the good work it is doing, give money, become a volunteer, use the services. Show immediately how taking the action will help the reader. The brochure may ask for financial support. Fundraising brochures require special attention. They will be discussed in Book 3.
- Use illustrations on the outside of the brochure as well as inside.
- Show people in the illustrations. Show them in action, not standing still staring at the camera.
- Make illustrations big. They may run across a fold into a second panel. Just make sure the fold does not pass through a major element in the picture such as an important face.

Further inside panels
- Continue relating information to the reader's interest.
- Give details of the results expected from your work.
- Continue to talk about individual people. Explain the work being done by one staff member or tell how one recipient of your service benefited. Use those people as representations of the organization and its work. Once you have the reader's attention by talking about one person, you can go on to talk about the organization as a whole.
- Continue using photographs or illustrations.
- Use positive comments made by beneficiaries and the endorsement of known experts about your work. Give the full names, and titles if appropriate, of the people who made the statements. Be sure that the words quoted are appropriate, real, and sincere, and sound that way. If possible, local beneficiaries too should be asked permission before printing their words.

Now I can read the bus numbers, so I can go to the shops. I can add up the cost of my vegetables.

This quotation from a speaker who has just learned to read sounds genuine. A more general, more formal statement would sound less credible – for example:

I have attained a reasonable level of literacy. Now I have many more opportunities.

- Include a form that people can send back to you showing how they would like to support your organization as volunteers, as donors, or in some other way. If you have a newsletter, you can ask if they would like to receive it. Plan the form carefully. Don't put your response form on the back of any information you want the reader to keep, such as the name and address of your organization. Print a dotted line to show that the form is to be cut off and where to cut.

Back panel
- Remind readers of what you want them to do. Sometimes this message is suggested on the cover or in the body of a folder but is never said clearly. If necessary, go back to the beginning and make the call clear. Repeat the request at the end.
- If the folder is to be mailed without an envelope, keep the back panel clear for the address. Leave enough space for stamps and for your return address.
- Make sure the full name of the organization, the complete address (including country) and ways it can be reached are prominent.
- Give the name of the executive director so that people can contact a real person.
- If there is room, include the names of important people associated with your organization such as board members.
- Put the charitable registration number or other official designation where it can be seen easily. Many agencies include their bank account number to increase their credibility and make it easy for people to transfer money as a donation.

Draw a thumbnail (about twice the size of your thumbnail) design of your plan so you can see exactly where each section of the text and each illustration will go. Then you can begin to think about design details.

• Indicate when the brochure is printed. If it is not important to readers, the date can be in small type in one corner. You may need this information in the future. We often forget how long a publication has been around and don't bring it up-to-date as often as we should. Or we confuse an old version with a new one and distribute out-of-date material. If you intend to use a brochure for several years, put the date in some kind of code. It is not good to let the reader know that a brochure is more than a year old.

Designing a brochure

Design and content in a brochure must be planned together. You need to know how many words you have space for. You also need to decide what is going to go on each panel and whether you have too many words to fit in the panels. Draw a design of your plan so you can see exactly where each section of the text and each illustration will go. Then you can begin to think about design details.

• Use standard-size paper folded in a standard way. That is the most economical format. Odd shapes cost more and don't fit standard envelopes.

• Use white paper or, if you have a little more money, use coloured paper if you are using only black ink.

• A second colour of ink may be useful and may not be too expensive. If you do use a second colour, try to use it throughout the brochure, not just on the cover or for headlines. You may use it for illustrations, but not for photographs of people. People look best in black or white. Make sure the second colour is dark enough to be read easily. Headlines printed in yellow, for example, are barely readable.

• Make sure the brochure has a family resemblance to other publications of your organization. It does not need to look exactly the same, but people who see it should be able to tell immediately that it comes from your organization.

• Use type large enough to be easily read. Don't crowd too much information into the brochure by making the type too small. Make the type no smaller than the type in this sentence.

• Don't be afraid to leave some space empty. A crowded brochure is not attractive, and looks difficult to read.

• Use lists, showing information point by point as in this book.

• Align the type across the top of the panels. Try to make each panel a complete unit. That's the way people read folders, one panel at a time.

• Don't let type run across the folds. Keep each panel separate.

• Don't worry if the panels are not exactly the same length at the bottom.

• Use headlines or symbols to break up the text.

• Don't use reverse type, that is, white letters on a coloured or black ground. This is hard to read.

20 Producing effective newsletters

Everybody is doing newsletters. Donors give money for newsletters so they can sustain giving money but the organizations cannot sustain the content. Ninety percent of material in the development sector is trash. Information that is available in the general press gets copied into newsletters. Most of them aren't read.

DR. SUDHIRENDER SHARMA,
ENERGY ENVIRONMENT GROUP, INDIA

Newsletters are published to promote the public image of an organization. They can also give details about programs and up-to-date information about activities and people. They are an important way of keeping in frequent, regular touch with supporters and people you want to be supporters. Newsletters supplement the annual report, which usually emphasizes overall accomplishments and provides financial information. Normally they are positive in tone.

A good newsletter is like a small magazine. It should be put together with the same imagination, planning, and attention to detail. Unfortunately, many newsletters show little evidence of editing.

Good newsletters have personality. They are put together by one person from one point of view, not by a committee. Their editors have the confidence to believe they know what their readers want. In many, the editor is visible, and talks with the readers in an editorial note. A newsletter can be more informal than a magazine or newspaper. It can also be more personal, treating its readers as part of a small, carefully chosen audience.

Before we look at what makes good newsletters, here are some characteristics of bad ones. They:
- contain out-of-date information
- ignore the future
- talk about policy, not people
- don't indicate graphically which of their contents are most important
- look the same every issue
- are written in a boring way
- have no personality, and seem to be produced by a committee

Take a look at the ones you receive to see whether they have these bad characteristics or the good ones listed in the next section. Do you want to read newsletters with even one of these bad characteristics?

Seven paths to effective newsletters
Here are some guidelines for producing lively newsletters, ones that will be read:

1 *Show by example.* Good newsletters are not about good organizations.

They are about the people who make the organizations good. Show what the organization is doing by giving examples and emphasizing people. Details and human beings add life.

An effective newsletter does not publish official, general, bloodless accounts that belong in an annual report. It singles out projects and personalities. It does not say, "Look at this long list of all the things we are doing in this broad field." Instead, it chooses one project or one person and concentrates on that subject as typical of the work under way. In the next issue it can go on to another project or person in the same field. If three or four

Vad minimsall veniam quis nostrud ellsuscipit vulputate velit esse milestie at consquat vel satillum dolore.

A good newsletter has its own personality. It does not look like every other newsletter its readers see. Nor does it look exactly the same every time it appears.

such articles appear in each issue, every project will be reported eventually – and the reports will be read.

Good newsletter editors find stories by leaving their offices, going out into the field, talking to colleagues. They know what is going on, and they are always alert for interesting examples.

2 Plan content well ahead of time. Editors know that certain events are going to occur. Good editors organize coverage beforehand. They arrange for photographs to be taken at an event or when a visitor comes. That way the photos are ready when they are needed. A wise editor also keeps a small stockpile of "insurance" material that can be used any time a planned story is not ready by the deadline.

3 Be different. A good newsletter has its own personality. It does not look like every other newsletter its readers see. Nor does it look exactly the same every time it appears. Or contain the same kind of information in each issue. Each issue should look distinctive. Otherwise recipients may say "I've already read that." One issue may start with three brief articles on page 1. Another may open with a large photograph. Some articles will be long (even 2–3 pages); some will be short.

4 Be selective. A good newsletter shows clear evidence that a human being has judged the material for importance and interest to the reader, and has organized it. The greatest failing of newsletter editors is in treating all articles as if they were equally important.

5 *Emphasize what is interesting and important. Give less space to what is dull but necessary.* Lively newsletters do not reprint news releases without editing. They avoid publishing speeches or long official statements word for word: instead they report only the most important points. They contain a minimum of administrative news. Newsletters published mainly for readers outside the organization may not even report staff news except for the most senior appointments or departures. Others publish brief administrative items, grouped under a single heading.

Interesting newsletters do not refer to the executive director or president of the organization in every article, or even in many articles in a single issue. Readers want to know about other people too. Frequent references to one senior staff member may simply make readers start to joke about the person's ego.

Many newsletters introduce humour when they can. It attracts readers.

6 *Edit tightly.* Newsletters are short on space. Their readers are usually short on time. Good newsletters don't waste words. The articles are written tightly and to the point.

7 *Capture readers' attention.* Use good headlines and interesting openings in the articles. If an editor can't find a good headline and opening, something is probably missing from the story. (See Chapters 12 and 16.)

Starting a newsletter

Typically, newsletters are 4, 8, 12, or 16 pages long – and rarely more. Shorter – 4 to 8 – is better. The most important readers are likely to be busy people. They are likely to set aside long newsletters and never read them, while short newsletters may be read right away.

Detailed planning is important in starting a newsletter. It is equally important to review that plan from time to time once the newsletter becomes established. Planning may follow six stages. The person who is actually going to prepare the newsletter should be involved in all of them.

1 *Make an overall plan.* Prepare a written statement of editorial purposes and policies. It should include:
- why the newsletter is being published: what goals it is expected to achieve
- the readers it is intended to reach
- the language best suited to reach them
- the nature of its contents: what will be published and what will not
- a clear statement of who has editorial control: the editor of the news letter, or the executive director? Is there to be an editorial committee, and if so what is its function?
- practical details, such as frequency of publication (at least four times a year is best), size and number of pages, probable circulation, preparation and methods of distribution, and schedules; if possible, the designer, if there is one, and printer should be included in this part of the

planning.

2 *Get the plan accepted.* Make sure the plan is understood and accepted by senior members of the staff and by the board before starting publication. There are many issues on which to secure agreement.

• Establish exactly who will decide what will be included in the news letter. The best editing is done by an individual, not by a committee. The person who is choosing and editing the material should have as much status and responsibility as possible.

• Tell the staff of the organization what will be needed from them – material, comments, ideas.

Use a designer to establish a standard format that the editor can follow most of the time. The editor may consult with the designer from time to time after that for help with problems or for comments on solutions.

• Develop some formal support such as an advisory board. It can include staff, board members, and volunteers. If at all possible, include one or two journalists who are not connected in any way with the organization. Their objective, professional viewpoints will be helpful. The ideal advisory board reviews each issue after it is published and offers comments on how future issues could be better. Some advisory boards think their job is to put each issue together. They want to decide what goes in and what does not and to examine every word. They become a publications committee. But committees produce bland publications, without personality, that no one wants to read.

3 *Plan the design.* Several options are open to you. Depending where you are and how much money you have, you may:

• Use a designer to lay out each issue. (This is unusual except in the largest organizations.)

• Use a designer to establish a standard format that the editor can follow most of the time. The editor may consult with the designer from time to time after that for help with problems or for comments on solutions.

• Use a designer to establish a standard format, which the editor can follow after the first issue.

• Use no designer: the editor creates the design and applies it. This may be the most common approach. The editor may use whatever design help is available on the office computers. If there is no computer, try typing the text in two columns to make it more readable.

Whatever option is used, several guidelines should be followed to make the newsletter as attractive and readable as possible.

• Establish a strong nameplate – the title at the top of the front page. Find a good name. Keep the nameplate the same and in the same place in every issue. It is your main identification. Include the date of the issue in the nameplate and don't forget to change it with each issue.

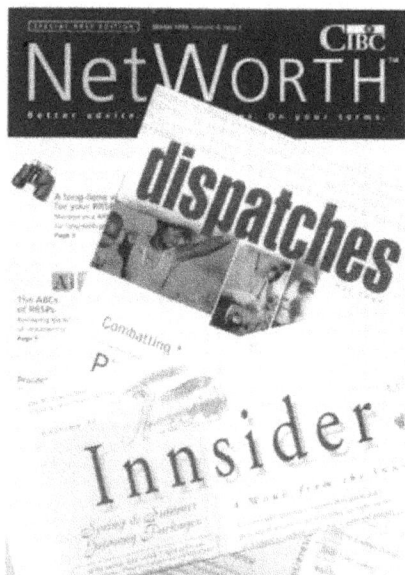

Establish a strong nameplate – the title at the top of the front page. Find a good name. Keep the nameplate the same and in the same place in every issue.

• Use illustrations, especially line drawings: they add variety and beauty.

• Give good photographs impact by making them big.

• Decide whether to have two or three columns of text on a page. Narrow columns are easier to read than text stretched across a full page. Extra columns also provide maximum flexibility in laying out text, illustration, and other elements.

• Place illustrations close to the text that they illustrate. Illustrations are best placed at the top or bottom of a page so the reader does not have to jump over them to read the words. Variety in placement is a good idea.

• Put the most important material at the top of a page.

• Leave lots of white space.

• Be tidy. Group small items under one heading ("Events," "New projects").

• Give each page a focus by using a dominant head, a large block of type, an illustration or photograph. In one place, provide:

• the name, address, phone, and fax numbers of its organization

• the e-mail and Web site addresses if the organization has them

• the name of the executive director and, if desirable, the board members, advisers, and fundraising patrons (if they agree to their names being used)

• the name of the editor of the newsletter

• how to reach these staff members

• an invitation to send in "letters to the editor"

• the frequency of publication of the newsletter

• the date and number of this issue if not on the nameplate

• how to send in a change of address

• how to contribute material

• the charitable registration number of the organization

• how to get on the mailing list

• the names of agencies that fund the organization, with appropriate thanks

• deadlines for the next two issues

• request for a mention of the newsletter if material is reprinted

4 *Plan the distribution.* Make sure all the people who should receive the newsletter are on the distribution or mailing list. Prepare the list methodically to include all the people who might be interested or whom the organization wants to inform and/or influence. Take advantage of the newsletter to reach groups outside the prime target readership. Send it to newspapers and other public media as part of a public relations program. Let them know they can quote from the newsletter.

Here is a short checklist of possible readers for your newsletter. It may be useful in developing an initial mailing list. Make it easy for people to get on the mailing list.

• staff
• donors
• volunteers
• newspapers, radio, television – local, national, international
• editors of newsletters of related organizations
• related organizations – local, national, international
• policy-makers – local, national, international
• funding agencies
• board of directors
• former staff members
• documentation centres/libraries
• universities/colleges – staff, students
• schools – staff, students
• visitors
• bookstores
• business people
• other newsletter editors
• people who appear in an issue
• people who contribute material

5 *Plan the budget.* Decide on the page size, average number of pages per issue, and design of the newsletter, how many copies are to be printed, the costs of distributing each issue, and how often it will appear. Prepare a total budget including the costs of:

• editorial time (allow enough hours)
• design
• photography
• typesetting and composition, halftones, paper, printing, and binding
• addressing, postage and other direct costs of distribution
• keeping the mailing list up-to-date
• regular evaluation of the newsletter's success

Plan a three-year budget. It will take that long for the existence of the newsletter to be widely recognized.

Think about selling advertising to local merchants. Charlene Hewat at Environment 2000 in Zimbabwe produced a small, quarterly newsletter she liked very much. It was plain, just black ink on white paper, but still not cheap to produce. When the publication started carrying advertising, it was filled with colour. And was produced at no cost. As a magazine, it was even sold in supermarkets. The magazine produced by Action for Development in Uganda also carries advertising. In addition, members must buy their own magazines. They also take 25 or 30 copies away to sell.

6 *Plan to review success.* Plan from the beginning to measure the newsletter's success.

- Build feedback devices into the newsletter. For example, include order forms readers can use to ask for more information or for your other publications.
- Sell or give away advertising space in the newsletter and ask advertisers to measure any response to the advertisements.
- Give the readers a chance to talk back. Encourage letters to the editor. Then print them.
- Survey readers to find out what they like and don't like and what changes they would like to see in the newsletter.
- Run contests for adults or children. Use puzzles, essay contests, art competitions, quizzes, etc.
- Make sure your own staff receive and read the newsletter. Ask for their comments.

The first issue

The first issue of a newsletter is always special. It gives the editor a chance to explain what the newsletter is trying to do. It also gives the editor a chance to introduce himself or herself, and to explain the benefits that come from the sponsoring organization. (Some of this can also be done any time a new editor is appointed.)

The first issue of a newsletter may:

- introduce the publication: its purpose and how it came to be started; what will be published in it; how often it will appear; who it will be sent to; its editorial committee and editorial responsibility; its correspondents.
- introduce the organization that is publishing it: its purpose; its size, scope, and capabilities; its major achievements, as part of a brief history; its director (introduced, perhaps, in a separate interview); its financial supporters; its relationships with other organizations. The introduction to the organization should be separate from the introduction to the publication. It could be included in an interview with the executive director; this would make the information more informal and personal.
- introduce the editor: give the editor's name and background, perhaps with a photo. Both the publication and the editor may be introduced in a personal column signed by the editor.

21 Annual reports that people want to read

Think very carefully about the plan for your annual report. Annual reports are necessary. Often they are the only way to keep in regular touch with people you care about. They can bring people up-to-date on the results of your work. They can make you look professional and well managed. They can reassure people that you are financially stable, with solid accomplishments. They are needed, but that does not mean that they need be expensive.

Annual reports are important. They are often the only tool. They are good for prospective donors. Show results, results, results.

Ms Malvika, South Asian Fund Raising Group, India

For most organizations, a big investment of time and money in annual reports may not return adequate benefits. Few people pay them the attention they deserve. Annual reports too often are boring. Most are not read. At best, readers glance through them, perhaps looking at the pictures, the list of donors (especially their own names if they agreed to their publication), and the financial summary. Many people don't even do that. Yet we continue to think that annual reports are an essential part of building credibility even if they merely languish on the shelves or in the files of everyone who receives a copy – if they don't go immediately into their waste baskets.

But annual reports, when they are well done and short, can be useful. They can make an impact. People will actually read them if they are interesting and attractive. How can you achieve that?

First, your report can look different every year. Some organizations issue reports that look exactly alike year after year except for the date. People may just put them aside, thinking they have already read them. Try to vary the presentation and appearance of the reports each year to keep readers interested. Try to overcome people's expectation that your annual report will be boring.

An annual report should not be a commemorative item. It should show the organization alive and well and with a future.

Some reports may have to follow the traditional order because the chairman says so. Otherwise, it is possible to experiment. Many organizations build each annual report on a single theme, which is different each year. They decide what has been the outstanding feature of the year and develop their report around that. They quote beneficiaries, and let them tell the story, with their pictures. They give the report a title that conveys the theme. They don't just call the document "Annual Report."

Consider how much you should invest in producing a report each year

153

and how you can get the most benefit from it. Look for ways to save money, but don't skimp on the design. Annual reports can be as short as one or two pages. Even then, they should be as attractive as possible. To save postage, send the annual report with something else. Make it part of your newsletter if you have one. That way, you can limit the annual report information to two to four pages. Or publish an annual report edition of your newsletter. Once you have printed the report, use it on every possible occasion. Hand out copies whenever you get the chance. Be sure that everyone mentioned in the annual report is given a copy.

The contents of the annual report

In Slovakia, an annual report, one of the basic tools contributing to the transparency of NGO activities, is issued regularly by only 3 per cent of organizations, occasionally by 14 per cent. The rest of the organizations confirmed that they are not preparing an annual report at all (37 per cent) or avoided answering the question.

Survey of NGO governance structures in Slovakia, Slovak Academic Information Agency, 1997

There are at least four major parts to an annual report:
  • the narrative about the accomplishments of the past year
  • the financial summary
  • recognition of support and service – donors, supporters, and volunteers
  • the list of officers and staff

The narrative: putting a human face on your organization

The narrative is often written or at least signed by the chairman. Its prose is usually lifeless and predictable, giving none of the flavour or excitement of your year. Readers often never get beyond the first paragraph.

1997 was an excellent year for WaterLink. Four projects were completed of the six currently under way. They were completed on schedule .... We ended the year in a stable financial position .... I want to thank the staff for their devoted service ....

If the chairman is a poor writer there are several options. If you write well, perhaps you can persuade the chairman to let you draft the report. Propose the newsletter format. Its limited space automatically restricts a wordy chairman. If you must print a standard, dull narrative, try to keep it short. Balance it with statements of results – the accomplishments of the past year – and make them prominent. The results can appear as a report from the executive director. Put the results in point form for easy reading.

During the past year we:
• *Doubled the amount of safe drinking water available to 2,000 people in four villages*
• *Halved the incidence of illness among children*
• *Installed the first irrigation wells in two villages, making it possible for people to return to their homes and plant crops despite the drought*

Switch the emphasis from the officers of your organization to the beneficiaries. Ask the people you serve to talk about what your organization meant in their lives last year. Ask your supporters – the mayor, a board member, a volunteer – to describe in simple language what the organization has meant to them. Use photographs with the comments if you can afford the cost. Make sure the comments sound appropriate, real, and sincere – as if they were said by the person quoted, not written by a bureaucrat.

The financial summary

Don't bore people or overwhelm them with too much detail. It is likely that you have audited financial statements prepared by an independent accountant. They are needed for donors, your board, and to meet various legal requirements. Most people, however, will be satisfied with a short summary of these statements, perhaps only ten to twenty lines. Offer to provide the full statements on request.

Saying thank you

Don't forget to thank:
- board members and committee members
- donors of all kinds
- staff
- volunteers

In many countries, people like to read lists of donors to see themselves and people they know. In others, people prefer their donations to be confidential. Be sure you have permission to publish the name of each donor, whether it is a person or company. If you publish such a list, don't limit it just to people or organizations who gave money. Put in everybody who did anything for you – a service, an in-kind donation, expertise. When you are saying thank you to people who have special roles, add something personal, something human about some of the people. You might refer to the good humour of the staff during a rough period, or to the early morning visits of the chairman. But be brief: unless you are one of the people being thanked, long thank yous are boring.

Finally, include a list of officers and staff.

"If we weren't so hung up on progress, the annual reports would be much easier to write."

Little extras

Think about making space for a coupon for readers to return to the organization giving their opinions, asking for information, offering help, or sending a donation.

Many organizations arrange for donations of printing or other publishing services as a way of paying for their publications. Selling advertisements or space for congratulatory messages can also help cover your costs and give the publication a more lively appearance. Look at the chapter on advertising in Book 3.

22 Obtaining good media coverage

Building credibility through publicity in newspapers, magazines, radio, television is always worthwhile. Good publicity alone will not produce credibility but, as a major part of a communications program, it can be tremendously effective.

A good relationship with the media is essential. It can come about if the editors and staff of the various media feel friendly towards an organization and its staff. For that to happen, the organization and its staff must feel friendly towards the media. If they expect media people to respond to their requests for publicity, they should answer requests from media people. Too often, people seem to expect good relations with the media as a right, rather than as something to be worked for. They approach the media only when they want something good reported, and then are angry when it isn't. An organization must also be prepared to deal promptly with bad news.

Even with friendly and positive relations, the competition for space and time in the mass media is intense. An organization is likely to have its activities reported only occasionally. And there is no way to control how the report will be worded. It is often more effective and efficient to reach for more specific, better-defined audiences through other channels that *can* be controlled, such as brochures, letters, posters, and advertisements.

Good media relations require imagination, quick action, hard work, persistence, an understanding that media people always need material, and an ability to sense when something is newsworthy. In the case study that follows, Wanlop Tangkananurak, now Senator Wanlop, used all these skills to establish the credibility of the Foundation for Better Life for Children in Bangkok, Thailand. (That he was later elected to the Senate of Thailand shows the success of his approach to gaining publicity.) The Foundation had one person when it started and by 1997 had 60 people on staff.

What did Senator Wanlop do right? He moved quickly. He didn't just talk. He used what he could put together easily – a simple leaflet – and went out to meet the public. He worked hard doing research so he did not waste time approaching the wrong publications or the wrong people. He persisted – going back and back to the media people until they not only accepted his opinions but actually came looking for them. Senator Wanlop knew media people need material, so he knew that if his writing met the needs of the editor it would be published. His research told him what was newsworthy. Finally, he was confident that he was proposing solutions to important national issues.

It is true that it is sometimes easier to get publicity for children's issues than for other causes. Certainly that was a factor in the Senator's success, but any organization can find a way to identify its particular cause with a cause that is popular with the public. To do that it must undertake the kind of study of the media that Senator Wanlop did.

When he began his campaign, he had not had media experience. He started from his feeling that he wanted people to know of children's problems. He analysed his society and realized there were many rich people who were building temples and giving money to the royal family. He wanted people to recognize they could do many other good things in their lives. At the very beginning, he stood in front of department stores and handed out leaflets about the Foundation and about children's rights. But he knew Thai people prefer not to be asked for money directly so he had to become expert at indirect appeals and approaches through the media.

Senator Wanlop found that building credibility through the media is not fast, especially when you have to rely on free coverage. It takes persistence, a variety of messages, and frequent repetition of core messages over several years before people even say, "Oh, yes, I think I have heard that organization does good work."

Magazines
Under the desks at the Foundation's offices are piles of magazines. When Senator Wanlop started the Foundation more than 18 years ago, he read all the magazines he could find – political magazines, children's magazines, women's magazines, etc. – to find out their interests and to see who was writing columns. He began sending letters to the columnists suggesting how they might link their writing to children's issues. He also started writing columns himself. Gradually, the magazines began calling him about children's issues. After several years he succeeded in getting the magazines to donate space for publicity about the Foundation. He also arranged to enclose a leaflet asking for support in copies of magazines mailed to individual subscribers. These relationships have been so successful that one magazine gave all the advertising revenue from its first anniversary issue to the Foundation.

Radio
The Foundation staff listen to all types of radio stations. At the beginning they made audiotapes about children's issues, including descriptions of how the Foundation works. They made 100 copies of the tapes and sent them to radio stations all over the country. Some were broadcast, because many radio stations are looking for useful material to fill air time. The Foundation also sent information to all kinds of people who talk on radio. It does not need to do that now. Like the magazines, radio comes to the Foundation.

Television
Senator Wanlop has also made good use of television. After any good program that touched on children's issues, he wrote or had someone else in the

organization write, praising the program and offering suggestions for future programs. After a while, he was invited to appear on a program or write a commentary himself. He is frequently called to comment on children's issues and how they should be covered on television. He suggested a program about two teachers running an orphanage. On the screen it said where donations could be sent. Money poured in.

Newspapers

Whenever a problem to do with children was covered in newspapers, Senator Wanlop never missed the opportunity it gave him to write to the papers. He always wrote right away.

The Foundation also produced stories for the media. Because the same story cannot go to 10 different newspapers or radio stations, one idea was written 10 different ways. He was concerned that poor children in Bangkok did not have a good diet. For a magazine read by young mothers, he talked about the nutritional needs of children, and how many children in the city did not have enough to eat. For a radio program heard by policy-makers, he talked about the need for government to consider a school feeding program for poor children.

What is clear from the Senator's program is that he knew exactly what he wanted to accomplish – to educate the public about the problems of children and the work of his organization in solving these problems. He studied all the media until he knew what each one wanted. He focused his energies on his goals and he persisted until he had done what he set out to do.

Financial support

Senator Wanlop believes fundraising and awareness building go hand in hand. He has changed his fundraising programs frequently, not just to keep donors interested, but also because new activities help to attract media coverage. At the start, Senator Wanlop's foundation had foreign funding. Now he does not accept it but he does act as an intermediary for foreign money given to other children's organizations.

Successful news releases

"News release" or "press release" are the most common terms for a written announcement sent to people who publish news on paper, over the air, and now on the Internet and the World Wide Web. A news release is the simplest, most effective, most reliable way of getting your news before the public. Most news releases end up in the trash. How can you keep yours on the editor's desk and then in the media? Here are some general rules for producing effective releases:

1 Before sending out a news release, visit your local radio and television stations and your local newspapers and magazines. Ask weekly newspapers and magazines about their deadlines, especially if the information you want published is about an event that will happen at a specific time; weekly publications may not use material that comes too late to meet their deadlines.

Ask what sorts of stories they are interested in and what they would like to receive from your organization. They will likely say they want stories about:

• significant achievements of your organization

> *Poor local children are gaining weight as the result of a one-day course in nutrition sponsored by the Association of Upper Egypt for Education and Development. The children told their mothers what they learned in the course. The mothers followed the simple rules, and as a result over the next three months the children gained three kilograms on average.*

• events that are happening, or are about to happen soon, in your area, such as the launch of a new program by your organization

> *A rally against military spending will be held Monday evening to launch a campaign organized by Volunteers for Peace. The organization says the government could buy 80 million textbooks with what it costs to buy a single fighter plane.*

• an unexpected development, or surprise

> *Poor children can gain weight by teaching their mothers how to cook better food. That is the lesson of a one-day course in nutrition given in local schools by the Association of Upper Egypt for Education and Development. The children carried home the simple rules taught by the course. Their mothers followed them. And over the next three months the children gained, on average, three kilograms each.*

• a new issue being raised

> *Every fighter plane the government wants to buy could pay for 80 million textbooks for our book-starved schools, according to Volunteers for Peace. The local branch of that organization will hold a rally Monday, part of a nationwide campaign against military spending.*
>
> *Other branches throughout the country will also be demonstrating for a shift in government priorities. At present, many schools have only one textbook per subject for an entire class, and in even the best-equipped schools most children must share a single textbook with two or three classmates.*

• an old question being answered

> *Many poor children go to school hungry, but that can change through education. One local group of poor children gained three kilograms on average over a three-month period after taking a one-day course in nutrition.*
>
> *The children learned a set of simple rules for better food and taught them to their mothers. The mothers followed the rules, and the weight gain followed. The course was sponsored by the Association of Upper Egypt for Education and Development.*

• individual people who have done something special or unusual, or who are being recognized for service to the community

> *Twenty volunteers who fought water pollution successfully will be honoured by the Mayor at a ceremony at City Hall at 2 p.m. Friday. Each of the volunteers spent at least one hour a week during the last year visiting local factories on behalf of Friends of the Environment. They asked the factory owners to reduce pollution in the water they are using in their factories before returning it to the river. More than half the factory owners agreed to take steps to remove contamination.*

It will be obvious from the examples that one story can be reported in several different ways. Choose the one you think will be most effective. Note that none of the stories began with the name of the organization concerned. People want news. They want to learn about people and benefits. They will not be interested in the name of the organization until they have learned what it has done and understand why they should be aware of its work. Note especially in the fifth example that the organization was not named until all the other key information was given.

Once you have started producing news, check back with editors from time to time to see how their interests have changed. Ask them also what you could be doing to provide them with better, more useful information.

2 Recognize two kinds of news releases and write them differently. One is a feature. It reports an ongoing activity – perhaps a research project that promises benefits or a training program that is helping people. It could be published tomorrow but would be equally valid three months from now. Avoid tying it to any specific date. Editors hold feature stories for times when they can use them.

The other is news. It is tied to a specific event that has just happened, is happening, or is about to happen. Make sure the time is clear and that it is now. News editors want news that is absolutely up-to-date.

3 Don't write too many releases. Only send out releases with stories that you would find interesting if you were a stranger to your organization. Ask yourself: "Would I read a story about this if it was in a newspaper? When did I last read a story like this? Did I find it interesting?" If you send too many trivial releases, the good ones will be ignored.

4 Write a good headline for the story. Some experts believe this is unnecessary, since the newspaper will probably write its own headline. But a good headline does capture attention and may make the editor's job easier. It is usually better to write the headline after you have written the release.

5 Capture the reader's attention in the first sentence. The first reader of a news release is likely to be an editor who (a) is busy and (b) receives many news releases every day. They don't have time to read past the first few words.

6 Give the main information in the opening sentences. The first paragraphs should answer all six questions. The order of the answers can change depending on the circumstances.
- *Who* did something significant?
- *What* did they do?
- *Where* did they do it?
- *When* did they do it?
- *Why* did they do it?
- *How* was it done?

Poor children [who?] can gain weight and improve the way their whole family eats. [what?] The Association of Upper Egypt for Education and Development [who? where?] gave a group of very poor children [why?] a one-day course on nutrition. The children told their mothers what they had learned [how?]. This week [when?], all the children were weighed. In three months each child gained an average of three kilograms.

You can test the opening with three other questions:

Is every word vital to the story?

Will the reader learn the main facts of the story from the opening?

Does it provide a summary of what we want to say?

7 Find a local angle if you can. A newspaper or a television station is more likely to be interested in a story if it is about a person or organization from its own region.

8 Remember that the release may be cut to fit a space on a page or on the air. Editors often cut from the bottom up. They expect news releases will be written so that they can be cut in this way. Never leave important facts to the last.

9 Only use quotes if the point made is especially interesting or tells something about the speaker that most people would not know. And always give the name and position of the person being quoted.

Poor children can gain weight and improve the way the whole family eats. The Association of Upper Egypt for Education and Development gave a group of very poor children a one-day course on nutrition. The children told their mothers what they had learned. In three months each child gained an average of three kilograms.

"Some of these families have four children. That often means each child gets breakfast only every fourth day. Even then, they are gaining weight. The improvement is wonderful." says Amin Fahim, the president of the Association.

10 Write simply, as though you are telling a friend exciting news. Don't start a news release with this style of presentation:

Emil Abad, executive director of WaterLink, announced today that his organization will clean up the riverbank in the next six weeks.

When telling another person, you are more likely to say:

We are finally going to have clean water. WaterLink is going to teach us how to do it.

So, write that way:

Hundreds of people will have clean water next year, thanks to training programs run by WaterLink. Training will begin next week, WaterLink's director, Emil Abad, told a Rotary Club lunch today.

11 Be accurate. If there are errors in even one news release, an editor may never use another release from that source.

12 Use short sentences and short paragraphs. That's what newspapers and most magazines like. Follow the rules for effective writing in Chapter 12.

13 Try to be objective. Write the release the way an editor would want to use it. Don't praise or flatter your own organization or its members. Keep to facts.

14 For newspapers and television, supply photographs if possible. Think of the photos you cannot resist looking at, active children for instance. Look always for action.

15 Follow the rules below to prepare a release that will be likely to be used by a busy editor.

- Type the release double-spaced with wide margins. Use only one side of the piece of paper. Correct any typing errors neatly.
- Make it clear the document is a news release.
- Make sure the editor knows where the release came from. Include the name and address of your organization, and the name, address, and telephone number of a person who can supply more information if the editor wants it. Make sure before you give out the name that that person has all the material, will be ready to talk, and will be available to reporters.
- Show the date the release is issued. Send it when you want the coverage, not too many days in advance.
- Make sure each page is clearly identified as part of the release. Each page should include a short identifying phrase and a page number: *Friends of the Environment volunteer awards page 2*
- Try to keep to two pages. If more space is needed, consider writing a "background release" or a "media note." That is a separate document that gives interesting but not essential information about the organization or about the topic of the release. Make sure it is clearly identified as connected with the main release. But in writing your release, don't assume anyone will read or use this material.
- Write "End" at the end. Staple the pages together.

16 Contact a person you already know at a newspaper or radio station when you especially want coverage. If one medium rejects your story idea or does not want to use your press release, ask yourself if you can improve your material by adding photographs or interesting quotes. Or try a different medium – perhaps radio instead of print.

17 In some countries, organizations must pay editors and reporters to get their news releases published. If this is common in your country, there is little choice but to pay the going rate.

18 Be patient. Releases with no time constraints have been published as much as two years after they were written. Better late than never, they still helped build a positive image for the institution that had issued them.

19 News releases about an event are not invitations to the event. They are for media people who will not be going to the event. If you want to invite reporters to an event, send an invitation along with the release, or send one separately. Call reporters to encourage them to attend. Explain again what the event is about and what will happen there, especially opportunities for photographs. Be sure the directions are clear. Have an escort ready to look after media people.

20 Don't send every release to everyone on your mailing list. Send a release only to the publication or other media you think will find it interesting. An editor who receives too many releases that can't be used from one organization stops reading any release from it.

21 Follow up with a phone call to any media people you feel are especially important or sympathetic to your cause.

22 Be cautious about holding a news conference. Most of the time, a news release is sufficient. Reporters won't come to news conferences if they

think they can get everything from a piece of paper. They will come if they think they will meet a newsworthy person, hear a story that can best be told in person, or see something or some person that will lead to a good photograph or a few seconds of pictures on a television program. If you hold a press conference:

- Make a list ahead of time of everything you will need, from pencils to a microphone.
- Start on time.
- Keep the press conference short – not more than half an hour.
- Distribute a press release that reporters can take away with them to ensure that they have accurate information.
- Have copies of other print materials available.
- Identify all the speakers.
- Keep a list of who attended.
- Follow up with reporters where needed.

23 Keep a log of your media activity including the name of the reporter, the date, time, who in your organization handled the call, etc. It is also useful to keep a written or taped record of your responses to media questions in case you are misquoted later or you want to check what you said to one reporter so that you will be consistent when speaking to others. Looking over the topics of past calls may suggest topics for future promotion.

24 Keep copies of all publicity materials, radio tapes, etc. for your files. Any time a photographer takes pictures or video or television footage, ask for copies for use in newsletters, annual reports, scrapbooks, bulletin boards, and as gifts to donors. Use them also in future publicity efforts.

25 Evaluate your news releases occasionally. Ask the people who receive them whether you are giving them what they need, in the form they need it. Are you giving too much or too little? How can you do better?

What to do when a reporter calls

Take or return any call from a reporter promptly. Reporters always have deadlines. Then:

- Ask who the reporter's audience is if you don't know. For example, will it be local? You want to talk for the right audience.
- Be positive, brief, and quotable.
- Have key messages well rehearsed. Insert them where you want to even if the reporter has not asked. Politicians are very good at this. When faced with a reporter's question about recent pollution in the river, they will start by saying something positive like, "Our government has made great progress in cleaning up the river. We are proud of our record." Once you have introduced your key message, stop acting like a politician. Answer the reporter's questions as clearly and truthfully as you can.
- Use facts that you are certain are correct to explain your point of view.
- Don't give your personal opinions. Give only the policies and positions of the organization.
- Don't argue with a reporter. Persuade with facts.

- Assume that reporters want to do a good job, to get the story right. Correct wrong or distorted information.
- In situations where people have been harmed or have suffered, show your deep concern.
- Assume a reporter may not know much about the subject. For example, very few journalists have a science background. They may have difficulty writing about agriculture, the environment, AIDS or other health issues. You can help reporters by giving background and context to the story.
- Even if you think a particular reporter is your friend, remember that, when a reporter is on the job (and often off the job), the story comes before the friendship.
- Always talk "on the record." Never ask to speak "off the record," meaning that you are talking confidentially to the reporter and not for publication. Some reporters will agree to hear things "off the record" but will later use what you said anyway.
- Never say "no comment." If you cannot answer, explain why. Offer to call back if you don't have the information.
- If the reporter misses some aspect of the story that you think is important, be sure to give the facts.
- If you find errors in the coverage afterwards, send a letter or call with a correction of the facts. Reporters rarely misquote people. My experience is that often people who complain about being misquoted just don't like what they had actually said.
- Don't expect to get on television. That is a bonus. Be happy if you are in print or on the radio.

Visibility can accelerate the downfall of an organization if it does not have clear goals and effective delivery.

MANUEL ARANGO, FOUNDER, MEXICAN CENTER FOR PHILANTHROPY

Turning bad news into good news

Once in a while you may attract bad publicity. That is one of the risks of working successfully at getting publicity for your organization. But you do have worthy goals and you do get worthy results. With that ammunition you may be able to turn what looks at first like a disaster into an opportunity to educate people about your organization and about the issue at hand. Publicity that starts out looking bad can turn out to benefit you in the long run if you handle it correctly. Here is a sample conversation with a reporter that does just that.

Q. Because all your money comes from overseas donors, you can do whatever you like. You don't have to answer to local people, do you?

A. It is true that we receive funding from overseas. However, our board of directors has ten members. The directors are all local people. They represent farmers, the business community, the schools, community groups, and the poor people we serve. They ensure that the needs of the community are met.

We realize the importance of local support. We have recently begun a campaign to raise money from local businesses, individuals, and government.

If you are facing bad publicity here is what to do: Above all, don't panic. Let only one senior person do the talking. Everyone else should refer inquiries to the designated person, who should follow certain rules.

- Be positive, brief, and quotable. Your statement may be all that is used by the reporter.

• Don't say more than you have to. If there is a silence, wait for the reporter to fill it. Don't feel you should. The reporter may know less than you think, and it is easy to say more than you want to.

• Use facts you are certain are correct to explain your point of view.

• If you or your organization were in the wrong, admit it openly. Then describe the steps you are taking to fix whatever went wrong.

• Don't argue about different opinions. Persuade with facts.

• Remember that even friendly reporters are always looking for a good story. When a reporter is on the job (and often off the job), the story comes before the friendship.

• Always talk "on the record."

• Write your own position on the issue as an editorial piece or as a letter to the editor. Show it to an outsider before you send it, to be sure the tone is right. Get it to the media quickly.

23 Planning and organizing public relations events

Events, new programs, promotional activities – all build credibility for your organization. They get people talking positively about your organization and, if you are fortunate, they attract publicity as well. This chapter is concerned with events that are not designed primarily to raise funds, though that may be an indirect benefit. Events specifically intended to raise money are discussed in Book 3.

While successful events have clear benefits, they can overtax the energy and the resources of an organization. They should not be attempted if the resources are not available or if many if the ingredients for success cannot be marshalled. You want as many as possible of the ingredients for success to be present. A significant occasion that will attract public interest is essential. Time for planning and promotion is also necessary. Other important ingredients are:

- helpful volunteers
- the right location
- lively, informative speakers
- interesting guests
- sufficient money to meet the requirements of basic hospitality
- enough imagination to make the event memorable
- a visual element that will appeal to reporters and photographers
- some entertainment or a "happening" designed to ensure that the whole event has a happy atmosphere
- staff or volunteers trained to mingle in a friendly way with guests

Take a look around your community to see how other organizations have attracted attention successfully. Look outside your community to the rest of your country. You will be successful in the long run if you stage an event that no one has done before, or if you carry out a traditional event in an unusual way. But if you plan to hold the same event regularly, you will need patience to get it established.

Several opportunities occur every year for holding special events. Here are a few.

Make the meeting special. Invite everyone your organization cares about or who you want to care about you. Invite the neighbours. Invite the people you serve.

Annual General Meetings

Many organizations think they have to have an annual general meeting, even if only to satisfy their constitutional requirements. Like annual reports, these meetings can be dull, dull, dull. What is to be done? You can keep them small and plain so almost no one knows about them. Many organizations limit attendance to members of the board and staff. Reports are given on the year's activities; the audited financial statements are approved; refreshments are served and everyone goes home.

Other organizations hold a board/management/staff retreat to coincide with the annual meeting. They meet somewhere outside the office – a hotel or conference centre – for a day or two. The combination gives both events more significance, increases the number of people who come, and brings staff and board members together for discussions without interruptions. Such meetings are not open to the public.

The most enterprising organizations make the annual meeting into a special public event that will enhance their credibility outside their organization. Here are some of the steps you can take to achieve such an event.

• Be positive. Many organizations expect that few people will come, so they plan an almost invisible annual meeting. Only board members and staff members will know the meeting ever happened. Think about going in the other direction. Think about having a very visible meeting. Is there an unusual or very public place you could meet that would draw attention to your work and perhaps attract publicity? What about a market, a park, a newspaper office, a school, or some other place where the public will see you? What about a business or university meeting room where you can put up signs and perhaps hold a reception? Could you have the meeting at the site of one of your projects that is easily accessible?

• Make the meeting special. Invite everyone you care about or who you want to care about you. Invite the neighbours. Invite the people you serve.

• Invite a local politician to attend and make some remarks. Invite the media. Politicians always want publicity, especially photographs, in the media. Give the politician something to do – plant a tree, cut a cake – that will make an action photograph. And send a framed copy of the photo to the guest afterwards with the name of your organization clearly displayed.

• What about unusual entertainment? Is there a music or theatre group that will perform? Is there a local celebrity whose presence would attract people? It should not be a person who has been invited to every event for years, but someone who is just becoming known.

• Give all speakers and performers clear, preferably written, instructions about where you want them to be, when they should be there, what you want them to do and for how long, and when they will finish. Make sure that they have information about your organization ahead of time. There is nothing more embarrassing to a speaker than getting the name wrong or revealing ignorance of the organization's activities.

• Get the people who come to write their names and addresses in a guest book. Add them to a list of people whom you will approach later for money.

Project launches

When you receive a grant for a new program or when you are starting a new activity, you have an opportunity to build morale as well as credibility. Make a splash. Have a party. Invite beneficiaries of your service as special guests. Plan it just as you would plan a special-event annual meeting.

If the project is costly, involves a whole new approach to your work, or is truly significant in some other way, it may be one of those rare occasions when you might think of inviting reporters. Set aside a special time to talk to reporters. Consider involving board members in the press interview.

At all these events the speakers from your organization should prepare their remarks ahead of time. Then they will be sure to cover all the points that need to be made, such as thanking the right people. They will be more relaxed because they are well prepared. And, very important, they can time their talk beforehand to ensure that it will be short.

Exhibitions

Taking a booth or stand at an exhibition can be an excellent way to display your organization – on three conditions. You need or want to reach the audience that will see it. The display will be eye-catching. Participation in the exhibition will accomplish a clear objective, not just some fuzzy public relations purpose.

Plan the display with the location in mind. Will it be laid out or stand on a table, or on a floor? Will you have walls to hang posters or pictures? How will you display your organization's name prominently? Think about the content of the display the same way you think about the content of a poster. The messages should be short, clear, large. Use large photographs or illustrations, your name, and your symbol – all large.

If you cannot afford a display for each exhibition, make three panels joined together that can be set up to form a widened U. The panels can then stand on a table. Put information on both sides. Such a flexible display can travel anywhere for years if it is well designed and sturdy.

Arrange for a knowledgeable, friendly person to be on duty at the display at all times. Have brochures available for distribution. Have inquiry forms so people can leave their names if they want more information. Have a donation box, perhaps a petition to sign, several chairs; make it a pleasant set up, perhaps with a few plants. If you fear that people will pass by without looking at the display carefully, add some action or colour – have attendants in costume, show slides or a video if there is electricity available, enlist a musician to perform.

Open days

Invite local people to visit your organization. You do not need to do anything elaborate or expensive but you do need to plan carefully how you are going to keep people interested. You want them to go away with a good impression of your organization – and with hard information about your programs.

• Prepare a budget for the open house publicity. Include expenses for posters, invitations, leaflets, programs, rentals of equipment, cleaning up and staff time. Include the cost of transporting people to and from the site.

• Limit the number of hours you will be open. You want lots of people at once. If there are only two or three people at a time, they will feel uncomfortable and the event will feel like a failure.

• Give the open house a focus. Have someone welcome the visitors at the door. Give an official welcome, perhaps several times during the open hours. Show photographs or slides about your work.

• Have the open day at one of your projects if it can be reached easily. Take people on a tour of one or more of your projects. Arrange for them to talk to the people you serve.

Recognition events

Even small organizations can honour a person or group that has made important contributions to the community or achieved something significant. This kind of recognition is valuable bridge-building to people you want on your side. The people being recognized will certainly feel good about it. By honouring them, moreover, you will be demonstrating your own concerns for the community. If you do it well, you will also get recognition for your organization in the media and with people whose good opinion you seek.

• Choose carefully the people to be honoured. They should be well enough known or have real and special achievements so that the ceremony will attract media attention.

• Give honours because they are well deserved, not because you expect or want some reward or favours from the recipients.

• Make sure the occasion includes some activity that will make good photographs. "Activity" is the important word. Giving an award certificate is common and not interesting. An unusual or original gift, perhaps something made by a member of your group – and big enough to be seen in the photographs you will arrange – is better. Find your own photographer. Copies of the photographs you order can be given to the media should no reporters or photographers come to the event. They can also be used in your newsletters and annual reports. Most people enjoy publicity, even though they will not often admit it.

• Think who you will invite. Ask people who are to be honoured for their suggestions. Start small. Invite only as many people as you can manage easily. Give the person being honoured a chance to speak to the gathering. This is another opportunity for publicity for the person and for your organization. Keep the events simple, short and appropriate. Have fun. Have music. Honour someone in this way every year, so that the event gradually gains a reputation and prestige – a local "Nobel Prize." That may take several years. Use what you learn each time to make the event better each year. You want people to look forward to it.

Special visitors
Whenever special visitors come from some distance, invite people you want to think well of your organization to come to hear them speak. The presence of the visitors honours your organization. It may also be newsworthy.

24 Making the Internet work for you

In Book 1, we talked about the isolation in which many organizations work. They don't know enough about what is happening around them and about what changes are on the horizon. For any organization with the necessary computers and connections, the Internet can end this isolation. Using the Internet, your organization can present itself as forward thinking, professional, up-to-date. It can be seen as a full member of its civil society.

This chapter gives some basic information, but is not a manual on how to use the Internet; it assumes you have some knowledge of the system. Rather, it gives tips on how to send e-mail messages that people will read and reply to. It also talks about how to use the Net to help you do your work without letting it take over your life.

The Internet is a computer network. It allows people to communicate with one another electronically through their computers.

The Internet

The Internet is a computer network. It allows people to communicate with one another electronically through their computers. The Internet has revolutionized the way the world does business. It can be especially useful to organizations with limited funds. The Internet gives an organization the potential to reach millions of people. Your computer can connect you to the world.

Within a few years, organizations will receive donations via the Internet. The process has begun in some countries, but is not widespread. Most people are not connected to the Internet. People who are connected need time to get used to such a new idea. The biggest hurdle to overcome, for people who could give money electronically, is the belief that financial information such as bank account and credit card numbers cannot be sent securely through electronic systems. However, no matter how far in the future electronic donations may appear to be for your organization, the possibility should be kept in mind. An organization that wants to be the first in its area to set up electronic giving and to promote it should be ready to move the moment it looks as though people are ready.

The Internet works at two levels. The simplest connection is e-mail or electronic mail. This works like a post office but without all that paper, all those dead trees, and all the delays in handling and transportation. Using e-mail you can receive messages directed to you and send messages to people you want to reach almost instantly. The second level is generally referred to as the World Wide Web (www). It works something like a library: you can use it to find information or tell people about your work. We will talk more about the World Wide Web further on.

E-mail

Using e-mail you can:

- send messages, formatted documents, letters, and data files quickly and cheaply all over the world
- send messages to dozens, even hundreds of people at the same time; these can be newsletters, bulletins, notices of events, your comments on a recent event or issue, announcements of new programs, news of changes in your organization
- promote your organization's work directly to the people you care about
- make contact with potential sponsors and supporters around the world
- reach potential donors
- subscribe to electronic mailing lists to receive useful information from people and organizations
- find volunteers internationally and locally
- exchange ideas about topics that interest you

E-mail messages are sent between people using computers connected to phone lines. An e-mail message is just like a letter, but better: it usually reaches its destination within a few hours, sometimes in a few minutes. E-mail costs much less than a fax or long distance telephone call because the information is compressed and takes almost no time to go over the phone line. An urban organization may pay only for a local call.

To take advantage of e-mail you need a regular supply of electricity, a recent model computer, e-mail software (Netscape Messenger or Eudora, for example), a piece of equipment called a modem, a phone line, an account with a service provider, and several books to try to calm your exasperation and help you figure out the whole system. In many places, you can also take advantage of e-mail with a cell phone, but for the moment this is expensive.

E-mail links a computer through a telephone line to an organization with a central computer that acts as a "server" or ISP (Internet Service Provider). Most cities in the world now have servers and they are being set up in smaller centres all the time. A server relays electronic messages. You will need to link up to a server in your region. When you send a message to someone else with e-mail, you will address it just as you address an envelope – but not with a number, street, and city. The address will include the name of the person or organization (or an abbreviation of the name, a nickname or alias). Next will come the symbol @, which means "at." After that is the name of the recipient's server (the "post office") and its location. If you send a message to that address, then next time the person you want to reach contacts their server, he or she will find your message.

You will likely pay a monthly fee to your server for this service. The cost can be quite low. Many servers are set up to enable non-profit organizations to use the Internet. These servers are free or charge very low fees. If you are a long way from a server, then you will pay long distance telephone charges for the time you are on the line with the server, just as you would pay to reach any other office in the same location. So get all your messages ready to be sent at once as soon as you dial and are connected.

You do not need your own computer to use e-mail. Many small communities now have centres where you can go to send and receive e-mail messages. The people at the centre can help you find e-mail addresses of the organizations or individuals you want to reach. They will give you your own e-mail address, a password, or both. Then when you visit the centre you can check your own mail, send replies, and print copies of whatever materials you need. Avoid exchanging e-mails on confidential topics when you are using a centre; people working at the centre may receive or see your messages.

For help in beginning with e-mail, see *@t ease with e-mail: A handbook on using electronic mail for NGOs in developing countries* in the list of "Suggested reading" at the end of this book. It is available both as a free printed book and from a Web site.

Making contacts by e-mail
You can start to build a list of e-mail addresses of people and organizations you want to tell about your organization, its program, its events. The same message can be sent to dozens of people at once. Simply put a comma between each address in the "To" section. But before sending information, ask people if they want to receive it. Sending unsolicited mail is called "spamming." (Spam – electronic junk mail – is named after the canned meat.) No one likes to be spammed. If you do it, you will make people angry and you will certainly lose their interest and possible support.

As you use e-mail more, you will find there are groups of people who talk and share information by e-mail in a discussion forum, mailing list or "listserv." You can "subscribe" to receive exchanges of messages automatically. And you can contribute or ask questions whenever you like. It may take some digging to find Internet discussion groups that fit your needs. At present two useful general directories of discussion groups are:
http://www.liszt.com
http://tile.net

Ask other organizations about how to begin. Joining one or two groups is all that is necessary if one of your first postings is a request for advice on what other groups to join. You will also find that organizations that give out useful information will put you on their e-mail distribution list. Sign up to one group at a time to be sure the information is useful to you. The number of messages can be overwhelming. You can waste a lot of money receiving them and a lot of time reading them.

Start your own group
You can go one step further if distribution of information is part of your mandate. You can start your own group where people can send messages to you and you will pass them on to anyone who is interested. Your organiza-

tion will then become a clearinghouse in your area of interest. Such a service is used, not directly to promote your organization, but to bring you useful recognition as a centre of expertise in certain topics. Creating an electronic discussion group for your constituencies is simple. You put together a message asking people if they want to exchange information. Then, instead of sending information to one person, you send it all at once to a whole list of e-mail addresses that you have on file. These people can sign up to be part of the group and, from then on, you will receive their messages and share them with the group. You can also add messages of your own any time you want to. Check with a dealer about programs that make managing a list relatively simple. Some services such as the "Liszt" site listed above may also allow you to establish a list.

Organizing and maintaining a group does take time and attention. For example, in many groups the person who forwards mail serves as a moderator, reading mail before forwarding it and enforcing rules about the subject and tone of messages to be sent to the group.

How to make e-mail messages effective

You will get a better response if you follow these general rules for Internet communication. Build your own system for dealing with e-mail messages so that none are lost.

- Read carefully all the instructions that come with your e-mail program.
- Don't feel you have to answer every message immediately. Take time to think over what you want to say. But don't wait too long. Internet users expect quick action.
- Don't file incoming messages until you have dealt with them; that way they won't get lost or ignored.
- Always write the specific subject of your e-mail in the space at the top of the message. That makes it easier for the recipient to keep track of messages.
- Check that your message is addressed to the right person. Fingers can move too quickly sometimes. A message sent to the wrong person might put your organization in an embarrassing position.
- If you are replying to a message but raising new matters, be sure to change the subject at the top to reflect the new topic.
- Don't use CAPITAL letters for emphasis. This is the e-mail equivalent of shouting and may be seen as rude.
- Keep sentences and paragraphs short, so the message is easy to read.
- When you reply to a message, the original message may show on the e-mail reply. Don't leave it there. It is better to summarize the first message in one or two sentences at the beginning of your message, should you need to ensure that the recipient understands what you are replying to. Reset your computer or delete the message you are answering.
- Unless the message is very short, if possible don't write it while you are connected to your server. For one thing, you will likely have to pay for the time you spend composing. Second, you won't write well if you are thinking about the cost instead of what you want to say. Some e-mail programs

do not allow you to write messages ahead of time. In this case, it is hard to avoid typing errors, unless you write messages in a normal document and then "paste" them into the e-mail later.

• Read over your messages before you send them. Because some e-mail programs don't allow you to check your spelling automatically, most messages have typing errors. People send messages too quickly. I rarely get an e-mail that does not contain several typing errors. The senders look less than professional as a result. Here are several sentences from an e-mail message I received:

> *Incidentaly, i participated in a seminar on finacial strtegic planning. Is was great! The facilators were from the state University, I was impressed. Most people that attended were lost however, this subject ares is a real paradigm shift.*

What is your impression of the writer?

• Use e-mail only for messages that won't embarrass you if someone other than the intended recipient reads them. People anywhere in the world can pick up your mail by typing in your e-mail address and your password on their computers. It is unlikely anyone would bother to do it, but it is possible. And this is only one way messages may become public. It is a good idea to stay away from making personal comments or sending sensitive information.

• Be cautious when sending an "attachment" – material stored in your computer that you "attach" to a message. When it is received, the recipient may not be able to open it without exactly the right program or version. Instead, you can break a long document into sections and send it as a series of three or four e-mail messages instead of as an attachment. However, some e-mail programs do not recognize boldface, italic, indented paragraphs, and so on. Therefore an e-mail document won't look as good as an attachment and won't be as easy to read. Saving documents that are to be attached as "RTF" (Rich Text Format) may solve the problem. Or, if you really care about how a document looks and attachments are a problem, send the document by mail or have it delivered.

• If you share an e-mail address, ask senders of messages to put your name in the subject line so their messages will get to you.

• If a message does not go through the first time, or the second or third, keep trying. But check to make sure you are using the correct e-mail address. E-mail systems can be out of order for weeks at a time, and some users rarely check their e-mail. It is good practice to ask the recipient to confirm receipt of the message if it is critical.

• Always include your e-mail address on your correspondence, stationery, etc., so that people can reach you that way if they choose.

• Don't let e-mail replace personal contact. E-mail is no substitute for face-to-face or voice-to-voice communication.

Setting up the signature

In many e-mail programs, you can use a "signature" to tell people about your organization. An e-mail signature is the electronic equivalent of a letterhead, except that it appears below your message. The text is inserted automatically at the bottom of every e-mail message you send. Without a signature, your e-mail message will be written on a blank electronic page.

Most e-mail software programs have a "signature" option. Select the help program in your e-mail menu and look up "signature." You will probably be shown a blank window or form where you can type your information, or you may simply type in a document and tell the program where to find it. This will become your e-mail signature.

A typical e-mail signature contains the name and the title of the person sending the e-mail, the organization's name, information about how to communicate with it other than by e-mail – that is, its street and/or mailing address, telephone number, and fax number. A slogan, brief mission statement, or one- or two-line description of the organization can also be included. With a signature, you will have a letterhead and a mission statement for your organization in every message you send. Use the signature to do small-scale fundraising or advocacy.

Other things to remember about "signatures:"

• Lay out your e-mail signature in five or six lines, not more. Put phone and fax numbers on the same line. Then you can spare a line or two to describe your organization.

• Send yourself a message to check whether your signature looks the way you want it to.

• Once you have written your e-mail signature, you may not see it within the messages you send. The program adds it when a message is being sent. Just because it's out of sight, don't let it be out of mind. Remember to check the text in the "signature" option window from time to time to see if it's still valid and current.

• When you don't have your own computer and are using a service agency instead, your signature may not appear automatically. So don't forget to type in a signature at the bottom of your message.

Using the World Wide Web
The World Wide Web is like a vast library packed with information of every sort. You will want to consider the uses you can make of this treasure house. Organizations all over the world now have what is called a Web site. A Web site is like a book in the library. It is an electronic presentation of an organization, a person, a cause, an interest – whatever someone wants to tell the world about. It sits on an electronic shelf in an electronic library waiting for someone to look for it.

When you look for a book, you may go to the library and either check the catalogue using key words, or browse through the shelves. When you publish a book, you think of who will read it and try to make it appealing to those people. The same is true of a Web site. But instead of a book you are looking for a "site" or a "page" or a "homepage." The term "page" is confusing. A Web page is not one computer screen of information; it is a part of a site, often with its own address. It may be the equivalent of many printed pages. It may contain both text and several types of graphics.

If you know the electronic address (the equivalent of a book title), you can go straight to the site you want (the "book"). Or you can hunt world-wide for information by topic. You may know what you want to find out but not who can give you the information. Searching for information by topic is called "browsing" or "surfing." It is the same as looking through the various subjects listed in a library catalogue, except you are doing it on your computer. You know, for example, that some international corporations have donations programs, but you don't know which ones. You can begin a search by topic – "corporate giving," "international philanthropy," "international fundraising," whatever seems useful. To start the search, you type these key words in a search engine.

Search engines are powerful tools that allow you to enter a key word and search through thousands of Web sites to find those related to the topic. There are many of these search engines; some are listed in a later section. Most Internet programs already have some installed. One site will lead to another and eventually you may find what you want. Search engines do not all use the same rules. When you begin using a search engine, take time to click on "help" or "more information" and learn how to use the program effectively.

Once you have information on your screen, you can read it and go on to something else. Or, like e-mail, you can download it, which means copy it into your own computer. You can then print it whenever you like. Searching can take hours. Most Web sites are difficult to use. However, you may be rewarded for your patience.

Using the Internet, you can hunt world-wide for information.

The Net has another dimension that gives it a power beyond any book. When you finish a book, it is hard to reach the author to discuss it. But the Net makes two-way communication easy. Many Web sites offer the opportunity to communicate directly with the organization that created them through what is essentially built-in e-mail. For example, a person looking at your Web site could ask for information or offer to be a volunteer right on the screen, without having to send a separate message.

Web site files – the computer files that are like library books – are usually stored on the "server" (computer) – the "library" – of an Internet Service Provider (ISP), the same organization through which you transmit your e-mail. When a Web site is stored in this way, anyone using the Internet can visit it. There is usually a monthly cost to store Web pages at your ISP. Often it will be part of the regular subscription price.

Most ISPs will provide you with statistics about how many visitors you have received at your site, from which countries they are coming, and which of your pages they are visiting. This information will show when you call up your own site. You can then see if you are reaching the people you want to reach.

Many people unfamiliar with the Internet assume that their Web homepages will be stored on their home or office computer and therefore make their computer and all its contents accessible to the world at large. This is not the case. The computer of the Web page owner is *not* connected to

the Internet. Only the server is connected to the Internet. Therefore, your computer is *not* accessible to others. It is not even necessary to have a computer to have a Web site.

Building the site

Using a Web site to heighten your organization's profile locally and internationally is a two-step process. First you must arrange for your own site, or "homepage." Then you have to let people know you have a site they will find useful. These jobs take skill and patience. You can do them yourself but that is generally not a good idea. Most people lack the knowledge and time to do a good job.

Unlike e-mail, which communicates only text, Web sites can include graphics – photographs and illustrations. A piece of equipment called a scanner is used to transfer illustrations and photographs into a computer.

You can save money by learning how to design a Web site, but it is best to hire someone who is experienced at setting up and promoting a site. Professional firms are springing up to provide this service. Such firms might reduce their fees or charge no fee at all to a non-profit organization. There may also be a high school, computer school, or college nearby where you might find students who would undertake the project as a class assignment.

Many countries have non-profit service providers. One example is SANGONeT, which provides an inexpensive service specifically designed to meet the needs of South African development and human rights organizations. It offers assistance with site design and with setting up and registering sites. It also offers training so organizations can create their own sites and keep their information up-to-date.

Your Web site needs the same thought you put into your brochure, your annual report, or your newsletter. Here are points to keep in mind when you are writing the script and when you talk to the person setting up your site.

• The person designing your site will ask you for the key words people may use in trying to find you if they are searching the Web. When I opened a Web site to announce this series of books on the Internet, I included the words "fundraising" and "philanthropy" in the text and in the title of the page. Then the designer asked me to give her other words that could direct people to my site even though they did not appear in the text. I added "international development," "international fundraising," "international philanthropy," "charity." The reason will become clear in the next section.

• Your Web address is called your Uniform Resource Locator (URL). An example is http://www.bluedogdesign.com. Your URL is your electronic address, the title of the book about your organization. It should be prominent in your printed materials.

• Make sure the title of your Web page reflects the content and that it includes the two major key words you expect your target visitor would use in a search engine.

• Give a clear, brief description of your organization's activities and services close to the beginning – perhaps your mission statement. First-time visitors may know nothing about your organization. Don't assume that just because they get to your homepage they know something about you, or even intended to reach you. One of the joys of the Web is what you find unexpectedly.

• Make it easy for people to use your site. Keep it simple. Put in only what is essential. Be sure each page includes the name of the organization and a link to the homepage, the introduction to your site.

• Use only the illustrations – photographs, logos, and other graphics – that are essential to your message.

• Give the user the option of a version without graphics. They look nice but often come up on the screen so slowly that people get impatient, especially if they are paying a lot of money for each minute they are using the phone line.

• Include the name and job title of everyone with an identifiable responsibility in the organization. This gives people a sense of the size of the organization and makes it seem less distant. Give clear directions about how to reach these people, especially by e-mail. This is rarely done but is important: it shows that your organization wants to build relationships with other people. And that, after all, is what fundraising is all about.

• Promise only information that is actually in the site.

• Use words that will be familiar to the audience you most want to reach. If it is corporate people, use the language of business. Include several languages if desirable. Write about supporting your organization as an investment in improving the community, about your productivity, your work and your ability to do it, and how you will achieve your goals.

• You may have already invested time in writing about your organization and in giving your publications an identifiable style. Your Web site should have the same style. The site can use the same illustrations and photographs you have already used in your brochure or other publications.

• Be sure the site reflects the whole organization, not just the interests of the person putting the site together. Show the material to several people in the organization to ensure objectivity.

• Use existing material. You can, on separate pages, include the annual report, recent press releases, articles from the newsletter, job openings, announcements of events. Because you don't have to wait for this information to be printed and distributed, it can be released much earlier than by traditional means.

• The content should be useful, not just a sales pitch. Include educational material that people really need so that people learn something useful.

• Say thank you to visitors to your site.

• Text that is too big or too small, or all UPPER CASE should be avoided. Upper case is HARD TO READ – use it sparingly. Background colours and background graphics can also make the text nearly impossible to read.

• If information changes frequently, plan how to ensure that it is always up-to-date. It is easy to change or add to your site – something much more costly with traditional printed materials. It does not make an organization look efficient, for example, if, under forthcoming events, it lists events that happened last month.

- Your goal in having a site is to involve people in your work. Every screen you build should have a big sign or button near the top that says, "I want to Help." People can click on that button to get information or offer help. Help may be a donation sent by regular mail, delivered personally, or sent by e-mail. Help may also be an in-kind donation, some expertise, or other volunteer service.

- Check all your material before and after it is transferred to your ISP's Web server. Use a spell-checker to catch misspelled words.

- Don't publicize your Web site address and the site itself until it is finished and presentable. People may not return to a half-finished site that says "Under Construction." Before you announce the site, ask others to try using it and tell you what they found difficult.

- Look up your own site regularly to be sure it is running. Mine disappeared for months without my knowing: I had not checked.

Promoting your Web site

Your Web site itself is only half the equation. Once the site is built and has been loaded onto your ISP's computer, the next step is letting the world know it exists. If people know your electronic address, they can go straight to the book, to your site. Always put your Web address on your correspondence and printed information so people can visit your site to learn more about your organization.

People can also find a site like yours by "browsing" or "surfing." Most visitors to a Web site find their way there through an Internet search engine Web site. For people who do not have your address to find you, you must be registered with the search engines. Have the person setting up your site register it with all the major Web search engine sites, directories, and Web yellow pages. As part of the registration, the person will register your key words. Choose these words carefully, for they are the path to your door. When someone searches for one of these words, your Web site address will appear on the list of sources of information. The major search engines (InfoSeek, Google, Excite, AltaVista, etc.) don't charge a fee for listings in their database.

Yahoo, one of the most popular Web directories for finding sites, gets more than 4,000 submissions each day for new Web sites to be included in its directory – 4,000 a day, 28,000 a week, 120,000 a month – and that's just the ones submitted to Yahoo. This suggests how important it is to get registered so that you have a better chance of being found.

Perhaps some far-off day you will be able to reduce the cost of printing brochures, notices of events, even annual reports because people will start looking at your Web site when they want current information about your organization.

Coping with bad news

When an organization is facing some bad publicity that could damage its credibility, it must be prepared to take its case to the public by all the means it has available. The Internet is one means of giving information, especially to journalists who may not be able to reach a spokesman for your organization.

Financing your Web site

Think about asking a local business to sponsor your organization's Web site – the design, setting it up on the Net, and paying the monthly fee to the server. Every voluntary organization serves an identifiable community. A business may be interested in reaching that same audience. Corporations are looking for ways to advertise their products. If your page happens to draw just the audience the corporation is looking for and attracts a lot of "hits" (people looking up the site), a business may be delighted to have its message seen by everyone who visits the Web site. Each person is a potential customer.

You can simply include a thank you for their help. But on many sites you will see one or more small advertisements, which a visitor can click to learn more about a business. At first glance, this may seem too commercial for many voluntary organizations. Think about it. In the changed climate in which organizations are now working, better relations with the business community are necessary. Two groups of people who respect each other's work can work out what each wants to get from having a Web site and design the site to meet both sets of needs. But it is important to ensure that the business sponsor does not have a veto on what the organization wants to say on its site.

More information

The list of Suggested reading and Web sites gives sources for additional information. You can, for example, learn more about using the Internet, get help in setting up a simple Web site (the European Foundation Centre at http://www.fundersonline.org provides a free toolkit and templates), or find lists in which you can publicize your organization by asking to be included (Idealist and One World sites).

Suggested reading and Web sites

Check with major aid agencies, foreign foundations, embassies, high commissions, large libraries, and your funders, who may have or be able to get some of these publications, especially the reference books. Many of the Web sites (including those listed with the books) include a variety of information for fundraisers. However, World Wide Web addresses change frequently; in this case a search engine may help. Since prices also change, they are not included. Books may be ordered by mail, by e-mail from the publishers, from Web sites, from some urban bookstores, or from a Web bookstore such as http://amazon.com or http://amazon.co.uk. See also the Web sites in Book 2, Chapter 24.

Alternative financing of third world development organizations and NGOs, Vols. 1 (445 pages), and 2 (300 pages), by Fernand Vincent. 1995. Geneva, Switzerland: Development Innovations and Networks (IRED), 3 rue de Varembé, P.O. Box 116-1211, Geneva 20, Switzerland. ISBN 2 88368 005 1
E-mail: ired@worldcom.ch

@t ease with e-mail: A handbook on using electronic mail for NGOs in developing countries. New York: The United Nations Non-Governmental Liaison Service and The Friedrich Ebert Foundation. 1998. Free from The United Nations Non-Governmental Liaison Service, Palais des Nations, CH-1211 Geneva 10, Switzerland. (Also available online; see list of Web sites below.) 130 pages. ISBN 0 9645188 5 6
Web site: http://ngls.tad.ch

Charity shops, by Hilary Bloom. London: The Charities Advisory Trust. 1995. London: Directory of Social Change, 24 Stephenson Way, London NW1 2DP, UK. 160 pages. ISBN 1 873860 77 3
E-mail: webmaster@d-s-c.demon.co.uk
Web site: http://www.d-s-c.demon.co.uk

Chronicle of Philanthropy, the newspaper of the non-profit world, published bi-weekly. 1255 23rd Street, Washington NW 20037, USA.
E-mail: subscriptions@philanthropy.com
Web site: http://www.philanthropy.com

Community participation and financial sustainability, compiled and edited by James Taylor, Dirk Marais, and Stephen Heyns. Action-learning series case studies and lessons from development practice. 1998. Published by Juta and Co. Ltd., Mercury Crescent, Hillstar Industrial Estate, Wetton, South Africa, 7780, in association with Community Development Resource Association, PO Box 221, Woodstock, South Africa 7915. 126 pages. ISBN 0 7021 4629 3
E-mail: info@cdra.org.za
Web site: http://www.cdra.org.za

Corporate responsibility: Philanthropy, self-interest and bribery, by Delwin Roy, former president of the Hitachi Foundation. 1999. Kluwer Law International, Distribution Centre, PO Box 322, 3300 AH Dordrecht, The Netherlands. ISBN 90 411 9645 5
E-mail: services@wkap.nl
Web site: http://kluwerlaw.com

Creating effective partnerships with business, a guide for charities and non-profits in Canada. 1996. Toronto: Imagine, a program of the Canadian Centre for Philanthropy, 425 University Avenue, Suite 700, Toronto M5G 1T6, Canada. 84 pages. ISBN 0 921295 37 7
E-mail: imagine@ccp.ca Web site: http://www.ccp.ca/imagine

The DIY guide to public relations for charities, voluntary organizations, and community groups, by Moi Ali. London: Directory of Social Change, 24 Stephenson Way, London, NW1 2DP, UK. 184 pages.
ISBN 1 873860 80 3
E-mail: webmaster@d-s-c.demon.co.uk
Web site: http://www.d-s-c.demon.co.uk

Face-to-face, how to get bigger donations from very generous people, by Ken Wyman. See list of Web sites below.

The five most important questions you will ever ask about your non-profit organization: Participant's workbook. The Drucker Foundation (http://www.pfdf.org) self-assessment tool for non-profit organizations. 1993. San Francisco: Jossey-Bass Publishers, 350 Sansome Street, San Francisco 94104, USA. 62 pages. ISBN 1 55542 595 X
E-mail: info@josseybass.com
Web site: http://www.josseybass.com

Fund-raising and the nonprofit board member, by Fisher Howe. A booklet in the governance series published by the National Center for Nonprofit Boards, Suite 510, 2000 L Street NW, Washington DC 20036-4907, USA. ISBN 0 925299 02 2
E-mail: info@ncnb.org
Web site: http://www.ncnb.org/main.htm

Fundraising for social change, by Kim Klein. 1996. Berkeley, California: Chardon Press, 3781 Broadway, Oakland, California 94611, USA. 350 pages. ISBN 0 9620222 3 3
E-mail: info@chardonpress.com
Web site: http://www.chardonpress.com

Fundraising ideas that work for grassroots groups, by Ken Wyman. See list of Web sites below.

The grass roots fundraising book: How to raise money in your community, by Joan Flanagan. 1992. Chicago: Contemporary Books, Inc., Two Prudential Plaza, Chicago, Illinois 60601-6790, USA. 332 pages. ISBN 0 8092 5746 7
E-mail: ntcpub@tribune.com
Web site: www.contemporarybooks.com

Guide to special event fundraising, by Ken Wyman. See list of Web sites below.

Managing your solvency, by Michael Norton. 1994. London: Directory of Social Change, 24 Stephenson Way, London, NW1 2DP, UK. 160 pages. ISBN 1 873860 25 8
E-mail: webmaster@d-s-c.demon.co.uk
Web site: http://www.d-s-c.demon.co.uk

Manual of practical management for Third World rural development associations, by Fernand Vincent. Vols. 1 (Organization, administration, communication. 240 pages. ISBN 1 85339 404 1) and 2 (Financial management. 208 pages. ISBN 1 85339 405 X). 1997. Originally published by IRED, republished by Intermediate Technology Publications Ltd, 103-105 Southampton Row, London WC1B 4HH, UK.
E-mail: itpubs@itpubs.org.uk
Web site: http://www.oneworld.org/itdg/publications

The raising of money: Thirty-five essentials every trustee should know, by James Gregory Lord. 1996. Third Sector Press, 28050 S. Woodland Rd., Cleveland OH 44124, USA. 128 pages. ISBN 0 939120 02 X
E-mail: quest@lord.org

Relationship fundraising, a donor-based approach to the business of raising money, by Ken Burnett. 1992. The White Lion Press Limited in association with the International Fundraising Group. White Lion Press, White Lion Court, 74 Rivington Street, London, EC2A 3AY UK. 330 pages. ISBN 0 9518971 0
E-mail: mikek@burnettassociates.com
Web site: http://www.burnettassociates.com

Successful fundraising: A complete handbook for volunteers and professionals, by
Joan Flanagan. 1993. Contemporary Books, Inc., Two Prudential Plaza,
Chicago, Illinois, USA 60601-6790. 306 pages. ISBN 0 8092 3812 8
E-mail: ntcpub@tribune.com
Web site: www.contemporarybooks.com

*Towards greater financial autonomy, a manual on financing strategies and
techniques for development* NGOs *and community organizations,* by Fernand
Vincent and Piers Campbell. 1989. Geneva, Development Innovations
and Networks (IRED), 3 rue de Varembé, P.O. Box 116-1211, Geneva
20, Switzerland. 225 pages. ISBN 2 88368 003 5
E-mail: ired@worldcom.ch

*The worldwide fundraiser's handbook, a guide to fundraising for Southern
NGOs and voluntary organizations,* by Michael Norton. 1996. London:
Directory of Social Change in association with the International Fund
Raising Group, 295 Kennington Road, London SE11 4QE, UK.
270 pages. ISBN 1 873860 75 7
E-mail: webmaster@d-s-c.demon.co.uk
Web site: http://www.d-s-c.demon.co.uk

Reference
*The directory of American grantmakers that fund charitable organizations and
individuals outside the USA 2000,* edited by Nancy Bikson and David
Wickert. Chapel & York Ltd., P.O. Box 50, Lingfield RH7 6FT,
United Kingdom. ISBN 1 90329 300 6
E-mail: info@chapel-york.com
Web site: http://www.chapel-york.com

Directory of international corporate giving in America and abroad 2000.
Tracks 650 companies with international connections. 75% give directly.
The Taft Group, P.O. Box 9187, Farmington Hills,
Michigan 48333-9187. ISBN 1 56995 336 8
E-mail: international@gale.com
Web site: http://www.taftgroup.com/taft/about.html

*The directory of international funding organizations, a guide for the non-profit
sector.* London: Charities Aid Foundation, 1997. Order from CAF, Kings
Hill, West Malling, Kent ME19 4TA, UK. ISBN 1 85934 031 8
E-mail: international@caf.charitynet.org
Web site: http://www.ngobooks.org

The European grants index. The first statistical analysis of the funding
interests of foundations and corporate funders active in Europe, as well
as Japan and the USA. Data said to be current, with 75 per cent of
listings containing information for 1996, 1997, or 1998. European
Foundation Centre: Fax: 32 2 512 3265.

E-mail: efc@efc.be
Web site: http://www.efc.be

Guide to funding for international and foreign programs, 2000.
The Foundation Center, 79 5th Avenue, New York City 10003-3076.
358 pages. ISBN 0 87954 903 3
E-mail: orders@fdncenter.org
Web site: http://www.fdncenter.org

The International Foundation Directory, 1998. Europa Publications,
P.O. Box 97974, Pittsburgh, PA 15227, US. Lists 1,500 foundations,
trusts and non-profit institutions in over 100 countries that operate
internationally. 817 pages. ISBN 1 85743 054 9
E-mail: sales@europublications.com
Web site: http://www.europapublications.com/

International fundraising for not-for profits: A country by country profile, by
Tom Harris. What a fundraiser must know when preparing for an
international fundraising campaign. 1999. John Wiley and Sons,
605 Third Avenue, New York, NY 10158-0012. 439 pages.
ISBN 0 471244 52 X
E-mail: catalogue@wiley.com
Web site: http://www.wiley.com

International grant guides. Foreign and international programs. 345 pages.
International grantmaking: A report on U.S. foundation trends, including
profiles of more than 500 leading foundations, 1997. The Foundation
Center, 79 5th Avenue, New York City 10003-3076. 170 pages.
ISBN 0 87954 760 X
E-mail: orders@fdncenter.org
Web site: http://www.fdncenter.org

The international guide to nonprofit law, by Lester Salamon. 1997. Analyses
the legal status of non-profit organizations in 22 countries. John Wiley
and Sons, 605 Third Avenue, New York 10158-0012. 400 pages.
ISBN 0 47105518 2
E-mail: catalogue@wiley.com
Web site: http://www.wiley.com

WWW.Grantmakers: directory of funders' Web Sites, 2000. Lists 1,000
organizations in North America and Europe that fund internationally.
Published by Chapel & York (See first reference listing). 109 pages. ISBN
1 903 903293 01 4.

Useful Web sites

Most sites in this list were suggested by Ken Wyman, a Canadian fundraising consultant. Many sites also have e-mail discussion groups that you can join.

www.charitynet.org
Information and financial resources for a better world. The voluntary action site of CAF (Charities Aid Foundation, UK)
http://www.CAFonline.org

www.charityvillage.com
One of Canada's – maybe the world's – most notable sites. How-to articles, current information on non-profit news, books, careers, professional associations, online publications.

www.chardonpress.com
Fundraising for social change is the theme of this American site from Kim Klein, publisher of the *Grassroots Fundraising Journal*, among other good print material. Online stories, free newsletter, non-profit links, and book catalogue where you can browse selections or search by topic, author, title, or organization.

www.charitychannel.com
Many non-profit discussion forums on specific topics, and Guestshare, a space to share documents among non-profit professionals trying to solve similar problems.

www.electroniccommunity.org
Intends to become the premier Internet portal for civil society organizations involved in the development of Africa. Interactive.

www.fundersonline.org
The European Foundation Centre provides a free toolkit and templates for setting up a Web site.

www.fundraising.co.uk
This Web site has developed a strong worldwide following based on its library services and in-depth coverage of events, jobs, news, grants, funding, compilation of sites. It also has a great feature called "stay in touch" which e-mails you about site updates.

www.fundsnetservices.com
Research and locate international funding: 1,500 sources are listed.

www.idealist.org
Rich collection of non-profit resources. Offers training for non-profit and community organizations on how to use the Internet.

www.ncnb.org
The National Center for Nonprofit Boards (in the United States) has extensive resources on board development including an answering service for e-mail questions.

http://ngls.tad.ch/english/pubs/at/ateng.html
@t ease with e-mail: A handbook on using electronic mail for NGOs in developing countries (see reading list above).

www.nonprofits.org
Huge site from the Internet Nonprofit Center with information for and about non-profit organizations.

www.nutsbolts.com
Practical "how-to" management tips. Browse some of the articles from current and back issues of their printed monthly newsletter, *Nuts & Bolts*, for the busy non-profit professional.

www.oneworld.net/production/supportcentre.html
Includes lists of organization whose lists you can join. The "support centre" offers help in setting up a Web site.

www.pactworld.org
Lists many useful resources. Look at www.pactworld.org/toolbox.html for development expert Richard Holloway's Civil Society Toolbox, including a section on financing civil society organizations.

www.pch.gc.ca/cp-pc/ComPartnE/pub_list.htm
Three excellent books to download, published on the Web by the Community Partnership Program, Canadian Heritage, Government of Canada:
Face-to-face, how to get bigger donations from very generous people, by Ken Wyman. 1993. 192 pages.
Fundraising ideas that work for grassroots groups, by Ken Wyman. 1995. 156 pages.
Guide to special event fundraising, by Ken Wyman. 1990. 170 pages.

www.philanthropy.com
Online source for Internet resources, and current and back issues of the American newspaper, *The Chronicle of Philanthropy*. Some information is available only to subscribers.

www.vita.org
Keep track of the plan by United States organization VITA, Volunteers in Technical Assistance, to bring low cost e-mail services to rural and isolated areas in developing countries.

List of Topics

This list contains page references to all three books. The Roman numeral is the volume number, I, II, and III. The Arabic number is the page number, e.g. III/224.

Acknowledgements

Many thanks for their ideas, information, and time, all given generously, to Sunil Abraham, Prof. Ely Acosta, Fitri Aini, Dr. Duri Samin Akram, Owais Aslam Ali, Gavin Andersson, David Arnold, Rick Arnold, Eugenie Aw, Darlyn Baconguis, John Baguley, Alec Bamford, Hilary Bloom, Ann Bown, Tim Brodhead, Patricia Bryden, Eka Budianti, Anne Burnett, Gladys Calvo, Crouse Campbell, Hur Badilles Camporendondo, Sharon Capeling-Alakija, David and Dorothy Catling, Junko Chano, Chanida Chanyapate, P. Chatterjee, Sergio Chavez, Mathew Cherian, Florence Chirozwa, Rick Christ, Gayle Gifford, Murray and Indira Culshaw, Katalin Czippán, Jane de Sousa, Virginia de Souza, Bianti Djiwandono, Debora Dunn, Robert Dyck, Chakib El Hakmaoui, Federico Espiritu, Amin Fahim, Jaime Faustino, Richard Fehnel, Richard Fuller, Helen Fytche, Nancy George, David Gillies, Thisbe Glegg, Patrick Sanjov Lal Ghose, Oded Grajew, Ruth Groberman, Shelter Guni, John Gwynn, Anne Hamilton, Em. Haryadi, Mahmood Hasan, Gary Hawes, Charlene Hewat, Richard Holloway, Beverly Howell, Prof. Stephen Huddle, Komsan Hutaphat, Vandana Jain, Dra. Hira Jhamtani, Amelia Jones, Fred Musisi Kabuye, David Kalete, Judy Kamanyi, Elizabeth Kane, Zandisile Kanisa, Amita Kapur, George Kassis, Gurinder Kaur, Christopher Kedzie, Daniel Q. Kelley, Renata Kiss, Kim Klein, Wayne Klockner, Francis Kumbweya, Lee Hui Lin, Christina Lavalle, Rodrigo J. Llaguno, Melchora Logronio, James Gregory Lord, Ezra Mbogori, Malvika, Miklos Marschall, Livai Matarirano, Paula McEvoy, Stephanie Melemis, Chinwe Mezue, Louis Mitchell, Mokhethi Moshoeshoe, Horacio "Boy" Morales Jr., David Morley, Mohini Mubayi, Richard Mugisha, Robbie Muhumuza, Jane Nabunnya Mulumba, Leslie Ann Murray, Milton Murray, Kumi Naidoo, C. Shekhar Nambiar, Peter Nizak, Michael Norton, Paul Themba Nyathi, Ada Obi, Bridgette O'Connor, Silas Omanyo, Ir. Katarina Panji, Prasart Pasiri, Tommy Phillips, Kenneth Phillips, Richard Phinney, Jennifer Pittet, Dan Pizer, Tony Poderis, Prof. Amara Pongsapich, Mary Racelis, Douglas Ramage, Niresh Ramklass, Padma Ratnayake, Thabiso Ratsomo, Lance and Pen Reynolds, Neni Rochaeni, Oscar Rojas, Angela Rosati, Romeo Royandoyan, G. M Row, Eugene Saldanha, John R. Samuel, Vijay Sardana, Tamás Scsaurszki, Michael Seltzer, Margaret Sentamu, Hasan Sharif, Dr. Sudirendar Sharma, Bruce Shearer, Jennifer and Wesley Shields, Rosanne Shields, Dan Siegel and Jenny Yancey,

Professor Esperanza Simon, Brinda and Tejeshwar Singh, Victor
Siburian, Ian Smillie, Barry Smith, Danilo Songco, Anne Speke, Per
Stenbeck, Pushpa Sunder, Gary Suwannarat, Louis Tabing, Richard
Tallontire, Martin Tanchuling, Senator Wanlop Tankananurak, Pam
Tansanguanwong, Lawrence Taylor, Mattana Thanomphan, Jennie
Thompson, Mark Vander Wees, Marianna Török, Sam Ugochukwu,
Veerachai Veerachantachart, Richard Vokey, Goh Ruoh Wei, Rob Wells,
David Wickert, Gordon Wilkinson, Ricardo Wilson-Grau, Judith
Wright, Ken Wyman, Kikis Zavala, Wang Zhenjiang, the Mesoamerican
partners of Horizons of Friendship.

These three books are partially financed by The Chronicle of
Philanthropy, Washington DC, USA. Corbin Gwaltney and Malcolm
Scully deserve special thanks.

   Many people are quoted in this series. Many others contributed
ideas and information. I hope I have done them all justice. I am grateful
for the support given to me by the Ford Foundation and by dozens of
organizations and individuals who are listed here and others whom I may
have inadvertently omitted. Many thanks to them all.

   I thank the cartoonists who gave permission to use their cartoons
originally published in The Chronicle of Philanthropy.

   Ian Montagnes gave excellent editorial comment and advice
throughout the writing of these books. Willem Hart brought his usual
commitment and imagination to the design of the series. My thanks to
both of them.

Elizabeth W. Wilson
Port Hope, Canada
March, 2001

About the author

Elizabeth Westman Wilson is a Canadian consultant and writer with many years' experience in fundraising and communications, both overseas and in Canada. While living in the Philippines in the mid-1980s she acted as consultant in communications and fundraising to the president of the University of the Philippines, carried out fundraising studies, and gave workshops in communications in eight developing countries. From 1989 to 1996 she was executive director, Developing Countries Farm Radio Network, and from 1975 to 1984 director, information services at the University of Toronto. Ms Wilson is currently president, Horizons of Friendship, a Canadian agency supporting organizations in Central America and Mexico. She is also the author of two books on oriental ceramics.

www.ingramcontent.com/pod-product-compliance
Lightning Source LLC
Chambersburg PA
CBHW080358030426
42334CB00024B/2923